Anna Mauranen

Reflexively Speaking

Developments in English as a Lingua Franca

Editors
Jennifer Jenkins
Will Baker

Volume 5

Anna Mauranen

Reflexively Speaking

Metadiscourse in English as a Lingua Franca

DE GRUYTER
MOUTON

Free access to the e-book version of this publication was made possible by the 16 institutions that supported the open access transformation *Purchase to Open Pilot* in collaboration with Jisc.

ISBN 978-3-11-161994-1
e-ISBN (PDF) 978-3-11-029549-8
e-ISBN (EPUB) 978-3-11-039515-0
ISSN 2192-8177
e-ISSN 2192-8185
DOI https://doi.org/10.1515/9783110295498

Library of Congress Control Number: 2022950103

Bibliographic information published by the Deutsche Nationalbibliothek
The Deutsche Nationalbibliothek lists this publication in the Deutsche Nationalbibliografie; detailed bibliographic data are available on the internet at http://dnb.dnb.de.

This volume is text- and page-identical with the hardback published in 20X3.
This book is published open access at www.degruyter.com.

Typesetting: Integra Software Services Pvt. Ltd.

www.degruyter.com

For Tapani's memory

Acknowledgements

Metadiscourse has been one of my research strands for a very long time, since my first work on it was published in 1993. The interest started already with my PhD. My supervisor John Sinclair didn't think much of the whole concept, but I wouldn't budge, so we ended up having quite a few debates around the matter. Therefore, I believe I owe my primary gratitude to John, who made the topic stick in my mind. Of course, he never backed down an inch on his position. Different views, however, came up around my first presentations on metadiscourse: I must thank above all John Swales for his enthusiasm and encouragement on my early work. Later, I occasionally continued with metadiscourse, or discourse reflexivity, in a small way in the 2000's, now concerning its use in spoken language. An important milestone was co-editing a special issue of the Nordic Journal of English Studies together with Annelie Ädel in 2010. Thank you, Annelie, it has always been great to share thoughts about reflexive metadiscourse with you! The first international conferences of Metadiscourse Across Genres were amazing, so thank you for organizing these, Erdem Akbas and Larissa D'Angelo! It was great to see how much interest there is in the topic across the world.

This book has been a long time in the making – I did the analyses long before writing it all up. The series editors Jennifer Jenkins and Will Baker deserve my warmest thanks for their incredible patience with the process. Similarly, the publisher's team, with Kirstin Boergen's lead, has done a really professional job, for which I am deeply grateful.

Finally, a different kind of influence has come from my family, my late husband and our three children. In addition to healthy nagging about my time-consuming activities in university management, they have maintained a supportive attitude to my research, and I believe they have some inkling about what metadiscourse means. . . Above all, they have been there. Thank you Tapani, Katariina, Julius, and Aleksanteri!

https://doi.org/10.1515/9783110295498-202

Contents

Acknowledgements —— VII

Chapter 1
Introduction —— 1

Chapter 2
Metadiscourse as discourse reflexivity —— 8
2.1 Metadiscourse and the ongoing discourse —— **8**
2.2 Metadiscourse as reflexivity and the rest of the discourse —— **10**
2.2.1 Texts and readers —— **12**
2.2.2 Prospection —— **14**
2.3 A cognitive viewpoint —— **15**
2.4 The active reader —— **17**
2.5 Interaction and the concept of metadiscourse —— **19**
2.6 Monologue and dialogue —— **22**
2.7 What discourse reflexivity includes —— **25**
2.8 Conclusion —— **31**

Chapter 3
Data and methods —— 34
3.1 Corpora and event types —— **34**
3.1.1 Event types in ELFA —— **35**
3.1.2 Event types in WrELFA —— **37**
3.2 The sample —— **39**
3.2.1 Seminar presentations and discussions —— **39**
3.2.2 Doctoral defences —— **41**
3.2.3 Blog comment threads —— **42**
3.2.4 Event types in different chapters —— **43**
3.2.5 Number of words in the sample —— **44**
3.3 Methods —— **44**
3.3.1 Process —— **47**
3.3.2 Categories —— **48**
3.4 The wider context —— **50**

Chapter 4
Discourse reflexivity in multi-party interaction — 52
4.1 Reflexivity in dialogic discourse — **53**
4.2 Managing discourse — **55**
4.2.1 Orienting — **56**
4.2.2 Retrieving — **63**
4.3 Managing situation — **75**
4.4 Conclusion — **80**

Chapter 5
Discourse reflexivity in dialogic writing — 83
5.1 The research blog as a concept and a genre — **84**
5.2 Blogs as dialogue — **89**
5.3 Discourse reflexivity in dialogic writing — **91**
5.3.1 Managing the discourse in blog discussions — **94**
5.3.2 Managing the situation in blog discussions — **101**
5.4 Conclusion — **105**

Chapter 6
Matching perspectives and co-constructing knowledge — 111
6.1 Prerequisites: matching perspectives — **114**
6.1.1 Clarifying — **116**
6.1.2 Negotiating viewpoints — **119**
6.2 Generating knowledge — **135**
6.2.1 Collaborating towards knowledge in spoken dialogue — **136**
6.2.2 Collaborating towards knowledge in written dialogue — **142**
6.3 Conclusion — **149**

Chapter 7
Discourse reflexivity in monologue — 152
7.1 Managing discourse — **156**
7.1.1 Contextualising — **157**
7.1.2 Commenting — **168**
7.2 Managing situation — **177**
7.3 Conclusion — **179**

Chapter 8
Discourse reflexivity across speech events — 184

8.1 Incidence and distribution of discourse reflexivity in the data — **184**
8.1.1 Rate of discourse reflexivity in spoken discourse — **185**
8.1.2 Rate of discourse reflexivity in written dialogue — **189**
8.2 Comparing dialogic and monologic speech events — **190**
8.3 Discourse reflexivity in spoken and written dialogue — **195**
8.4 Conclusion — **199**

Chapter 9
Conclusion — 204

9.1 What have we learned from dialogic data? — **205**
9.2 Other interesting findings — **207**
9.2.1 Co-presence in speaking — **207**
9.2.2 Embodied vs disembodied communication — **209**
9.2.3 Long discussions — **210**
9.2.4 Social asymmetries — **211**
9.3 What were the commonalities? — **213**
9.4 Where next? — **214**

List of figures — 219

References — 221

Index — 233

Chapter 1
Introduction

Ten years ago, I remarked on the surprisingly small proportion of metadiscourse studies that investigated spoken discourse compared to the total amount of metadiscourse research (Mauranen 2012). This is still true, even though much more research has been devoted to spoken discourses since then. The proportional gap remains enormous. If we look for studies addressing not only speaking in general, but speaking in dialogic interaction, the result is hardly visible to the naked eye.

The ultimate reason for studying metadiscourse has not changed. It is the intrinsic fascination of this fundamental characteristic of human language: the ability to reflect on itself. This inbuilt capacity in our languages is an indication of a more general capacity of the human mind to monitor its own operations, that is, metacognition. We can think about our own thinking, and we can talk about our own talking. Language is nevertheless not only an instrument of cogitation, but of communication. Dialogic speech is where cognition meets interaction; metadiscourse is one of the resources that language has for increasing the transparency of our intended meanings and communicative intentions to our interlocutors. It builds on our theory of mind, which makes assumptions about what our interlocutors or audiences know and think, and thereby helps us design our talk for our recipients accordingly. Importantly, metadiscourse is a discourse phenomenon, therefore not reducible to individual words or phrases, and even when individual metadiscoursal expressions coincide with a word or phrase, it is their status in the discourse that matters. Therefore, counting 'metadiscourse markers', useful as it may be for comparisons, generally makes for conservative rather than innovative research.

Speech is foundational to language, unquestionably its most ubiquitous and constant mode of use, and can with a high degree of confidence be said to be its original mode (possibly vying for first place with sign language); spoken interaction is what language is fundamentally about. Passing it over in studies of metadiscourse is a major omission.

Two things, then, motivate writing a book on metadiscourse in spoken interaction: metadiscourse research has all but ignored spoken interaction, and spoken interaction research has all but ignored metadiscourse.

What reason do we have, then, for assuming that investigating dialogic speech might bring new understanding to the study of metadiscourse? Most studies comparing written and spoken metadiscourse, or only studying the latter, have found no major differences. The early studies that compared metadiscourse in speech and writing discovered only minor differences (Luukka 1995; Ädel 2010), and although

https://doi.org/10.1515/9783110295498-001

some more recent studies have begun to challenge their similarity somewhat more (Lee & Subtirelu 2015; Liu 2021), they have not come up with radical departures either. Even without direct comparison, studies of spoken academic monologues like lectures or presentations have applied analytical models built on written texts and found largely similar metadiscourse (e.g., Rowley-Jolivet & Carter-Thomas 2005; Webber 2005; Pérez-Llantada 2006; Fernández Polo 2018), with some scholars observing more colloquial expressions (Flowerdew and Tauroza 1995; Zareva 2011). More recently, these more traditional academic speech genres have received an addition from a short presentation type, the three-minute pitch, or three-minute thesis presentation (3MT), where doctoral students present their research in competitive settings. The 3MT has become a popular topic for metadiscourse research (Zou & Hyland 2020; Hyland & Zou 2022; Qiu & Jiang 2021; Liu 2021) and other kinds of discourse studies. Again, the studies have applied Hyland's (2005) writing-based model with no major alterations or additions, and again the mode is monologic.

New light is thrown on the question in Zhang's (2022) recent large-scale multidimensional study on reflexive metadiscourse across spoken and written registers. The study includes dialogic, that is, conversational registers, and unlike the monologue-focused earlier studies, finds a major divide between speech and writing. Zhang shows that spoken registers, unlike written, use metadiscourse markers to explicitly emphasize interaction between the addresser and addressee. That is, conversational speech typically displays frequent occurrences of metadiscourse markers relating to addresser, addressee, saying and arguing, receiving and understanding, in addition to defining and explaining, which it shares with other registers. The study thus reveals significant differences between dialogic and monologic registers: what Zhang calls markers of 'participant interaction' are frequent in dialogues but not in monologues. At the same time, what he calls markers of 'discourse presentation' show no significant difference between dialogues and monologues. The cross-modal similarity found in previous studies may thus to some extent be explained by characteristics of monologues.

While dialogic speech has remained a rare option in metadiscourse research, it has not been entirely non-existent. In addition to Zhang's (2022) inclusive comparison, McKeown & Ladegaard (2020) studied metadiscourse and dominance in multi-party discussions, and I have also carried out a few smaller-scale investigations (Mauranen 2001, 2003, 2010, 2012). To my knowledge there is even less on written dialogic metadiscourse, with the exception of three studies of digital dialogues, Smart (2016), Biri (2021), and Mauranen (2021b).

Given that there is so little research on spoken dialogue – including polylogues – the question of how it might differ from research based on monologic discourse, whether spoken or written, is motivated on that basis alone. Dialogue is synchronous joint activity, which can be symmetric, that, is, participants can perform similar actions. By contrast, monologic speaking is asynchronous, performed by a single speaker, the activity thus neither joint nor symmetric. Many intriguing questions arise regarding the effect that the joint, synchronous, and symmetric activity, the simultaneous presence of interlocutors and the rapid pace of turn-taking in dialogue might have on metadiscourse.

Interacting in real time means that participants in a dialogic exchange need to share their representations of the situation to a sufficient degree to be able to carry out a meaningful dialogue, that is, they must 'match their perspectives', or, in Pickering and Garrod's (2021) terms, they must be aligned. Does metadiscourse play a role in this? If there is little time for pre-planning, and a pressing need to attend to what interlocutors are saying to make the speaker's own speech relevant to how the interaction is going, or to steer it to their preferred directions, how, if at all, might metadiscourse come into it? Will new functions or uses emerge, beyond possibly some new expressions or well-known features of speaking, like hesitations or colloquialisms? How do monologues, spoken dialogues, and written dialogues compare? Spoken monologues and dialogues are both embodied and fast unlike written dialogues, while all dialogues have at least two active participants, which implies that the outcomes and directions of the discourse are far less predictable than in monologues of any kind. Can we find social or other situational parameters that affect metadiscourse in interaction?

Clearly, the distinct character of metadiscourse in the conversational register compared to other registers (Zhang 2022) adds to the interest value of discovering what could be behind the finding on closer inspection.

Previous research into spoken metadiscourse has not only been heavily biased towards monologic genres, but also favoured academic discourses. There are some exceptions to the academic emphasis that I am aware of, like Ilie (2003) on parliamentary debates and Malmström (2014) on preaching, and hopefully there are more to come. Studies on metadiscourse in the digital media have shown signs of opening towards other domains, like notice boards (Smart 2016), social media (Biri 2021), advertisements (Delibekovic Dzanic and Berberovic 2021), and vlogs (Ädel 2021). The academic bias is nevertheless true of metadiscourse research overall, perhaps reflecting its roots in student writing in Crismore's (1983) and VandeKopple's (1985) work. All the studies mentioned above on monologues like lectures, conference talks, and 3MTs have taken their data from the academic domain.

In this book, I intend to tread the same path. This may at first sight look like a strangely limiting choice: surely ordinary conversations are more fundamental to dialogic speaking than academic discussions? There are nevertheless two good reasons for doing this. The first is that in extending a well-charted research area like metadiscourse studies towards new territory, it makes sense to keep some basic parameters intact to be able to relate the results to previous findings. This means that any new insights from the dialogue focus can be seen against the background of what we already know about metadiscourse. The second reason is that academia overall is highly reliant on not only writing but on the spoken word. Although in many experimental and laboratory sciences, the core research may not appear to depend on verbalisation, much of it actually does so. Laboratory science depends on collaborative work that requires speaking; from planning, designing, and monitoring experiments to interpreting observations depends on talk before writing it up, like sociologists of science found long ago (e.g. Gilbert & Mulkay 1984; Latour & Woolgar 1986). Speaking is thus ubiquitous in academia. The speaking and writing phases involve very different discourse orientations, as shown in Gilbert and Mulkay's (1984) seminal research, which led to the notions of 'contingent' and 'empiricist' repertoires.

My present data comes from corpora that represent English as a Lingua Franca (ELF), which in the contemporary world typifies the reality of academic English (Jenkins 2014; Mauranen 2012; Jenkins & Mauranen 2019). Academic conferences, university programmes, scientists and scholars have adopted English as the default language of collaborative international research and international study programmes (Franzmann et al 2015; Wächter & Maiworm 2014). ELF has been a controversial matter in applied linguistics, especially in its early days some twenty years ago (Jenkins 2000; Seidlhofer 2011) but has since been accepted by the research community. It is typically seen as part of the multilingual turn that has characterised the research field more broadly (see, e.g., Jenkins 2015). ELF is now the mainstream, the new normal in English. It is clear that ELF is not 'simplified' or otherwise deficient English, but a driver of linguistic change (Laitinen & Lundberg 2021) and equally complex as other kinds of English (Mauranen 2021a). Fluent speakers of ELF also process the English that they hear in essentially the same way as speakers of English as their first language (Dobrego, Konina & Mauranen 2022). Possibly the principal and most enduring contribution of ELF research will turn out to be not the study of English, but a more general one: how we see language and its role in human communication. Research on ELF has opened the eyes of linguists working in English and also in other languages to look at languages as interconnected, drawing from a common pool of communicative resources. We are learning to appreciate the change that follows from the presence of second-language speakers and ubiquitous language contact.

The combination of ELF and metadiscourse is also interesting in its own right, a strand of fundamental research into human language: if speakers engage in metadiscourse when they do not speak their L1 (although some speakers in this data, do, of course), then metadiscourse is a general property of human communication, not limited to a particular language or group of languages. It helps establish to what extent metadiscourse is like, say, discourse marking, which

McCarthy (2001) suggests is a universal feature of language. Such ordinary features of speaking, metadiscourse or discourse marking, tend to pass unnoticed in descriptions of general or universal features of language because they are discourse phenomena rather than part of sentence grammar, but they certainly should be taken on board along with more traditional linguistic categories insofar as we are interested in the fundamental character of human language.

My approach to metadiscourse is reflexive, as it has been from the start (Mauranen 1993a). Metadiscourse, or *discourse reflexivity* in a nutshell is discourse about the ongoing discourse. This is to say that metadiscourse stands in a 'meta' relationship with the discourse that it is part of in an analogous way to metacognition, which stands in relation to cognition while being part of it, and orients to being cognisant, or aware, of cognition. Metacognition is part of cognition and metadiscourse part of discourse. To be as clear as I can about this, I investigate discourse reflexivity, discourse about discourse, that is, discourse that talks about itself. I discuss the concept in more detail in Chapter 2, and its methodological implications in Chapter 3.

At this point it may be useful to point out that many scholars now accept that there are two approaches to metadiscourse: alternatively termed as a 'thick' and a 'thin' one, or a 'narrow' and a 'broad' one. The epithets 'thick' and 'narrow' are usually connected with the 'reflexive model' of metadiscourse, associated with scholars like Ädel (2006), Smart (2016), and me (Mauranen 1993a), while 'thin' and 'broad' are most closely connected to Crismore (1983), VandeKopple (1985), and Hyland (2005). Clearly, there are many overlaps in all these models, as well as variation in what individual scholars include or focus on, but the main distinction lies in how much material is subsumed under metadiscourse that goes beyond the core concept of discourse about the ongoing discourse. For example, are hedges, expressions of stance or engagement, or all self-mentions inherently part of metadiscourse? In the reflexive approach they are not. Some studies also mix parts from the two approaches (e.g., Bouziri 2021). In addition, different methodological choices tend to be associated with the two main schools of thought, though in reality the connection is more tenuous. For example, most metadiscourse studies of any persuasion employ elements from quantitative and qualitative methods.

In the approach that I have adopted, the elements included in *discourse reflexivity* must stand in a 'meta' relationship to the ongoing discourse. My methodological approach is thick in that it is predominantly qualitative and contextual, with some numerical support.

The general methodological perspective in this book is, then, discourse analytical, as is usual in metadiscourse research. Discourse reflexivity is a discourse phenomenon, rather than, say, grammatical or lexical. Because the focus is on spoken dialogues, co-present social interaction occupies centre stage. There is also a cognitive thread that goes through the book, based on the understanding is that human cognition is interactionally oriented, because we are so inalienably attuned to our fellow humans, especially to their speech.

Towards the end of the book, where the import of analyses from different chapters are brought together, the findings are related to three kinds of parameters: *discourse*-based, *external* constraints, and some *social* parameters that seem relevant for making sense of the variability found in the different event types investigated.

The book is organised so that it begins with a general theoretical underpinning of the approach in Chapter 2, where the nature of spoken interaction is described as dynamic, co-present, collaborative, embodied, and fast. The chapter discusses the specific contribution that reflexive metadiscourse makes to the unfolding of discourse in interaction along with other linguistic cues. Prospection is a central concept in depicting the role of discourse reflexivity, and it is argued that reflexive discourse updates and changes the ongoing discourse with a specific contribution to predicting the discourse ahead and interpreting and confirming its import up to the point of the utterance.

Chapter 3 describes the research material, above all the event types that are analysed, the sample, and the methodological approach adopted: a data-driven, exploratory bottom-up analysis of discourse reflexivity in context. It also discusses analytical principles such as categorisation as well as taking on board the wider situational context with its different constraints.

Spoken dialogues are analysed from the bottom up in Chapter 4, which makes several pivotal distinctions that are applied in subsequent chapters to other spoken discourses and written dialogues and modified as the need arises. It shows how discourse reflexivity is involved in the distributed, collaborative discourse between interactants and how fundamental participants' orientation to each other's speech is. Reflexive metadiscourse in spoken interaction replaces previous notions of metadiscourse, which have primarily depicted it as helping predict the current speaker's (or indeed writer's) upcoming speech, with a more nuanced picture, where participants actively engage with each other's contributions and relate their own to collaborative development of the evolving discourse.

Analysing the dialogic mode continues in Chapter 5, which takes up the written medium and explores discourse reflexivity in online comment threads on research blog sites. Digital dialogues are well positioned to unravel effects of medium (speech vs writing), channel (online vs co-present) and genre on dialogical reflexive metadiscourse. The analytical approach is top-down, imposing the framework developed in Chapter 4 and testing how far it fits the data. Discourse reflexivity turns out to be as important in online dialogue as it is in spoken dialogue, and most categories are very similar, but the medium and the channel have their own effects, comparatively small but distinctive and not unimportant.

Dialogues continue to be in focus in Chapter 6, which investigates the interactive co-construction of new ideas, thoughts, and knowledge in dialogic interaction. Knowledge construction is envisaged as intersubjective and collaborative, inherently dynamic, with outcomes that can be unpredictable. Reflexive metadiscourse plays important roles in bringing this creative collaboration about. The categories of discourse reflexivity follow those outlined in chapters 4 and 5, but the angle from which the discourse is viewed highlights different aspects of it, especially those that make thoughts or ideas more readily shared.

Chapter 7 switches to a different mode, monologue, while maintaining the spoken medium and the co-presence of speakers and listeners. Not unexpectedly, this data brings more notable changes to analytical categories developed for dialogues, but overall, the most fundamental functions of discourse reflexivity are shared across the modes. The most striking differences between monologic and dialogic modes relate to tasks that are either carried out by a single participant (as in monologues) or interacting participants in a distributed fashion (as in dialogues). Organising the discourse falls on the sole speaker in the monologic mode, as do various commenting activities. Reflexive metadiscourse in spoken monologues would seem to resemble written monologues, as previous research has shown, but it also shows effects of the co-presence of the audience, evincing the social and situational sensitivity of speech.

Although qualitative analysis is the main approach in the book, a numerical tally of discourse reflexive expressions is held throughout. Chapter 8 presents an overview of the incidence of discourse reflexivity in monologic and dialogic modes and in dialogic modes across the spoken-written medium divide. The most striking differences are again found between dialogic and monologic modes, but there is considerable variability beyond this discourse-related division. The chapter discusses other discourse-related factors that may explain such variability as well as factors that do not directly reflect the discourse but may rather be reflected in it, such as external constraints and social parameters. In general, the overview supports the observations made in the qualitative analysis but brings up new insights and points to unanswered questions.

Chapter 9, finally, wraps up the book, discusses the main findings and their import and suggests ways forward. It shows how important it is to include dialogue in metadiscourse research, what we have already learnt from it, and how much there still is to be discovered about reflexive metadiscourse.

Chapter 2
Metadiscourse as discourse reflexivity

Our understanding of humans as a unique species has received serious blows over the last hundred years or so. Other species build sophisticated dwellings and complex social systems, benefit from symbioses with other species, use and make tools. In important respects the distinction between humans and many other species looks like a matter of degree, including communicative systems (N. Lee et al. 2009; Tomasello 2014;), as recently posthumanism has emphasised, including linguistics (Evans 2014; Pennycook 2017). Some traits are nevertheless particularly highly developed in humans and characterise our species: the tendency to collaborate more than other species, and the tendency to communicate more than other species. Both characteristics relate to the fundamentally social nature of humans, and the vital importance of social interaction to their life and success. Many researchers in different fields have made similar observations about collaboration, and Mercier and Sperber (2017) make both.

Communication is thus inextricably intertwined with collaboration. We need to understand, or make good guesses about, each other's intentions, meanings, and emotional states to collaborate successfully. Not only that, but above all, we need to work towards shared and new meanings jointly, largely if not exclusively through language, in other words collaborate to communicate and create new understanding and knowledge in the process. In brief, we must communicate to collaborate, and collaborate to communicate. To achieve this, we rely on communicative resources that are sophisticated, flexible, and amenable to change and adaptation. One of the properties of human language that may not find equivalents in the communication systems of other species and may therefore give us some communicative advantage is its capacity to talk about itself self-reflexively while the same system can also be used for talking about other matters. There is a meta-level of communication, a reflexive possibility in human discourse that enables us to indicate how we intend our interlocutors to take what we are saying and how it relates to what they are saying. This, in short, is the domain of discourse reflexivity, or reflexive metadiscourse.

2.1 Metadiscourse and the ongoing discourse

The idea of metadiscourse has not been without its critics. Objections have been raised to the concept altogether. One is that the whole notion is trivial, the other that it is misuse of the prefix *meta*-. The triviality objection holds that there is

https://doi.org/10.1515/9783110295498-002

nothing remarkable about discourse talking about itself, because we can speak about language just like we speak about anything else. This is of course true in that everyday talk is concerned with language as a matter of course: not only do we talk about different languages we know or have encountered (*we all speak one language which is Swahili*) or what is talked about (*we mostly speak about politics)* but we also make category distinctions (*creative language, technical vocabulary*), pass evaluative comments (*rich vocabulary, funny expression, heavy accent*), or talk about rules and rights of using language (*you can't talk about content without talking of a process; women couldn't speak in church*), or address the complicated relationship between a referent and its linguistic expression (*can 'Bildung' be translated in any other language?*). Besides, we can deliberately exploit metalanguage for instructional purposes, and use it to talk about texts in a writing class, for example (Myhill et al. 2020). While these examples illustrate just a few of the purposes for which language is talked about, they indicate an awareness of language in our ordinary lives. Language is not only a transparent means of communication, but also an object of thought in itself, a site of emotional and aesthetic responses, as well as of linguistic theorising. Abundant vocabulary and terminology exist for talking about language, and we can call it *metalinguistic* speech. This way of talking about language does not, however, capture the reflexive potential of language.

Reflexive metadiscourse is distinct from mere references to and comments on language: it is a way of speaking about the ongoing discourse that organises, specifies, and modifies the discourse at hand. Thus, we can insert linguistic comments directly into the ongoing discourse by performing a number of discourse regulating acts, such as indicating what we are going to say (*I'm going to talk about; I'd like to say that . . .*), monitor the way others may understand our communicative intentions *(that's not what I was going to say; I want to ask what you mean by that)*, prompt others to speak (*what were you about to say; do you want to answer the question*) and regulate our interlocutor's speaking (*we can't just pass it and talk about these; can you please speak louder*). What we see in these examples is a different kind of awareness of language from the metalinguistic comments above, and an engagement with language as an ongoing process rather than as a separate object.

Reflexive metadiscourse is part of the discourse that is being (co-)created, updating and changing it in the same way that any other part of the discourse does, but its distinct contribution is to promote specific perceptions about the state of the discourse up to the moment of speaking and the discourse ahead. Even if the boundaries between metalinguistic comments and discourse reflexivity may occasionally become blurred, the difference remains clear: reflexive discourse is discourse about the ongoing discourse, while metalinguistic comments refer to 'language objects' outside the current discourse.

Seen in this light, as an integral part of the discourse it participates in while simultaneously creating a new layer onto it in a kind of self-aware commentary, reflexive metadiscourse is part of our more general capacity to reflect upon our own experiences and actions. We are able to distance ourselves from immediate experiences, identities, attitudes, and gut reactions, and subject them to conscious reflection and monitoring (e.g. Bandura 2000; Fleming & Frith 2014). Even though the processes we can bring to consciousness are only fragments of our entire mental activity, we are nevertheless able to think about our own thinking, that is, to make thinking an object of thought itself. This constitutes *metacognition*. It can be divided into implicit and explicit metacognition (Fleming & Frith 2014), the former of which is available to infants as well as animals, again reminding us of how thin the line is that divides humans from other living things. Processes that allow us to talk about our talking are analogous to metacognition: we can be aware of our verbalisations, and we can indicate this by means of the very act of verbalising.

A second objection to metadiscourse applies to the term, notably by Sinclair (e.g. 2005), who contends that this is a misuse of the prefix *meta-*, which, as the argument goes, usually refers to something external to a notion or object, or an abstraction from it, a higher-order concept. In this philosophical sense, then, if we postulate an object language, which is used for talking about the world, then a metalanguage would be a separate system for talking about that object language. Basically, this implies metalanguage is a formal language for analysing an object language. This sense of *meta-* is employed in some disciplines, so that we speak of the 'metalanguage of mathematics', for example. Analogously, we might talk about formal systems of linguistic analysis or the terminologies of theoretical linguistics as the metalanguage of natural language. This is not how we usually talk about metalanguage in linguistics as already noted, and neither is the *meta-* prefix limited to the metalanguage of describing objects or systems in other sciences. For example, in cognitive sciences we find not only metacognition, but concepts referring to its subsystems like 'metamemory', which refers to our awareness of our memory processes. In biology the prefix is used quite differently again, and *metapopulation* refers collectively to dispersed but interacting populations of a species (Hanski 1999). Thus, although Sinclair is undoubtedly right in arguing that there is no way of getting outside language by using language, it is not possible to get outside cognition to contemplate on one's cognition, either.

2.2 Metadiscourse as reflexivity and the rest of the discourse

If we take metadiscourse to be part of the discourse in a self-referential sense, similar to metacognition, discourse reflexivity can most naturally be conceptualised as discourse about the discourse it participates in and is constructing. If we put the idea as briefly and generally as possible, discourse reflexivity is discourse about the ongoing discourse. Definitions of metadiscourse along these lines have been put forward in approaches that talk about "text reflexivity" (Mauranen 1993a), "discourse reflexivity" (Mauranen 2001, 2003, 2012; Smart 2016), or "reflexive metadiscourse" (Ädel 2010). As a group they have been called the *reflexive model* of metadiscourse. *Reflexivity* captures the conceptualisation of metadiscourse as self-reflexive discourse. It is an expansion of the notion of ´text reflexivity´ that I used in 1993 for expressions in texts that refer to the texts themselves as opposed to expressions that refer to other texts for, say, analytical or critical purposes. From another angle, we can draw an analogy with the logical modalities of *de re* and *de dicto*, where references to texts other than the one currently unfolding are *de re* from the point of view of the current text (thus metalanguage), and those referring to the current text itself are *de dicto* (thus metatext) (Mauranen 1993a).

Clearly, most discourse is about *de re*, that is, matters other than itself. This has not been an issue in metadiscourse research, whereas where to draw the line between metadiscourse on the one hand and the rest of the discourse on the other has been a major concern. Hyland (2005) notes, quite rightly, that separating the 'propositional' and the 'meta' has been difficult for most researchers. It has nevertheless been attempted all along. Underlying the distinction seems to be a false dichotomy between 'the interactional' and the 'propositional' (or 'ideational', or some other similar term more linguistic and less directly derived from truth-conditional semantics than 'proposition'). In the early days of metadiscourse research in applied linguistics, Crismore and Farnsworth (1990: 120–1) distinguished the referential or informative plane, and the expressive, attitudinal plane, which they took to correspond to Halliday's ideational and interpersonal metafunctions. However, their classification divides metatextual subcategories into Halliday's textual and interpersonal metafunctions. This is at odds with Halliday's concept of 'textual', which includes thematic development and other organising and cohesion-creating language (e.g. Halliday 1985; Halliday & Hasan 1976). Metadiscourse has no place in Halliday's system, which probably explains the confusion among scholars who have sought to fit their models into his theory. Some Hallidayan categories are nevertheless included in metadiscourse approaches of the 'broad' kind. These include conjunctive relations, which are part of his textual metafunction, and modality, which he subsumes under the interpersonal function.

The issue of 'meta' vs. the 'propositional' has not been confined to confusions about Hallidayan categories. Mauranen (1993a), Hyland (2005), and Ädel (2006) have each discussed it in turn along very similar lines. The early scholars' idea that metadiscourse was separate from a 'primary' propositional discourse cuts no ice with any of them. Rather, they see metadiscourse as an integral part of the text, on a par with the rest. Similarly, all three argue for a functional interpretation whereby metadiscourse is 'meta' relative to something else in its specific co-text, not a set of inherently metadiscursive items. Finally, all three have drawn a distinction between 'content' and 'meaning' so that 'meta' elements are recognized as contributing to meaning, while not necessarily to content. The total meaning of the text, then, is understood to be holistic and to consist in the interplay of all its elements. These notions seem to be now widely accepted in metadiscourse research at a general level, but the issue of what constitutes 'the rest' in the text, the 'other-than-metadiscourse', is less clear and less consensual, as is evident from different scholars' choices of the linguistic elements they subsume under metadiscourse.

2.2.1 Texts and readers

The conundrum of the content-metadiscourse dichotomy relates to two things: the nature of text, and the role of the reader. Let us try to untangle it by starting from the text and postpone tackling the issue of the reader to Section 2.4. For the sake of simplicity, I will confine the discussion to written text in this section, because the discussion around metadiscourse vs. the rest of the text have hitherto been predominantly concerned with writing.

To try to envision metadiscourse as part of the text, it is perhaps useful to start by a brief look at what texts do in the bigger picture – how they interact with their readers. Many texts of course inform their readers about something and could on that basis be regarded as having propositional value (indeed, in the age of disinformation and 'fake news' this is constantly an issue). It is nevertheless not easy to find texts that merely inform us, with no additional purposes – such as regulating our behaviour by instructing, warning, or advising us about something, persuading us to buy products or services, or to accept research findings. Texts conform to tacit rules about what is relevant to talk about, such as being useful, newsworthy, surprising, scandalous, or awe-inspiring, or, at the very least, filling a gap in our knowledge. If you ask people to summarise what a text said, they tend to report not only what we might call its content matter, but usually merge this with its illocutionary force (*We must wear safety helmets when we go down; Neanderthals had a sophisticated culture*). Texts thus build up shared experience (Sinclair 1981[2004] between the writer and the reader, but more things than the 'content' contribute to this shared experience.

The unspoken rules that guide our reading of a text result from our socialisation in literate societies into the world of texts from an early age. Such tacit rules, like social norms generally, are acquired through observation, experience, and education. Well socialised competent members of literate communities come to know to expect certain things from texts. They are, in other words, primed to read texts in certain ways (Hoey 2001). Like other social norms, text norms change with time and vary with circumstances, and our expectations adapt accordingly. Similar expectations hold for text-external matters, which orient our reading before we even start. Texts appear in various physical and visual contexts: pinned on noticeboards, printed on menus, leaflets, stuck on doors, printed in books or learned journals, digitally on webpages or social media. Our actual reading is further guided by images, subheadings, abstracts, tables, captions, translator's prefaces, footnotes, diagrams, bullet points, or font style alterations. There is evidence of the visual context affecting the ease of anticipation of how a text continues (Ankener, Sekicki, & Staudte 2018).

In the text itself, as we read it from left to right (or depending on the writing system, in some other order) some of the reader's experience at any moment builds directly on the wording of the text, while a substantial proportion emanates from the pre-existing mental representations the reader brings to bear on the process. The text material guides the reader's meaning-making in countless ways, many already revealed in early text linguistic research. Some are simply common patterns we expect to find, like cause and effect, general and specific, claim and denial, or temporal sequencing (Winter 1977; Hoey 1983). Among pioneering studies on relevant linguistic indicators that trigger expectations in readers, Winter (1977) identified lexis that helps anticipate the pattern of the rest of the text, and Tadros (1985) detected *advance labelling structures* that involve lexical and grammatical elements for similar purposes. Many other scholars have followed suit, for example Hoey, who in his later work informed by cognitive science (2005) returns to the central role lexis plays in recognising and anticipating what a text is going to be like and how it will continue. Various sequencing and ordering practices, such as theme-rheme order and other coherence and cohesion-creating means (e.g. Daneš 1974; Halliday & Hasan 1976) depend on linguistic cues involving the level of text and discourse rather than only smaller units like the sentence or parts of it. In brief, then, texts are imbued with external and internal cues that guide our reading, help us make sense of them, anticipate what they are going to be like and how they will continue once we have started reading. Metadiscourse is one of them, but by no means the only one. Its unique qualities are fascinating, but it is important to bear in mind that it combines with a myriad of other cues that mediate writer-reader interaction.

2.2.2 Prospection

At this point, it may be useful to take speaking on board along with written text, alternating or integrating them as the topics allow. A fundamental higher-level concept that articulates the basis of the reader's textual anticipation is *prospection*. This concept applies to writing and speaking alike, and it was first put forward by Sinclair as early as 1966, but elaborated mainly in the 1980s and 1990s (see, e.g. Sinclair 2004). His claim is that "a major central function of language is that it constantly prospects ahead" (2004:12). This implies that the state of the discourse at any point is contained in the current utterance or sentence, and as he puts it, "the scene is set for each new utterance by the utterance that is going on at the moment" (ibid.:13). This dynamic view of discourse was (and still is) virtually entirely missing from other approaches to text analysis, and many scholars have instead emphasised the nature of speech as dynamic in contrast to the written text, which is static (e.g. Halliday 1985; Chafe 1980; Brazil 1995). While true in the physical sense, the recipient's experience may not be static in either case. Sinclair started from speech, but subsequently extended the notion to written text (e.g. 1985[2004]; 1993[2004]), calling for an integrated description of the two.

Prospection has not been widely adopted in language studies, apart from a related concept of predictive activity in spoken interaction, *projection*, which was later developed in Conversation Analysis (CA) to refer to the way conversational participants predict conversational structures (Schegloff 2013). Projection is also studied in Interactional Linguistics (IL), (e.g. Auer 2005; Couper-Kuhlen & Selting 2018), which largely overlaps with CA, but with a specific interest in language, while CA's prime concern is the structuring of social interaction. In these twin research traditions, projection is what enables a conversation participant to predict the completion of a conversational structure by foreshadowing its later trajectory on the basis of its earlier part (Couper-Kuhlen & Selting 2018). Like prospection, projection is understood to operate at different interdependent levels of language (Schegloff 2013), of which Auer (2005) distinguishes several, all supporting a holistic view of anticipating what is to come in the ongoing discourse: action projection, sequential, content-based, syntactic, and phonological projection. A further similarity is that like prospection, which is not normally assumed to make an exact set of predictions, but to function as a practical aid to quick and efficient interpretation, like a heuristic (Sinclair & Mauranen 2006), projection is understood to work in the same way (e.g. Couper-Kuhlen & Selting 2018). Where CA seems to come closest to metadiscourse is in 'projector constructions' (Pekarek Doehler 2011), which seem to overlap with certain kinds of metadiscourse.

Prospection and projection do not differentiate between the speaker's (or writer's) and the hearer's (or reader's) perspectives, that is, between production and reception. In cognitive linguistics, the related term concerned with the processing of ongoing language is *prediction*, which refers only to the recipient's processing. It would seem to clarify matters to make a distinction between the speaker's and the hearer's perspectives. In the first case, we talk about what we can see in the language, in the second, what we can observe in the human listener. I will therefore talk about *prospection* when properties of the stimulus, i.e. language, are concerned, and about prediction when the hearer's processing is in focus. It follows that metadiscourse is what we find speakers use, and insofar as it facilitates listener processing this means it helps them *predict*.

2.3 A cognitive viewpoint

When text linguistics first began to embrace a holistic understanding of text, similar thinking was gaining ground in cognitive research. These developments took place around the same broad time frame, the 1970s and the 1980s, but they seem to have developed largely independently (though with some exceptions, e.g. Sanford & Garrod 1981), judging by the almost non-existent inter-references between the two fields. Holistic and top-down ideas must somehow have been in the air, even though the general concepts of Gestalt theory date back to early twentieth century, and one might have thought it was staple in the study of cognition. Notwithstanding, schema theory (Rumelhart 1975) and other related concepts like scripts or frames influenced thinking in the 1970s, as did experimental findings showing that connected sentences, or texts, are remembered better than series of unconnected sentences (Kintsch 1974). Texts were seen to represent a higher level of psychological organisation than less structured collections of language items. Some researchers began to investigate both top-down and bottom-up processing in text comprehension (e.g. Morgan & Sellner 1980), which meant a reorientation from the previous exclusive attention to sentences and their structural permutations. At the intersection of cognitive and linguistic interests, text grammars began to emerge, some influential ones based on generativism (e.g. van Dijk 1972), thus quite disconnected from the purely linguistic and mostly functionalist developments based on the Prague School (Daneš 1974) and Hallidayan functionalism (Halliday & Hasan 1976). Perhaps it was in American functionalism, or "West Coast functionalism", that the cognitive determinants of discourse became most prominent. Narratives became a central topic of research, and notably Chafe (e.g. 1980) investigated their production in speech. Much of his work sought to analyse consciousness and language in an integrated way and take temporal development on board in both, and he has continued to develop the notion of linguistic and cognitive temporality in his later work (e.g. Chafe 1998[2014], 2018). However, neither cognitive nor text models in the 1970s generally assumed Chafe's perspective of temporal flow or Sinclair's dynamic, prospection-based orientation. Talking about top-down processing has largely given way to predictive processing in more recent cognitive approaches to language, but arguably the concept is the same (see, Seth 2021).

Although Sinclair's notion of prospection arose purely from contemplating discourse theoretically, independent developments in experimental cognitive linguistics and cognitive neuroscience emphasise similar activity in brain functioning. In these fields, processes of prediction and anticipation have surfaced at the centre of interest in recent years, although they have paid little attention to authentic natural language. Many neuroscientists now emphasise the proactive nature of the brain (e.g. Friston 2010; Willems 2015; Northoff 2018; Buszáki 2019), meaning that the brain reaches out to predict, to anticipate, and to test hypotheses, instead of being essentially a reactive organ that solely responds to external stimuli, as it was largely depicted until quite recently. As Clark (2013) puts it: the brain is a prediction machine. Researchers talk about predictive processing (Friston 2010), or predictive coding, assuming that since the brain operates in uncertain conditions, it is likely to maintain probabilistic models of environment, updating them on the basis of sensory information (Hari et al 2015:183). This probabilistic view of prediction falls particularly well in line with the notion of prospection. Interestingly, it has recently been shown to be a relevant concept to language processing. Heilbron et al.(2022) showed that the brain spontaneously predicts upcoming language at multiple levels of abstraction. Although their data was read-aloud text, it gives a fair indication that processing authentic speech may be similar.

Anticipation and prediction are thus well-established perceptual processes, but the predominant research interest in the cognitive and neurolinguistic study of language has been restricted to very small units (phoneme, word, syntactic structure) in constructed examples, and until recently, continuous language or natural language use has been dismissed out of bounds. It seems, however, that in processing conceptual stimuli, including continuous events, humans are likely to rely on top-down, or predictive, processing that integrates the representation of the current event with previously stored knowledge (Kurby & Zacks 2008), and recent studies of more naturalistic, continuous discourses such as narratives, have provided evidence of the brain's predictive activity under continuous language comprehension (e.g. Willems et al. 2015), for example by relying on situation models similar to those in processing continuous event stimuli (Kurby & Zacks 2015). *Situation model* is a term typically used in reading research (Sandford & Garrod 1981; Van Dijk& Kintsch 1983) and recently also applied to dialogues by Pickering and Garrod (2021) and is essentially coextensive with *event model* (Radvansky & Zacks 2014). I shall mostly employ the term situation model in this book, because it fits both dialogue and monologue.

These lines of research resonate also very well with for example Chafe's pioneering work (e.g. 1994, 1998[2014], 2018) analysing discourse from a cognitive viewpoint, but once again, there is surprisingly little interconnection between experimental cognitive neuroscience and recent developments in linguistics, with few exceptions, such as Tomasello's (2014) "cognitive-functional perspective" (see also papers in Tomasello 1998[2014], 2003[2014]). Metadiscourse is of course consonant with the processes of anticipation and prediction, as one of its generally recognised functions is to provide explicit clues about how the current holder of the floor envisages the discourse moving on. Characteristically it performs communicative acts that set up expectations of what is going to happen next in the discourse (*I'm going to talk about . . .*). These contribute to recipients' predictive processing, their hypotheses about which way the discourse is moving. Much of processing consists in confirming hypotheses – or discarding them, in which case we need to update our event or situation models (e.g. Radvansky & Zacks 2014; Pickering & Garrod 2021). It is likely that metadiscourse supports the formation of felicitous predictions and pertinent situation models.

Metadiscourse can also serve for example to confirm readers' or hearers' interpretations of what has passed (*as I said*) as one of its roles in the communicative dynamism of language interaction. Moreover, it involves a perceptible element of planning. Planning, again, is a particularly pronounced cognitive activity in human behaviour (e.g. Radvansky & Zacks 2014: 169) compared to other species. Among other things, it includes breaking down larger goals into smaller sections, which has also been evinced in metadiscourse research (see also Chapter 7).

2.4 The active reader

Let us now return to written text and the role of the reader for a moment, to address the role of the reader in relation to discourse reflexivity as anticipated in Section 2.2.1. A corollary of predictive discourse processing is that we must assume reading is a proactive process like listening. Adopting this active predictive conceptualisation would require a change of viewpoint in typical metadiscourse research, where the presumed reader-writer interaction in effect stays entirely in the writer's court, and the reader, by implication, is allocated a peripheral, receptive role. Research is heavily based towards the writer's use of metadiscourse while the reader's uptake is usually simply assumed.

If we wish to understand how texts mediate interaction and how metadiscourse comes into the process, we must adjust our models of both text and the interactive process. For text, it is essential to acknowledge the complexity of interpretation and the multiple levels at which we accomplish it, instead of simply positing the existence of metadiscourse and 'the rest'. I see no major principled disagreement about this in the research community, but a more nuanced understanding of what role metadiscourse plays in text requires more serious thought than a cursory reference to holistic meaning or an unsupported prioritisation of metadiscourse as the principal or even sole carrier of the interactional potential of text (note that throughout this book, I am not making the distinction between 'interactive' and 'interactional' that Thompson (2001) makes, though relevant to written monologue, because my main focus is on speaking). Metadiscourse must eventually be seen in the context of other textual means that writers employ to influence, convince, or relate to their readers. For the interactive process, a deeper understanding of the interaction between readers and writers and the various means that affect readers requires rethinking the reader's role. Hitherto, the reader has not only remained an imaginary creature, but also been assigned a perplexingly reactive, almost passive role in the literature. Metadiscourse is generally conceptualised as the writer facilitating the reader's task: helping, assisting, guiding the reader. While all this may well take place, such a view also entails a reader who is constructed as somewhat helpless without explicit guidance from the writer, thus essentially reactive. What comes across is a kind of 'needy reader'.

The alternative is to posit an *active reader*. If we do this, then other clues in the text besides metadiscourse are potentially equally – or more – relevant to the reader. This is also in line with current neuroscientific research. Assuming an active reader shifts our angle and necessitates reconsidering the place of metadiscourse relative to the whole text and invites us to revise our current models accordingly. For one thing, such revision would lead the way towards more reader-oriented metadiscourse research by adding the reader's perspective to the much-investigated writer's perspective. For investigating the writer's activity, the implication is that in principle any means of organising or patterning discourse can be taken to manifest recipient design or interactionality, which the active reader may or may not engage with.

The active reader (or their brain), then, seeks out multitudinous clues in the text in order to reduce uncertainty and prospect ahead in anticipation of what is likely to follow. For proficient readers this will be successful most of the time. Fluent reading consists largely in confirming hypotheses based on the evolving representation of the text in the reader's situation model. Surprises also occur: the text can contradict the reader's expectation and necessitate immediate updating of the representation. Surprises momentarily raise the cognitive load (e.g. Frank 2013), but can also be pleasurable, as in reading fiction. It is not self-evident that maximal guidance is the optimal solution for the reader.

One of the assumptions often made in text analyses is that readers expect point-to-point signalling, for example with metadiscourse, of how the text is going, or what the argument is. Actual readers may not, however, read all of the text, let alone in the order in which it is presented, but often simply look for something specific, and then move on to other texts (e,g, Edge 1986). This is, of course, quite common with academic texts. They may also abandon reading in the middle if they realise they are not members of the intended audience, or if they disagree with the premises, the viewpoint, or the argument. Altogether, as Hoey (2001) points out, texts gain their meaning from readers' interactions with them. In this sense, the reader is as important to the text and successful interaction as the writer.

2.5 Interaction and the concept of metadiscourse

From the position of the writer, the reader of a published text (as opposed to, say, a personal letter or text message) is of course an imagined reader, or an implied reader. This is the case in Hyland's conception of metadiscourse, even though the cornerstone of his model is "writer-reader interaction". It would seem to be something of a misnomer, being more like writer-*to*-reader interactive signalling. Hyland is well aware of the reader's position as the writer's construction but supports his notion of interaction by arguing that the writer constructs their awareness of the audience in a relevant way based on their previous knowledge of similar texts and circumstances (e.g. Hyland 2005:12). While it is reasonable to argue that such audience awareness lies behind recipient design when speakers or writers shape their discourse, it is less reasonable to predicate actual interaction on one party alone.

The lack of bidirectionality is an important issue: to what extent can we postulate interactionality in communication if our knowledge about the uptake is missing, and one of the parties not only silent but unknown? One answer is to pin it onto recipient design, like Hyland (2005). Recipient design is central to other accounts of interaction and communication, and it is posited as a universal of language use in conversation analysis and interactional linguistics. Couper-Kuhlen and Selting (2018) point out that it is not limited to the most evident expressions like those referring to person, place, and time (e.g. Sacks & Schegloff 1974), but "present in all linguistic forms for building turns and implementing actions in talk-in-interaction." (Couper-Kuhlen & Selting 2018: 554). Seen in this light, recipient design implies a holistic approach to text: while it is possible to identify specific elements with particular functions, the whole act or its total effect emerges from their complex interactions. Recipient design is also recognised as an aspect of interaction in cognitive neuroscience of language. For example, Baggio (2018: 214) describes it as adaptive signalling behaviour on the part of the sender, or mentalising (Baggio 2018: 237), that is, forming an idea about what the receiver does or does not know. As an umbrella term for this activity, we can talk about the *theory of mind* that a speaker or writer forms about what their audience has in mind, knows, or does not know. In terms of both cognitive neuroscience and interactional linguistics recipient design can be seen as a facet of ongoing social interaction with co-present interlocutors, "the particular other(s) who are the co-participants," as Sacks & Schegloff (1974) put it.

Of course, it is possible to extend the notion metaphorically to a collective, imagined recipient as in writer-to-reader interaction, perhaps along the lines of Goffman's (1981) 'bystanders', but the nature of this latter, unidirectional interaction, is dramatically different from one where two or more parties relate to each other alternating in the roles of speaker and hearer. Moreover, non-verbal cues from listeners are available to speakers even in monologic situations (see Chapter 7). The speaker's theory of mind about their hearer(s) can therefore continuously adapt to the dynamically unfolding situation, which is of course inaccessible to a writer.

If we cannot reduce writer-to-reader interaction to metadiscourse but have to recognize a plethora of linguistic phenomena involved in bringing it about, then investigating this interaction exclusively through metadiscourse, however broadly defined, becomes restrictive. Alternatively, if we broaden the scope of metadiscourse to include all possible interactionality in text, the concept becomes either empty or redundant, because we could just as well say that we investigate writer-to-reader interaction mediated by text. Even if we should add a reader perspective onto the research agenda, it is still asymmetrical as well as asynchronous: the actual readers are not the ones the writer envisages, and the processes of composing and reading are separated in time.

Metadiscourse does not, then, equal interactionality in writing, because it covers too little, and is therefore too narrow. To say something meaningful about explicit (usually forward-looking) metadiscoursive commentary on the text, the comprehensive conceptualisations of Crismore, Vande Kopple, Hyland etc. are too broad. If we want to capture the particular kind of contribution that is conveyed through the self-commentary of text to its interactionality, we have to define it more precisely. For this purpose, the concept of discourse reflexivity is more appropriate. It is better suited for grasping a specific facet of discourse – its capacity for reflexivity – than a broader, unfocused one, which nevertheless ignores much of the interactive potential that language bestows.

The broad notion of metadiscourse is also problematic in that unlike reflexivity, it does not stand in a 'meta' relation to the discourse, that is, it is not about the ongoing discourse in a way that is analogous to how metacognition or metamemory relate to cognition and memory. If we consider discourse elements like hedges, boosters, and attitude markers, they can certainly be conceived as interactional, but not reflexive in the 'meta' sense. Finally, the broad notion misses out on the complex interactions between elements of different kinds, that is, effects that interactionally relevant text elements can adopt in combining with each other. For example, hedges tend to co-occur with metadiscourse (Mauranen 2001). This is intriguing, because metadiscourse arguably narrows down interpretation options for the reader or listener (Mauranen 2001) to the point of expressing speaker dominance (McKeown & Ladegaard 2020), while hedges convey epistemic openness (e.g. Mauranen 1997; Hyland 2005). Lumping together too much in a single concept thus leads to a failure to perceive interrelationships between different interactionally relevant elements, while there is the possibility of unintentionally excluding those elements that are not regarded as part of metadiscourse. As we saw in 2.2.1, numerous textual elements and properties have been discovered that can reasonably be regarded as relevant to writer-to-reader interaction, but which are not in a meta relationship to the rest of the text.

The idea of depicting the written text as far more rhetorical and interactional than previously thought was a major step forward in the early 1990s, inspired by a shift in linguists' attention towards speaking and spoken interaction over the previous couple of decades. This was part of a general 'interpersonal turn' in applied linguistics. In studies of research-related texts, which was common in metadiscourse scholarship, a further source of inspiration came from the revolutionary ideas put forward in the new approach to science studies: the sociology of science (Gilbert & Mulkay 1984; Latour & Woolgar 1986). This new discipline challenged the traditional fields of the philosophy of science and the history of science, which had largely sustained the idea of science being pursued almost untouched by the human hand. Now research was scrutinised in the daily toil of researchers and research publications were viewed through the lens of rhetoric, persuasion, and audience awareness. The shift of perspective was substantial in applied linguistics, too, but analysing written text from a more interpersonal angle overlooked some essential limitations that follow from exclusively attending to the written medium.

Clearly, we must assume all communication is interactional, because without interaction there would be no communication or even a need for it. If utterances are not taken up, they do not communicate, however skilfully formulated. Interaction is fundamental to all human language use and meaning is co-constructed by communicating parties. So far speaking and writing are alike. However, while spoken interaction negotiates meanings between co-present participants, writers and readers are separated from each other, and the interaction is in a significant way disembodied and unidirectional: writers do not know how, when, where, or whether their text will be read and what meanings may be made of it. Readers make their own meanings from the text, but the outcome is not negotiable with the writer, who will by and large not be aware of readers' reactions. The writer can construct a target recipient in their mind, and the text may imply one, but the actual readers of a text cannot be conjured up by the author's imagination.

They may be unexpected, outside the intended audience, located anywhere, and are inevitably removed from the author in time.

Time on shorter scales also constitutes a relevant difference between the spoken and the written medium. Temporal rhythms in co-present social interaction and written communication are substantially dissimilar: while face-to-face interaction unfolds in hundreds of milliseconds, written communication proceeds in seconds or more (Hari et al 2015). If we add to this the larger scale asynchrony of written communication, the temporal discrepancy between the two modes of communication gets even more striking. There are thus severe limitations to writer-to-reader interaction: the disembodied nature of the communication, the lack of bidirectionality, the discrepancy between imagined and actual readers, and the temporal mismatch.

2.6 Monologue and dialogue

The considerations of linguistic and cognitive factors hitherto point towards the possibility that not only writing and speaking, but also monologue and dialogue present seriously different challenges and affordances to discourse reflexivity. They have important contrasting characteristics (e.g. Chafe 2018). 'Dialogue' in the present context is used as an umbrella term, subsuming dyadic as well as polyadic spoken interaction. Human language emerges from dialogue, that is, verbal interaction in the first place: N. Lee et al (2009) talk about the *interactional instinct*, which Tomasello (2003, 2014) assigns to an innate drive to communicate. Thus, spoken interaction is where language originated for the species and where it originates for every individual. *Mutatis mutandis*, the same applies to interactive sign language. This central position of dialogue in shaping language and social interaction was the point of departure for conversation analysis in the 1970s and more recent thinking along similar lines has sparked off fresh theoretical and empirical approaches in many other strands of linguistic research, such as dynamic systems theory (N. Lee et al 2009), usage-based linguistics (Du Bois 2014), and construction grammar (Goldberg 2019). The notion of 'distributed cognition' (Clark 1997) is also readily applicable to dialogic interaction, since "interactive language use is 'distributed cognition' par excellence" as Levinson (2013: 158) puts it.

In usage-based linguistics the dialogic turn has meant for example conceptualising linguistic constructions as by-products of ongoing dialogic interaction: interlocutors cooperate to achieve intersubjectivity and produce linguistic functions and forms in joint activity. Importantly, alignment and priming are crucial components of the joint construction of linguistic expressions and meanings (Pickering & Garrod 2021; Tantucci 2021; Tantucci & Wang 2022). We can also envisage them as indicators of these processes.

As speakers engage with each other's talk, they mesh their own contributions into the evolving discourse, which progresses from its initial settings towards unforeseen outcomes. In this way, we can envision dialogic speech functioning as a dynamic complex system. The question for metadiscourse is how, if at all, it participates in such co-construction of linguistic form, function, and meaning.

First engaging with dialogic data in the then incipient MICASE corpus, I observed that uses of discourse reflexivity went beyond those familiar from written discourse, and I divided the principal ones in terms of *targeting*, i.e., whose discourse they seemed to be talking about or aiming at (Mauranen 2021b). The tentative labels *reflexive, dialogic*, and *interactive* were perhaps not the most fortunate, but the attempted distinctions hold up reasonably well (see Chapter 4 for elaboration).

Long conversational turns can occasionally acquire monologic characteristics, but in academic discourses monologues and dialogues tend to be kept apart by genre conventions. For monologues, the speaker has normally prepared for an extended delivery, and others are restrained from taking the floor during the presentation. The speaker's challenge is to keep listeners interested, sufficiently updated, and reminded of the goals of the presentation as well as how what is being said at a given moment fits into the whole and is relevant to it. This can include reminders or brief summaries at interim stages, to maintain listeners' interest and signpost their navigation through the course of the speaker's delivery. The listeners, in turn, predict the continuation of the delivery by all available means, many of which overlap with those used in reading, but where paralinguistic means like prosody, gestures, or voice quality not only substitute some written text devices like punctuation, but add to and modulate the meanings that can be constructed from the talk. Sustained attention during listening to long monologues is an arduous task and augments the listener's cognitive load.

Temporality functions differently from the written mode, since references to previous stages of the discourse cannot be retrieved verbatim unless very recent (up to about 10 seconds ago), and there is no going back: new speech is continually streaming in, replacing the previously heard. By contrast, in dialogic interaction the roles of speaker and hearer keep alternating, and each participant may find themselves occupying either role in rapid succession. From a neuroscientific viewpoint, Hari and her associates emphasise the swift pace of interaction, which includes temporal overlap:

> True social interaction occurs at a fast pace and the responses can overlap in time. Examples include the very quick turn-taking during conversation and the unconscious mutual adaptation during a joint motor task, such as carrying a big heavy object. (Hari et al. 2015: 185).

In embodied interaction individuals communicate not only with language, but through paralinguistic means like prosody and multiplex nonverbal ways such as facial expressions, gestures, and glances. We even respond to our interlocutor's blinks quite sensitively, as neurocognitive processing reveals (Mandel et al. 2015).

Mutual expectations in spoken interaction require constant updating for effective functioning. Mercier and Sperber (2017) approach updating from the angle of the characteristic flexibility and creativity of humans in their coordination activities. These properties enable the fine-grained coordination that underlies the multifarious forms of cooperation. To achieve this, mutual expectations must be constantly updated so that they remain reliable (see also Hari et al. 2015; Pickering & Garrod 2021). Pickering and Garrod (2021) argue that interlocutors' representations of the language as well as the situation must be aligned for successful dialogue. If this be the case, both parties need rapid updates of the discourse at all levels as it develops.

If we think of a context like academic discussion, which can be cognitively quite demanding to follow or participate in, we see a prime example of discourse in need of constant updates. The processes can be particularly complex in the polylogues that academic discussions typically are, with or without regulated turn-taking. In unregulated turn-taking, like everyday conversations or informal discussions, participants attend to the interaction itself simultaneously with incrementing shared experience, to keep the conversation going, and to follow or initiate new directions as the need or opportunity arises. Regulated turn-taking, like in moderated conference discussions, does not necessarily lighten the participants' cognitive load: prospective speakers will have to wait for their turn while simultaneously attending to the intervening speakers so as to fit in their own turns with not only what they originally had in mind but also with what has occurred between that point and their turn to speak. For this, they must attend to the twists and turns in the interaction more intensely than when listening to extended monologue.

Any means of facilitating this complex processing and updating are eagerly taken hold of. As discussed, language has many means of making this happen. Among them, reflexive metadiscourse is a good candidate for managing ongoing updates by relating the current state of the discourse to what has preceded and what is likely to follow. It is the current speaker who articulates reflexivity, but it is their interlocutors who update and adjust their expectations to align with the speaker's reflexive remarks. In other words, speakers make prospections and hearers make predictions. At the same time, it is possible that discourse reflexivity may also help speakers themselves to stay on course, by punctuating longer stretches of speech, as self-reminders of where the argument is heading, or perhaps playing for time at difficult junctures.

Academic discussions may be particularly demanding for rapidly updating situation models. They are unpredictable like any discussions, in addition to which they have specific properties, including co-constructing knowledge by bringing together different findings, interpretations, and viewpoints. This incorporates offering and seeking clarifications, showing respect to other viewpoints while holding one's ground, and seeking to resolve mismatches and conflicting evidence or interpretations while presenting one's position as consistent: in short, negotiating perspectives.

In brief, then, spoken interaction is embodied, very fast, and a joint achievement of co-present participants. We may reasonably expect that it offers such roles for discourse reflexivity as may not be evident in monologues, be they written or spoken.

If we accept that spoken interaction is fundamental to human language and substantially different from writing, is this not something that has been well known and thoroughly studied in linguistics for a few decades now? There is no shortage of research into dialogue and social interaction. An abundance of studies has been and is being devoted to the progression and contingencies of conversation, while the roles of repetitions, repairs, particles, structures, and a myriad of constructions are being scrutinized in a vast number of languages and in an enormous range of contexts. We are learning that nonverbal signalling like blinks have interactional significance (Mandel et al. 2015), as do phenomena on the borderlines of the verbal and the nonverbal like hesitation markers (Clark & Fox Tree 2002). There is, however, a notable gap: metadiscourse has not been investigated in dialogic discourse, with a mere handful of exceptions, as we saw in Chapter 1. There is thus a huge space to be explored of discourse reflexivity in interaction.

2.7 What discourse reflexivity includes

At his point, operationalising the notion of discourse reflexivity in dialogic interaction is in order. The analyses in the chapters that follow will show how it works, but to go about the analyses, a baseline is needed to pin down the phenomenon that will be observed in different types of events. At this stage the question is, then: what goes into discourse reflexivity? A complete model or a full taxonomy of reflexive expressions is not attempted, first of all because it is not possible even in principle to provide an exhaustive list of all language that can be used in a discourse reflexive function. Importantly, this is unlikely to be the case with any linguistic phenomenon because linguistic categories are inherently fuzzy, which analysts of natural language must take into their stride. The crucial matter in exploring discourse manifestations of a category that is definable and identifiable at an abstract level is to prioritise the search for prototypical cases (Rosch 1978) instead of seeking to satisfy the formal rules of classical categorisation and focus on the necessary and sufficient features that determine sharp boundaries. For metadiscourse specifically, it is generally agreed that is not reducible to a closed class of expressions but is inherently context-dependent (e.g. Mauranen 1993a; Hyland 2005, 2017; Ädel 2006; McKeown & Ladegaard 2020; Zhang 2022).

The second reason for not attempting even a rough taxonomy let alone an exhaustive list in this chapter is that my analytical approach is exploratory and data-driven, and therefore proceeds from the bottom up: categorisation develops reflecting the data. The material that I use is selected for exploratory research, for capturing different uses in different kinds of discourse – spoken and written dialogue, spoken monologue – and is therefore not suitable for imposing an a priori taxonomy. An exploratory approach is motivated by the novelty of the topic area.

Previous research on spoken metadiscourse has, understandably, largely resorted to writing-based categorisations, because it has mainly investigated monologues. It has nevertheless provided interesting insights into the divergent weighting that categories adopt under varying circumstances of speaking. Most studies of monologic speech add some subcategories of their own, even though overall, the research has not come up with many entirely novel categories. By contrast, what I want to do here is to start from the pivotal data, spoken interaction, derive tentative categories from its analysis, and compare it to other datasets adjusting the categories to fit the new samples as the need arises. The data selection and more detail about the analytic procedures are discussed in Chapter 3, and an overview of the major categories in the whole data with cross-sample comparisons is drawn together towards the end of the book (Chapter 8). At this point, I am setting the scene by a general outline of what is included and what is ruled out.

Discourse reflexivity, then, addresses the ways in which elements of discourse are used for talking about the discourse that is currently unfolding. The conceptualisation rules out metalanguage about discourses other than the ongoing discourse and corresponds to the reflexive model of metadiscourse (see, Mauranen 1993a, 2010, 2012; Ädel 2006, 2010; Smart 2016; McKeown & Ladegaard 2020; Zhang 2022). In contrast to my own earlier operationalisation of the concept (Mauranen 1993a), the present framework excludes instances of 'low explicitness' such as conjunctions even if their scope extends beyond sentence boundaries, as well as instances of writer-reader or speaker-audience interaction that do not clearly contain an explicit reference to the discourse *qua* discourse, that is, unless in Ädel's terms, the action is "carried out within the world of discourse" (Ädel 2006:30). Both subtypes are similarly excluded in Smart (2016). Moreover, the distinction between high and low explicitness may not have been very felicitous to begin with (see also a recent critique of its questionable applicability to speech in McKeown & Ladegaard 2020), and I would rather talk about reflexive items in terms of their relative context-dependence.

The point of departure is, then, the reflexive approach to metadiscourse, as explained above in Section 2.2 (in contrast to the 'broad' view, see Section 2.5): discourse about the current discourse. 'Current discourse' in the prototypical case means a continuous speech event with a beginning and an end. Since many academic events have a composite or chain-like character, which maintain manifest continuity despite temporal distribution over smaller sub-events, they can arguably be seen to constitute one *macro-event*. On this basis they can be regarded as shared experience by participants in the event incorporating the current moment of speaking, and we can assume that material from these events are incorporated in the participants long-term working memory in a similar way that such material works in reading long texts (see, e.g. Ericsson & Kintsch 1995). Typical macro-events would be conferences or conference sections, term-length university courses, or Internet discussion threads (see Chapter 3 for more detail). Clearly, the participants in macro-events may in reality vary to some degree, but the default is that they remain constant (see Chapter 5).

The domain of discourse reflexivity is thus bounded by time and continuity. Metalinguistic references made to the present discourse fall within it, while those made to non-present discourses remain outside (Figure 2.1).

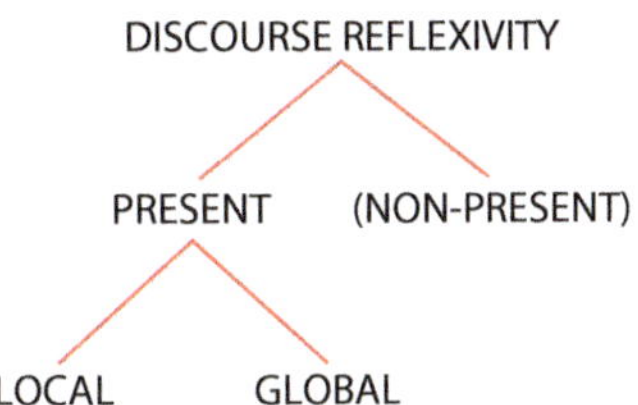

Figure 2.1: Discourse reflexivity as discourse about the ongoing discourse.

Example (2.1) illustrates the principal distinction. *I say this* encapsulates the speaker's (or, in this case the blogger's) previous several sentences, and is unmistakably about the ongoing discourse, while *the discussion* refers to non-present (*many high-traffic sites*) discourses.

(2.1) ***I say this*** without fear of being crucified by my LHC colleagues, since *the discussion* has been raging on many high-traffic sites for a while.

Within a discourse event's bounds, we can discern varying timescales ranging from different parts of a macro-event ***(the last presentation** on on **on Tuesday er we heard** that there's still a very strong fixation in the region*) to event- or sub-event internal, shorter timescales. These can anticipate local or immediate continuation (*I just like to make a brief comment on this***)** or longer-term, global prediction (*my talk is going to be on women and politics in Iran*). In principle these are further divisible along finer scales, as it seems that speakers can fine-tune the span of their reflexive comments quite flexibly (see Chapter 7). Local and global reflexive expressions can appear alongside each other in longer discussion turns or monologic presentations, where multi-span structuring supports coherence and clarity, much in the way similar devices work in written text. But they can also structure dialogic event types. For example, some PhD examiners like to explain their overall plan before starting (2.2) and as the examination progresses, provide more local indicators of how the discourse is moving along its path (*yes and now we come to the the really difficult questions*). Structuring of this kind is reminiscent of what we are used to seeing in written texts, for example towards the end of research article introductions.

(2.2) <S3> . . . *we start erm with* the central questions . . . *then* that *in the second step we discuss* the theoretical framework *then in the third step we discuss* the methodological approach . . . and *then we we finish* with er part four which is erm a discussion on the findings and the conclusions . . . </S3>

How do we recognise a discourse reflexive expression when we see one? While some expressions seem immediately identifiable as reflexive wherever they appear, with others, making them out is less straightforward. Overall, longer utterances tend to make their reflexive import fairly clear (***here we are discussing** a missing link; this is **as I've already pointed out** an issue which . . .*). However, identifiability can hinge upon the effect of an individual item within the broader co-text (DISCUSS; LECTURE). Some items are relatively context-independent or *context-creating* and play a key role in their immediate environment for providing clues to meaning-making. Typical examples of discourse reflexive verbs would be SAY, SPEAK, MENTION, TELL, TALK, ASK, ANSWER, COMMENT, CLARIFY, REFER, DISCUSS, or LISTEN. Typical nouns include QUESTION, COMMENT, PRESENTATION, LECTURE, SPEAKER, DEBATE, or TERM. That said, it will not take long for anyone to find counterexamples where any of these items are used in a non-reflexive manner. Their contrast to highly *context-dependent* items is nevertheless clear: some items, especially verbs known as 'light' verbs can be reflexive in co-text, but on their own will not contain much that would help construct reflexive meaning. Their contribution overall to meaning construction is slight: verbs like GO, COME, GET, PUT, HAVE, TAKE, or

GIVE do not give much indication of how to interpret them, but *get the point, have a question,* or *put it this way* already do. Some nouns show similar characteristics (THING, POINT). On the whole, the import of individual elements in longer expressions which function as one unit is best viewed as a cline, where the end points are most clearly seen in verbs such as SPEAK, ASK, or ANSWER at one end, and light verbs like HAVE, GET, or GO at the other, but where most items (FOCUS, MEAN, DEFEND, ADD, or EMPHASISE, for example) fall in between.

Thus, even though it is possible to enumerate a small set of individual items that are particularly likely to signal discourse reflexivity, in an overwhelming majority of instances it is longer, multi-word units, clauses, sentences and beyond, which more reliably indicate discourse reflexive functions. Even typical context-creating items depend to some degree on their co-text for their interpretation. It is therefore vital not to rely on decontextualised items for analysing reflexive discourse. As we argue with Ädel (Ädel & Mauranen 2010, see also Chapter 3), how we approach context is a crucial dividing line between 'thin' and 'thick' approaches to metadiscourse. A thin approach, which begins from a set of potential metadiscoursal items, has been defended on the grounds that an initial search for potential items can be manually weeded out afterwards by contextual cues. This can work well for context-creating items, but the further we go towards context-dependent items, not to speak of rare and innovative expressions, the more unattainable the goal becomes. In line with the thick approach, the point of departure in this book is qualitative and context-sensitive in analyses and category formation.

Context-dependence renders discourse reflexivity somewhat blurred on the edges, but fuzziness in the sense of incomplete determinacy is the rule rather than the exception in language as already discussed. Moreover, expressions can play multiple roles and flip across boundaries. Speakers apply their language resources creatively, which implies that categorisation in natural language must allow the possibility of category flipping.

Moreover, for reflexive metadiscourse, inherent fuzziness is not limited to context-dependence or category flipping. A phenomenon worth noting is what Smart (2016: 229) discusses as "pragmatic reorientation" (Butler 2008) whereby the pragmatic function of a semifixed phrase such as *it's possible to say* gets to overshadow the original literal discourse reflexive meaning. Its interpretation as an instance of discourse reflexivity is therefore not straightforward, despite the presence of a strong cue in the typically context-creating *say*. What we see here is a process of language change whereby items undergo semantic bleaching (Hopper & Traugott 2003) or *delexicalisation*, which also relate to Sinclair's late work on 'meaning-shift' (e.g. 2007; Cheng et al. 2009). The process of delexicalisation is developed in detail in Vetchinnikova (2019: 212–216) as one where words through frequent co-occurrence get associated with a specific communicative function. In this process, the individual words start losing their core meanings and adopt the role of one holistic 'meaning-shift unit' (Cheng et al. 2009). How this relates to borderlines in discourse reflexivity can be illustrated by considering example 2.3 where SAY THAT is used three times.

(2.3) . . . did I understand you correctly when *you said that* . . . then *one can say that* Russia is a kind of unitary actor is it is it true er maybe *maybe you can say something more about that*

The first instance (*when* ***you said*** *that*) is undoubtedly discourse reflexive, as is the final one (*maybe* ***you can say something*** *more about that*). Both refer to the discourse at hand, and a co-present addressee. The middle one, however, (***one can say*** *that*) is less clear, because it is a fixed multiword unit similar to *it is possible to say* and has undergone a measure of delexicalization. The reference in both cases is to a generic or abstract entity, which can be seen as resulting from a depersonalisation process. Whether we regard *one can say* as discourse reflexive is an analyst's decision, and likely to be made differently by different analysts – even differently by the same analyst in different contexts. The reference is not explicitly to the current discourse, but it does mark the onset of a general statement within the ongoing discourse, and thus feeds into prospection, at the same time indicating the discourse function of the upcoming statement as the speaker's assessment of the state of affairs (as opposed to, say, a statement of fact). In this context, even though it is in the middle of a longer discourse reflexive utterance, I am inclined not to regard it as discourse reflexive, but I can see that another interpretation could also be defended.

In addition to delexicalization, a similar, if seemingly reverse process is in evidence on the borderlines of discourse reflexivity, namely *relexicalization*. In this process, a multi-word unit that has become to be associated with one holistic meaning with its parts semantically bleached, is broken down so that the constituent parts of the unit are used as independent items with their individual senses. Relexicalisation has been observed in ELF writing by Vetchinnikova (2019), and earlier in ENL by Partington (2006), who shows how it is used for humorous effect. Along similar lines, Pitzl (2015) talks about creative 're-metaphorization' in ELF. But if exploiting relexicalization for humorous effect is deliberate, both Vetchinnikova (2019) and Pitzl (2015) note that relexicalisation or re-metaphorization can also take place unconsciously, and that this is what seems to be happening in ELF contexts. To complicate matters further, delexicalization and relexicalization are tendencies rather than fully fixed phenomena and appear mostly as preferences (or dispreferences) for a whole with a given sense. If we take a frequent fixed expression like *generally speaking*, which usually means that a statement holds at an abstract level, disregarding particulars or exceptions, its frame *-ly speaking* can also be adopted for productive use. The productive option is not very common, but in ELF contexts speakers seem to exploit the possibility fairly freely (e.g. *historically/ linguistically/ legally/ formally speaking*) without showing a clear preference for *general* in the frame (Mauranen 2012). Nevertheless, most linguistic processes take place in the same way whether speakers are using their first or their additional languages. Thus, we can also detect collective fixing (see Vetchinnikova 2014) on certain novel preferences in ELF, for instance *(saying) some words about X* instead of *(saying) a few words about X* (Mauranen 2012).

Altogether, then, fluctuating processes of change, such as delexicalization and relexicalization, are constantly going on in language, facets of its indeterminacy. The ensuing ambiguity with regard to interpreting specific instances as discourse reflexive or too much semantically bleached, or too unusual, does not, however, shatter all boundaries in metadiscourse any more than other manifestations of the inherent fuzziness of linguistic categories do; it is the prototypical instances that matter most. Certain boundaries are more determined than others, but hardly any are absolute. For example, references to non-present discourses are out of bounds for reflexive discourse, but there are situations where this is difficult to determine. What we should take away from this is that we should indeed take context seriously and approach large-scale quantitative findings and inter-study comparisons with some caution. Additionally, most analyses even on a smaller scale contain some measure of inaccuracy.

2.8 Conclusion

This chapter has outlined the concept of discourse reflexivity adopted in this book. The term discourse reflexivity has been used in part synonymously to the term metadiscourse, but where it has been deemed necessary to make a distinction between broader, and in my view less motivated usages of the latter term, discourse reflexivity or reflexive discourse have deliberately been chosen to refer specifically to discourse about the ongoing discourse. Reflexive discourse was further contrasted to metalanguage, which also talks about language, but in the sense of referring to 'language objects' outside the current discourse.

The specific contribution of discourse reflexivity, or metadiscourse, to speech and writing was discussed in relation to other linguistic cues that also provide stimuli for anticipating what is to come in the discourse. It was noted that a myriad of clues has been identified in both conversation and written text that help communicating parties make sense of what they read or hear, and that meanings arise from communicative collaboration as co-constructed by participants. There is thus no opposition between metadiscourse and the rest of the text, often somewhat misleadingly conceptualised as the propositional content, because discourse is a holistic entity where complex interactions of a plethora of elements come together in sophisticated collaborative meaning making. Discourse reflexivity is one among them. Discourse, including reflexive metadiscourse, works at all levels of language.

To capture the specific contribution that reflexive discourse can make to the ongoing discourse, it was necessary to consider cognitive processing. Readers and listeners come to discourses with expectations that build upon their accumulated experience and the context in which the discourse takes place. They take an active role in making sense of the discourse, with prediction as a key concept in the process. Predicting ahead (or anticipating, projecting) is what readers and hearers engage in, making probabilistic guesses amongst all the uncertainties of linguistic communication about what is likely to follow. The predictions may or may not be confirmed and need to be frequently updated. Altogether, the picture emerges of a dynamic process which requires active participation of all communicating parties. Discourse reflexivity contributes to generating expectations of what is likely to follow, how it is meant to be taken, and confirming or altering predictions.

Interaction has been a basic notion in metadiscourse studies throughout, and of course there is no communication without interaction. This chapter raised questions about the usefulness of positing metadiscourse as essentially writer-reader interaction because written communication is asynchronous, disembodied, and unidirectional. Authors may envision a target audience of their texts, but that need not be the actual audience. Moreover, readers do not participate in the interaction. In fact, we know very little about readers and metadiscourse. We should posit an active reader and re-orient attention from the exclusive interest in the text to find out more about what readers do with regard to metadiscourse.

Above all, metadiscourse research should also embrace spoken language more seriously. Not only do speech and writing differ on many vital accounts, but there is reason to believe that so do monologue and dialogue. Spoken interaction is co-present, embodied, and very fast. To get a grip on how metadiscourse is involved in typical bidirectional interaction, dialogic interaction must be taken on the agenda.

How discourse reflexivity is to be delimited for analysis hangs on the conceptualization of discourse reflexivity as discourse about the discourse it participates in and is constructing, in other words as part of the discourse that is currently being co-created by interacting parties. Reflexive discourse updates and changes the ongoing discourse with its specific contribution to predictions about the discourse ahead and interpretations and confirmations about its import up to the point of the utterance. It is important to bear in mind that reflexive discourse cannot be reduced to a closed class of expressions, because it is inherently context dependent. Some expressions are more readily recognizable as instances of reflexivity than others. The borderlines remain fuzzy on account of contextual interpretation and the continually changing nature of language, but prototypical cases of discourse reflexivity are identifiable and separable from those that are less typical, like for example metalinguistic or delexicalized expressions.

Chapter 3
Data and methods

Investigating discourse reflexivity in spoken interaction obviously requires data from dialogic speech. In addition, it is useful to compare the core material to datasets from related sources from suitably different angles so as to suggest how dialogic speech differs from for example monologic speech or dialogic writing. The source domain in all of the material remains constant and is rooted in academia. Academia has remained at the heart of the study of metadiscourse since its inception, and therefore provides a well-researched backdrop to the current inquiry. The furthest away from the core academic context that the material strays is to research blogs, which are on the borderlines of traditional academia, but increasingly a normal part of university and research group genres. Being longer and less ephemeral than the ubiquitous tweets, they offer a dialogic genre which resembles conversations within academia better.

The other important general point about the data is that it consists entirely of English, specifically of English used as a lingua franca (ELF). This reflects the reality of English use today when most of its speakers use it as an additional language and those who have it as their first language, or one of their first languages, also speak it with others than first-language speakers. In the academic domain English as a lingua franca is the dominant global language in publications (e.g. Lillis & Curry 2010; Hyland 2015), and equally in spoken language in the everyday work of research groups and international conferences (Franzmann, Jansen & Münte 2015), in student and staff exchanges, and international study programmes (Jenkins 2014; Wächter & Maiworm 2014; Jenkins & Mauranen 2019). The natural choice for exploring metadiscourse use in contemporary academic English speech is therefore ELF.

3.1 Corpora and event types

The data comes from two databases of contemporary academic English. As befits the current use of English in academia, both databases represent ELF: the ELFA corpus and the WrELFA corpus. Since the book is mainly about metadiscourse in speaking, the central source is ELFA, which is a speech corpus, and since the focus lies particularly on dialogue, WrELFA is drawn on for written dialogue to complement the picture and tease out possible indicators of 'dialogicality' independent of the medium. Both corpora are freely available for all research purposes. They are outlined broadly here, with details available on their websites (www.helsinki.fi/elfa).

https://doi.org/10.1515/9783110295498-003

3.1.1 Event types in ELFA

ELFA, the corpus of English as a Lingua Franca in Academic Settings, was compiled during 2001–2008, and comprises a million words of spoken English in university and conference contexts. It consists of academic speech events in four Finnish universities (the University of Helsinki, Tampere University, the Technological University of Helsinki, and the Technological University of Tampere), together with events from international conferences held in these universities. The discourses are weighted on dialogues so that dialogic events account for approximately two thirds of the events. Speakers come from 51 different first language backgrounds.

The corpus consists of speech events which represent what we might call 'folk genres', that is, event types labelled and defined by the members of the speech community themselves, such as 'seminar', 'lecture', 'symposium', 'thesis defence'. Similar terms are widely used across academic institutions. In compiling the corpus, prominence was given to event types that are widely shared and could thereby be regarded as prototypical academic speech genres. Data selection was based on 'external' criteria (Sinclair 2005), which reflect relevant social uses of language rather than language-internal ones. The only selection criterion that can be seen as linguistic is the strict requirement of authentic speech, that is, speech that has not been elicited for research purposes, but which has been recorded in its normal environment as unobtrusively as possible. No other linguistic criteria were applied in the selection, for example such that might concern register, correctness, or proficiency, for example.

The basic unit of sampling was 'speech event type', a term that was preferred to 'genre', because it is a looser concept, and more appropriate for a database where some discourses have a more firmly established status as genres (e.g. lectures) than others (e.g. panel discussions). Many event type labels are identical across most universities in the world ('seminar', 'lecture', supervision'), but what they actually mean or expect from their participants can vary widely according to their local contexts (e.g. Mauranen 1994). They may therefore not readily lend themselves to reliable comparisons in databases compiled in different contexts, but the ELFA corpus is compiled in Finnish universities with essentially uniform definitions of the genres.

International conference discourses also display diverse event types, but these would seem to follow the traditions of research fields and in this sense be more global than university discourses with their local flavours.

Some academic event types are one-off occasions, such as PhD defences, which, although common enough and closely regulated in their local contexts, occur independently of each other. More typically, though, many academic events follow the arrangement of interlinked components, for example in lecture series or seminar courses, or conferences that take place over several days. Lectures and seminars or tutorials may also be connected to each other so that for example lectures may act as input to seminar sessions. These various chainlike events represent a kind of *macro event* type, as already explained in Chapter 2. They are subject to further variations and divisions, so that for example conferences are typically subdivided according to their internal criteria, and fall into types like symposia, thematic sections, or panels within a larger conference. This means we have two kinds of macro-events: the conference, and the sections or strands within it. Thus, academia abounds with composite event types, and the corpus seeks to reflect this by including interrelated events such as macro-events of interconnected monologues (say, presentations in the same conference) and dialogues (the discussion section following presentations), whole thematic sections in a conference, or a few consecutive sessions in a seminar or lecture series.

In terms of disciplinary domains, a balance was sought between the major types of SSH and STEM areas, although it must be said that there is hardly a 'natural' balance that could easily be determined – should it reflect some aggregate global distribution of subjects in all institutes of higher education, for example, or the grand total of publications, or the overall amount of research actually carried out? In ELFA the shares are close to even, with Social Sciences and Humanities (SSH) covering 46% of all speech events, Science, Technology and Mathematics (STEM) 42%, and the remaining category of disciplinary areas that seem to fall between these in being divided between 'soft' and 'hard' paradigms, namely economics and administration, altogether 12%. The decision to aim for a relatively even balance between STEM and SSH is of course arbitrary in the absence of any obvious or straightforward criteria of what the balance should be. It is clear that STEM areas dominate globally in terms of numbers of publications, but if pages or words were counted, the picture might be different. In all, an even distribution would seem to be more relevant to linguistic research, but even that may be more of a convention than a reflection of the activities actually going on.

The corpus is deliberately biased towards the dialogic mode of speaking, which in practice means polylogue, since one-to-one sessions, for instance supervisions, are not included. Dialogic events account for 67% of all speech events and the remaining 33% represent the monologic mode. It should be noted that graduate seminars and PhD defences in the Finnish university system (as in many others) are predominantly dialogic, and together account for 53% of the data. This balances out some of the heavy monologic bias of conferences, where presentations tend to take up many times the number of minutes allocated to discussion time. The bias cannot entirely be overcome, and of course it also reflects the current reality of academia. The result is that although far more individual dialogic events were recorded, the total minutes of monologic speech and the total number of words in them were higher (see Section 3.2.5 below). Any event sampling from the corpus needs to take this into account.

3.1.2 Event types in WrELFA

It follows from the present focus on dialogues that the effect of the medium on dialogue becomes interesting: how does metadiscourse change, if at all, if we take written dialogues under scrutiny along with spoken? Written, digital dialogues have become a daily experience to us all over the last couple of decades. Linguistic scholars have shown lively research interest in various characteristics of digital dialogues, but they have not been included in most corpora, certainly not generally available reference corpora. Therefore, their import on register analyses (e.g. Biber & Conrad 2009; Zhang 2022) has been non-existent, although they are likely to have been part of the text mass in studies of Internet registers, which included blogs (e.g. Grieve & al. 2011). Moreover, digital dialogues have not been studied with metadiscourse in mind, apart from Smart's (2016) pioneering study on message board dialogues. For our present interests, the value of written digital dialogues lies in the light they may shed on discourse reflexivity in speech vs. writing

Thus, the written counterpart of ELFA, the WrELFA corpus, Written English as a Lingua Franca in Academic Settings was drawn on. It is the first corpus of written ELF, completed 2015 at the university of Helsinki, with 1.7 million words of written English as a Lingua Franca. This does not sound like a very large corpus if compared to other databases of written English, but since it is based on careful selection of lingua franca discourses in the academic domain, its strength lies in its representation of these written discourses in unedited form. Unedited texts are always hard to obtain, and the very large corpora of written texts, especially academic texts, tend to be based on published, thus edited material. For ELF writing, this would be particularly unhelpful, because only unedited texts give us access to the writers' original products.

The WrELFA compilation principles were also external and in general followed ELFA guidelines in all but the focus on dialogues, which, of course does not typify academic writing. There is, nevertheless, one section which includes dialogic academic writing: the research blog corpus. In all, WrELFA consists of three subcorpora:

(1) PhD examiner's reports
(2) Research blogs with their comment threads
(3) Academic research articles (the SciELF corpus)

Like ELFA, WrELFA represents both STEM and SSH fields, with as much of a balance between them as was feasible to obtain. The observations concerning the balance that were made in the previous section on ELFA are valid here as well. The objective was to capture both high-stakes genres and more relaxed ones for variability. PhD examiner's reports and research papers are both high-stakes event types, while blogs are less so. While examiner's reports are typically single-authored and by definition unedited by outsiders, research papers before any kind of language brokering are hard to find. The PhD examiners' reports are all from the University of Helsinki, where they range from three-four to 15 pages, and are not written to a strict format, even though they are to answer questions concerning the academic value and acceptability of the thesis. The point to note about them is that the process consists of two steps: pre-examination before the public defence of the thesis, where the examiner can ask for revisions and corrections, and which therefore tend to run into some detail and be fairly long, and the examiner's final report after the public examination, which tends to be much shorter, perhaps just one page. The examiner's reports collected for the corpus were of the former kind, that is, pre-examination reports. The other high stakes genre was the research article, and this subcorpus is an independent, self-standing part of the whole, the SciELF corpus, which was compiled as an international collaboration.

The blog subcorpus consists of blogs that are kept by researchers, not for example science journalists, and consists of the blogs themselves together with their comment threads. The blog comment threads are the only section of WrELFA used for this book. Comment threads are asynchronous dialogues, where each commenter's contributions come in at different times, and get interlaced in the discussion. When compiling the WrELFA corpus, we noticed what Mahrt & Puschmann (2014) had already pointed out: most research blogs do not receive any comments. Many attract only a handful. By contrast, some blog sites are lively discussion sites, and they can have long interlocking discussion threads where the discussants engage with each other's comments in addition to the blog. The corpus was compiled with the L1 status of the blogger in mind (no monolingual L1 English speakers), but obviously the commenters' L1 status cannot be ascertained, as they mostly write under pseudonyms, and rarely make references to their first languages unless they write in a second language. The language backgrounds in the blog comment threads are therefore multifarious, and the shared language on the sites is English, which renders them typical English as a Lingua Franca environments.

3.2 The sample

The source corpora were sampled for suitable types of events and discourses for delving into spoken academic dialogue in search of discourse reflexivity, and for outlining its characteristics against two kinds of comparisons: spoken academic monologues on the one hand and written academic dialogues on the other. All transcripts and texts were included whole, without extracting passages from them. The analyses are performed on different selections from the corpora in each chapter.

Overall, conference presentations and their discussion sections were included in their entirety, as were doctoral defences. For the rest, monologic and dialogic data were sampled separately. With regard to both, I started with conference data, which taken as a whole constitutes a reasonably sized sample (see section 3.2.5). This meant beginning with 'mature' academic discourses as the primary data, assuming that this roughly represents target behaviour in academic discourses. Seminar presentations and discussions were sampled, and so were blog discussion threads. The sampling is described below.

3.2.1 Seminar presentations and discussions

Graduate seminars contribute a student perspective to the discourse selection. They are typical macro-events, in this case serial events, which run for one or two terms in the Finnish university system. Their purpose is to support students in researching and writing their master's theses. Sessions normally last 90 minutes, typically include one or two shortish (about 15 to 30 minutes) student presentations of their plans and findings, and a longer discussion of the presentations among the participants, who usually number between six and ten. Seminar presentations were analysed with the rest of the monologue sample, the discussions with the dialogue sample.

Academic institutions regulate and determine their practices in many ways, but also allow for a fair degree of 'academic freedom'. Thus, while some norms and practices are imposed upon seminars by the institution, others the group can decide for itself, and yet others are tacitly understood and evolve in the course of events. Evaluation criteria, required outcomes, and the language are institutionally determined, while things like selecting a chairperson, the desirability of interruptions during presentations, or first-name use may be negotiated *ad hoc*. More subtle norms of language use tend to be tacit, a matter of linguistic self-regulation within the group. Graduate seminars thus operate within layered structural frames coming from the institution as the outer layer and from practices that the groups have established for themselves as the inner layer. Within those limits, the discussion is co-constructed by participants fairly freely at any point and can develop into many directions. Unpredictability is thus quite characteristic of these discussions along with a degree of informality, which imparts more of a conversational flavour to them than we see in the relatively structured dialogues of conference or doctoral defence discussions. As comparatively self-organised multi-party discussions, graduate seminars open an interesting view on discourse reflexivity, involving as they do frequent turn shifts, overlaps and situational interaction management.

The seminar sample was made by first selecting a set of presentations, from which the related discussion sections followed. The corpus has 27 seminar discussions in all, of which a sample of 10 was made based on the following criteria:

(1) selection on 'external' grounds, based on metadata information
(2) maximal disciplinary variation
(3) maximal L1 variation
(4) followed by a discussion as far as possible
(5) the duration of the talks roughly comparable

Adhering to these principles, the resulting sample consists of the following presentations:

Forestry (L1 French, female)
Virology (L1 Rumanian, female)
Biology (L1 Portuguese, female)
Biology (L1 German, male)
Philosophy (L1 Hindi, male)
Political science (L1 Lithuanian, female)
Political science (L1 Chinese, male)
Education (L1 Dutch, male)
Political history (L1s Czech & Polish, male)
International relations (L1 Finnish, female)

The sample thus consists of four instances of natural sciences and six of social sciences and humanities, which reflects the distribution of the whole corpus quite well. Two subjects, biology and political science are represented twice, others once. The language selection is wide, with all speakers from different first language backgrounds. The duration of the presentations varies from 14 to 34 minutes. In addition, gender balance among presenters was sought if possible; it was not a major priority but resulted in five females and five males. It is worth noting that there were no seminar events from language subjects in the sample, nor seminar events with English as the object of study in the whole corpus.

This sample then served as the basis for selecting dialogues with the aim of getting ten discussion sections on these presentations. It turned out that two presentations (in biology) were followed by one joint discussion, resulting in a total of only nine discussions. Their interrelatedness nevertheless means a good balance and comparability across the two samples and is similar to the conference and doctoral defence data where the presentations and discussions come from the same events and the discussions relate to the presentations. The total time in seminar presentations is 3h14min, while the time spent in the corresponding discussions is roughly twice as long. The aggregate number of speakers is obviously lower (10 vs. 79) for presentations.

3.2.2 Doctoral defences

This event type was included as a whole from the corpus. All the defences were recorded in Finland and followed the Finnish academic system. Since doctoral examination systems have quite localised traditions in different countries, the event type needs a brief description here.

In Finland, doctoral examinations are organised as traditional academic disputations, that is, as public debates between one or two opponents (the examiners) and a defendant (the candidate). An audience is also present, which usually comprises academics and fellow PhD students in the field, as well as the candidate's friends and family, which means the audience is fairly heterogeneous, much in the way of audiences in inaugural or valedictory lectures. The disputation is formally presided over by a *kustos*, usually the supervising professor, whose role is limited to opening and closing the event with predetermined phrases and allocating turns from the floor when the actual disputation between the opponents and the defendant is over and the audience is invited to join into the discussion. Whether the audience joins in varies but has become increasingly common.

The defence begins by a 15-minute presentation (*lectio praecursoria*) by the candidate about their doctoral research. These are not in included in the present data, although they are in the corpus. Following that, the opponent (or one of them) presents a brief statement as an overview of the thesis and its place in the field. This is a short monologic section in each examination and included in the data. The dialogic examination then begins, which may last from a minimum of one hour up to four hours. In this material, the events last on average 112 minutes. The examiner and the candidate (opponent and defendant) organise the talk between themselves, but it is to a notable extent constrained by their predetermined institutional roles which means the examiner has the initiative, asking questions and making critical points about the thesis.

The data consists of 14 doctoral examinations, with the fields somewhat biased towards technology:

Information technology (4)
Materials engineering
Industrial engineering and management
Automation engineering
Internal medicine
Mathematics
Social policy
Translation studies
Journalism and mass communication
Political science
Education

3.2.3 Blog comment threads

Unlike the other event types in the data, which are central to academia and the university system, research blogs remain comparatively peripheral. Their inclusion is motivated as representing written dialogue, and in addition, by ongoing changes in academia with its growing emphasis on outreach. The digital age has expanded openness and meant the blurring of some boundaries between academia and the more general public. Research blogs are an early manifestation of this, with other fora of social media providing additional sites for publicising research projects and findings together with debating research-related issues.

A previous definition of a blog by a group of corpus linguists was adopted as a point of departure: "A blog, short for a weblog, is a website containing an archive of regularly updated online postings." (Grieve et al. 2011: 303). Blog texts are open, contain links to other Internet sites, and terms like "updated" and "regularly" in the definition point to frequent appearance of new items. Both features, openness and regular updating, are quite distant from traditional academic publication, which is nevertheless absorbing some of the more recent practices as best they can, along with developing new forms altogether, such as video journals. From a genre theory perspective, the blog can be seen as a cluster of genres (Mauranen 2013a) that includes the research blog, which in historical terms has long roots in print genres that promote the advancement and public dissemination of science and scholarship. The target genre here, as already noted, is the research blog kept by active researchers who write about their own work, and the comment threads that the blog entries generate. Blogs and their comment threads thus fall into the chain-like macro-event model that typifies many academic discourses. Interconnectedness within discussion threads is strong, as the comments concern a given blog posting or previous comments to it.

The material was selected from the Blog subcorpus of WrELFA. The current interest in dialogic discourse led to excluding blog posts themselves and focusing on discussion threads. The selection for research field and L1 was based on the blog and the blogger's L1. The bloggers engage actively in the discussions, since many questions are directed at them. Theirs is the only L1 that can be ascertained. As with seminars, ten discussions were the target, and the criteria applied along similar lines:

(1) external' selection, based on metadata information
(2) maximal disciplinary variation
(3) maximal L1 variation, excluding monolingual L1 English bloggers
(4) maximal discussion length

The whole blog subcorpus contains a wider variation of research fields and blogger L1s than are represented in this sample, but the requirements for the presence of discussion and its duration limited other choices quite drastically. However, prioritising them was vital for capturing a good amount of blog dialogue. The sample therefore includes research field repetitions and even in one case two separate discussions from the same blog site that carried out particularly long and intense discussions on various topics within quantum physics.

We thus have two samples from the largest blog set in the corpus, that is Physics (Czech), three blogs from Medicine (including two different Bengali blogs), two from Molecular Biology (Dutch and Spanish), one Ecology (Italian), one Sociology (Italian), and one Political Science (Rumanian):

Ecology – Italian
Molecular biology – Dutch
Molecular biology – Spanish
Medicine (1) – Bengali
Medicine (2) – Bengali (different blog)
Medicine (3) – Dutch
Sociology – Italian (two bloggers)
Political Science – Rumanian
Physics (1) – Czech
Physics (2) – Czech (same blog)

3.2.4 Event types in different chapters

The analyses drew on different corpus samples, apart from Chapter 8, which discussed them all in a general overview.

Conference discussion sections and seminar discussions: chapters 4 and 6.
Blog discussion threads: Chapter 5.
PhD defence discussions: Chapter 6.
Conference and seminar presentations: Chapter 7.

3.2.5 Number of words in the sample

The data drawn from the two corpora amounts altogether to roughly half a million words, with a heavy bias on dialogues. The precise figures are as follows:

Conference Monologues	94,360w
Conference Dialogues	74,057w
Seminar Monologues	24,901w
Seminar Dialogues	51,873w
PhD defences	217,701w
Blog discussion threads	33,301w
∑	496,193w
Monologues	∑ 119,261w
Dialogues	∑ 376,932w

As already noted, different chapters used different sections of the data for analyses. How the diverse parts of the data compare to each other in terms of the incidence of discourse reflexivity will be discussed in Chapter 8, which presents an overview of the numerical findings from the analyses with regard to the word numbers.

3.3 Methods

Since the objective is to explore new territory in a well-researched area of language use, the methodological approach is exploratory and qualitative. It starts from a theoretical position and is thus guided by a general concept of the phenomenon investigated, but few assumptions are made about what all the relevant linguistic manifestations may be. Since it is of course not possible to apply pure induction, without any theoretical beliefs or biases, the aim is to make as few a priori assumptions as possible about categories or uses beyond the general concept. Importantly, no a priori lists of items or categories are applied.

Metadiscourse research is inherently co-text dependent, a discourse phenomenon with identifiable uses, and in this sense could also be seen as a functional rather than a formal category or a fixed set of expressions. Even its prototypical manifestations may have non-metadiscoursal interpretations in different contexts (see, Chapter 2, section 2.7). For example, a verb like CALL can be used either in a discourse reflexive way (. . . *is now trying to provide a low-cost I would* ***I would call*** *it sub-PC something* . . .) or in a non-reflexive way (*the little money that goes in that* ***is called*** *government fund to the institutes* . . .). In this way, the approach is both theory-informed and *data-driven*. Corpus linguists can perform analyses that are data-driven to a greater or lesser degree, although the principled distinction between corpus-driven and corpus-based approaches (Tognini-Bonelli 2001) has been a bone of contention in corpus linguistics. A corpus-driven approach has been dismissed by some scholars as intuitive, in contrast to more rigorous statistically or theoretically motivated research (e.g. Gries 2010).

The debate is reminiscent of older distinctions between inductive vs. deductive reasoning and research, but no unequivocal superiority of one over the other is possible to establish independently of the objectives of a particular study or the data available to it. To confuse matters further, many empirically oriented language researchers prefer to steer clear of 'intuitive' analyses, because intuition is associated with notions like 'native speaker intuition' (which, contrary to common belief, is far from infallible or immutable, see e.g. Pickering & Garrod 2017). It is, however, important to maintain a clear distinction between intuition as used in data analyses in general and irrespective of the research field, and intuition as referring to a speaker's sense of grammaticality or acceptable expressions in their first language or a language they know well, which is specific to certain schools of linguistics. Analysing data, such as discerning categories, inevitably relies on the analyst's judgment and decision, which is ultimately based on intuitive assessment of the evidence. A recent example of a largely corpus-driven analysis of metadiscourse is Zhang's (2022) multidimensional register analysis. It started from a set of identifiable metadiscoursal expressions, and for this part was corpus-based, but the functions of metadiscourse in a large database of a broad range of registers were identified in a corpus-driven fashion as they arose from dimensions found in the factor loadings and cluster analysis.

It is also useful at this point to remember the distinction Annelie Ädel and I drew between *thin* and *thick* approaches to metadiscourse (Ädel & Mauranen 2010; see also Chapter 2, section 2.7). We pointed out that the thin approach regards certain items as inherently metadiscoursal, and in this way reflects the primacy of the linguist's intuition. It also can overlook context by resorting to corpus searches based on predetermined lists of items. In this way, it bestows a bird's eye view of item distributions, but with uncertain precision, because the items, though in principle context-creating, may not serve metadiscourse functions in their actual contexts, unless the retrieved material is manually checked. Conversely, such an approach is bound to overlook expressions which are atypical or based on context-dependent items. By contrast, what we called a thick approach is data-driven, discourse analytical, and emphasises the context as essential to interpreting an item, which mostly is a longer unit than a single word.

Both approaches have their strengths: the thin approach lends itself readily to quantitative comparisons across genres, registers, disciplines, cultural divides, novices vs. experts, and so on. It can rely on lists and provide useful overviews of where discourse reflexive expressions cluster across divisions built into the research design. The thick approach relies more on qualitative analyses, and as an inherently context-sensitive perspective, can delve deeper into less obvious uses of metadiscourse, above all discover new expressions not found in lists, and capture more elusive context-dependent instances such as light verbs (see Chapter 2, section 2.7). A thick approach is also important because language is inherently variable, indeterminate, and in a continual state of change. In addition, because ordinary everyday language is highly creative (Carter 2004), we need thick approaches to capture this. ELF is particularly open to unconventional, nonstandard, and creative uses (Pitzl 2015), and obviously it would mean a great loss if only typical standard expressions were included (Mauranen 2013c). This and the boundaries of reflexive metadiscourse are discussed in more detail in Chapter 2.

The thin and thick dichotomy is not always as categorical as this, but it is a reasonable depiction of the big picture. In practice, many who carry out corpus studies on relatively small corpora supplement corpus searchers by checking the items manually. Likewise, it is possible to run numerical counts in data that has been first explored qualitatively or check qualitative findings against large databases. While these methodological possibilities thus soften the dichotomy, they do not remove it: if lists are adopted as the point of departure, or an "opening exploration" (Hyland 2017), it means that some items are likely to be discarded after a check, but new ones unlikely to be added, because a list already constrains the material that is taken up for scrutiny. By contrast, starting from a qualitative approach precludes the use of very large corpora, and analysing even a corpus of half a million words, which is the basis of this book, is laborious and time-consuming. Qualitative research can be supplemented by numerical counts or checked against larger data. The approach I adopt in this book is a thick one, and the analyses employ qualitative methods, supported by basic numerical data (see Chapter 8) for working out the incidence of metadiscourse in the material. I talk about 'numerical' rather than 'quantitative' research here because I do not perform complex statistical analyses on the data. This is, however, normal practice in metadiscourse studies: usually the incidence of 'metadiscourse markers' are presented in terms of raw numbers, markers/N words of running text, and percentages, in other words, not on statistical analyses. My focus is on close reading of the discourse.

The numerical results were based on counting each individual, independent expression of metadiscourse separately, irrespective of its length. Some are shorter (*you said that*), others longer (*so I was wondering if you could explain a little bit more*). Discontinuous expressions were counted as one if they were part of the same functional unit even if interrupted by other material (***first I'd like to say that** as a . . . **I have a number of comments to make***) All such occurrences were then assigned to the categories that were emerging from the analysis, and some undecided cases left out. Precise numbers are shown in Chapter 8, and in the running text of the analytical chapters I have also given percentages or sometimes rounded figures for ease of focusing on the big picture.

The ideal solution for getting the best of both thin and thick approaches would be to train a tagger on manually analysed data and apply a semi-automatic or, even better, a fully automatic procedure based on machine learning. So far, this option does not seem to be available, perhaps not even in the near future. Programs based on machine learning have become adept at finding expressions and even complex interconnections between them but dealing with expressions with similar or related functions or effects is still beyond them and requires a human analyst.

3.3.1 Process

As is common in qualitative explorations, the analysis proceeded in consecutive subsamples from the data. The same steps were followed for spoken and written discourse: first a confined sample was drawn, with all its discourse reflexive expressions noted and classified for best fit with the data. This preliminary set of categories was then imposed on the next sample and adjusted as necessary. The procedure was repeated until a saturation point was reached, that is, the categorisation fitted new samples without requiring further adjustment, and the remaining data was analysed with these categories.

The analysis began with conference discussions, that is, a dialogic event type with mainly experienced academics as speakers. The assumption was that this is the kind of speaking that roughly equals target behaviour in academia, and the categorisation could serve as a basis or preliminary guideline to subsequent analyses of similar event types. It served as a point of departure for helping refine principal conceptual issues and establishing tentative functional categories. It also helped look into boundaries and borderlines for classification of discourse reflexive expressions, though indeterminacies of boundaries and a focus on finding prototypical cases were primary (see Chapter 2, section 2.7, and section 3.3.2 below). Graduate seminar discussions were similar to conference discussions as event types, albeit in an educational rather than a research context, and the proportion of discussion vs. presentation time was the reverse of conference time allocation: presentations were short, discussions long. The participants, apart from seminar leaders, were academically novices. The analyses of their reflexive metadiscourse use benefited directly from the initial work on conference discussions. Conversely, the seminar discussions were a good testbed for the conference dialogue categories and led to adjustments in the framework so that it fitted the whole data.

Monologue data comprised presentations from conferences and graduate seminars, and again the analysis started with the more senior academics' discourses. Their analysis followed along the lines of dialogues: spoken monologues by senior academics were first studied from the bottom up, the categorisation then tested on the second set of data from graduate seminar presentations and adapted where necessary.

After establishing the categories in spoken monologues, they were compared to those in spoken dialogues, and the frameworks were harmonised with each other where this was possible (see section 3.2).

The only written event type was the blog discussion thread, that is, written dialogue. The analysis again set out bottom up from the similarities observed in the uses. The tentative categories were then combined towards a bigger picture, and compared to the categorisations of dialogic speech, then monologic speech.

3.3.2 Categories

The overall objective was to achieve a general categorisation of discourse reflexivity that would, if possible, apply to both dialogic and monologic speech as well as to written dialogue. The assumption was that written monologue could eventually be subsumed under the same system, even if such material was excluded from the current database. Working towards this end meant adjusting the tentative categories that resulted from the bottom-up analyses for each separate broad event type – spoken dialogues, spoken monologues, and written dialogues. Comparison and possible matching started from the top down, that is, from the principal categories. Dialogues were compared first, followed by monologues. The main categories were adjusted where this seemed motivated, but most of the time this was either not necessary for the higher-level categories or not motivated, because the most important principle was to reflect the data as accurately as possible. The lower-level categories, which bifurcated much more, were thus left intact. In this way, the result was a combination of bottom-up and top-down categories.

Matching top-level categories represent the major types for each speech event group and enable comparability across the groups (speech, writing, dialogue, monologue) as well as provide a general scaffolding for minor categories. The minor categories in turn are sensitive to the special features of the event types and reflect their contrasting aspects and specificity.

Discourse categories typically maintain a measure of fuzziness, and the borderlines can be debatable. As already discussed in Chapter 2 (section 2.7), this is not a problem, since slightly indeterminate outer boundaries do not alter categories substantially, and therefore drawing the line precisely is not of prime importance. We can simply note that some instances are more, others less prototypical (Rosch 1978; Lakoff 1987). Where precise category boundaries are needed is in the case of what is known as classical categorisation. Classical categorisation is based on pinning down sufficient and necessary criteria for classes of items and becomes a requirement in exact quantitative measurements. It comes to its own as a basis for quantitative analyses because significance measurements require exact figures. As already pointed out, this is not the approach adopted here, where analyses are qualitative and depend on only basic numerical data, such as occurrences per 1,000 words and percentages, which nevertheless suffice to discover the incidence of reflexive metadiscourse within and across event types. While our categories are not 'natural categories' in Rosch's sense, but analyst's categories, the notions of prototype theory have informed the approach to categorisation.

Categorisation was thus built on the basis of use in context, which meant that individual expressions could take different shapes and forms, but to be subsumed under the same category had to serve the same kind of purpose in their contexts. Expressions also varied considerably in their span, from just two or three words (*good point; as I said*) to two dozen or more (*. . . okay er let let me also then and now we're coming back to the question I said I wanted to discuss me and you or rather that you maybe wanted to discuss with me namely about the question of* modernising). Moreover, the exact boundaries of individual cases may not be clear-cut, because reflexive expressions can incorporate non-reflexive items, like *political culture* in *should I first say that you also refer to* ***political culture****, in one of your answers*, or they can themselves be incorporated in longer passages, interspersed with non-reflexive items, as in (3.1):

(3.1) <S24> yeah *I would just like to push a little bit further his suggestion* because I think that *what he was suggesting* (xx) with I-Ps you have this er incentive er objective but in traditional knowledge you don't have it *as he said* and maybe maybe the I-P type of protection is not at all the right kind of protection for traditional knowledge </S24>

Would such instances be most fruitfully seen as one long discourse reflexive passage, or several shorter items, each counted individually? Items must obviously be counted as consistently as possible, which implies a uniform decision on delimiting their extension. The solution adopted here is that each continuous or discontinuous (i.e., interspersed with non-reflexive items) expression with an identifiable discourse reflexive function of its own counts as one. In the present analysis, then, the above passage (3.1) has three separate discourse reflexive expressions: *I would just like to push a little bit further his suggestion; what he was suggesting; as he said.*

Another issue is the multifunctionality of individual expressions. For example, *good point* indicates primarily an evaluation while it also refers to an interlocutor's turn. In cases where two functions seem to be inextricably intertwined in the same expression, with neither clearly primary in view of the context, the expression has been counted twice. This was generally avoided in the analyses and settling on a primary function was preferred wherever possible.

3.4 The wider context

Identifying and categorising each case separately is thus required for teasing out relevant expressions to ascertain their incidence and comparability, but in addition to that, there is an intriguing question of how such items, once identified, work in longer discourse extracts: how are they employed for complex purposes, and in what kinds of sequences do they accumulate in unfolding discussions? For questions of this kind, it is vital to look into longer passages than the immediate co-text of each expression. The extended extracts that were sampled for closer scrutiny were drawn from the entire dialogic databases from ELFA and WrELFA in places where at least one reflexive expression was spotted, and discussion threads around them were inspected for more. This sampling of long passages of discussion was done independently of that described above (section 3.2), where each discourse reflexive expression was counted in the files that had been sampled.

As a consequence, there was no inherent or principled overlap with the samples analysed for individual expressions and those that were sampled for probing discourse reflexivity in extended development. There was nevertheless bound to be some incidental overlap, and to avoid counting the same items twice, the extracts for analysing reflexive metadiscourse in extended passages were not included in any counts. They were analysed and discussed in a chapter (Chapter 6), which deals with co-constructing knowledge, and negotiating difficulties and uncertainties over several turns.

When we compare the functions and the incidences of discourse reflexivity across event types, we begin to see how various constraints apply to the different kinds of events. These may suggest explanatory factors to why reflexive metadiscourse is used more in some circumstances than others (see also Mauranen 2003). To get a handle on what factors might contribute to the variation found in the data I looked at some parameters of the broader context: external constraints, discourse characteristics, and social parameters. These are taken on board in chapters 4, 5 and 6 and discussed further in the general overview in Chapter 8. Clearly, this analysis is tentative and not the main focus of the present study, but it points to a need in metadiscourse analysis to extend the concept of context.

Chapter 4
Discourse reflexivity in multi-party interaction

As we engage in ordinary conversations, we perform a complex linguistic and interactional task with our interlocutors. We contribute to our accumulating shared experience while maintaining interaction, alternate in speaker and hearer roles in rapid succession, often overlapping but not too much, take and concede the floor, relate our turns to those of others – in short, we generate meaning and interaction as joint activity. We excel at coordinating our actions in complex ways verbally, paralinguistically, and non-verbally. All means verbal and non-verbal are undoubtedly involved in the self-regulated, coordinated activity of co-constructing meaning and interaction in all spoken interaction, but their relative importance varies in different situations and during conversations, so that sometimes we rely more heavily on verbal and sometimes nonverbal cues. Paralinguistic cues accompany all verbalisation.

Academic discussions would seem to locate themselves at the verbal-heavy end of the scale. They also tend towards more institutional regulation than everyday conversations: as discussed in the previous chapter, academic discussions range from the formal and highly regulated, like meetings or doctoral defences, to more self-regulated graduate seminar or study group discussions. Yet even the most informal kinds like students' teamwork are based on pre-set goals and usually (certainly in the ELFA corpus) organise themselves by for example selecting a chairperson to help them keep focused on the task. This sets the discussions clearly apart from self-regulation in everyday conversation, where habits, norms, and conventions set the frame, and even these are open to negotiation.

In these circumscribed academic circumstances, one might imagine that discourse reflexivity is not greatly needed, because discussions progress in a predetermined fashion. Particularly at the formal end of the scale, specially appointed persons invested with the authority to utter certain stipulated speech acts regulate the discussion. Nevertheless, we already have evidence that metadiscourse is used in academic speaking, although we know very little about how this manifests itself in different types of speech events, and how social parameters like the formality of the occasion might influence its usage.

While we may thus assume that discourse reflexivity is, at least to some degree, used in discussions within academia, it would also seem likely that it is put to new uses beyond those established in research on monologues. A silent audience facing a monologic presenter has been replaced by a group of fellow participants, who have their own interests and agendas, and who may turn the discussion to unexpected directions.

https://doi.org/10.1515/9783110295498-004

4.1 Reflexivity in dialogic discourse

Let us start the exploration into dialogues with an example. Extract (4.1) comes from a conference discussion section. The session is attended by 39 conference participants, one of whom (S11) has given the final talk in a longer session on the same topic, with alternating presentations and discussions. At this point five people take an active part in the discussion, one of whom (S18) is the chair. The passage has been shortened by removing a good deal of such content that is presumed to be uninteresting to the readers of this book and irrelevant to reflexive discourse. The same practice is applied throughout in the examples.

(4.1) <S32> ***can i ask*** <S34> sure </S34> so do do you see there some some fundamental difference between these undevelopment countries and development countries because i i ***i could ask the same question*** of of the use of the mold- mobile phone of my own children <S11> mhm-hm </S11> is is there they're really used and what is the [benefits] <S11> [mhm-hm] </S11> and do they have the understanding and skills to use the real benefits of the of the mobile phone so so what is the fund- what is the fundamental <S11> mhm </S11> difference here and why it is ethical question </S32>
<S11> er ***we could say*** that er that the difference exists . . . not beneficial i'm ***i'm not saying*** that that people have to be prudent . . . and we can afford to allocate them whatever i ***i agree*** that there's there's also problem . . . </S11>
<S18> okay and then <NAME 31> ***had a comment or a question make it short please*** 'cause there's couple of others </S18>
<S13> ***okay i'll be very brief*** er i mean <NAME S31> go ahead </S13>
<S31> yeah <S18> yeah </S18> erm *i think* ***this connected with to your question also*** er ***let's keep talking on*** mo- about mobile phones er erm i think every technology all all technologies have the those er bad side effects <S11> mhm-hm </S11> and er you ***you spoke about*** er how to react to . . . </S31>
<S11> . . . so that's ***that's what i mean*** that we have to look at all the sides of these issues </S11>
<S31> er actually i was maybe a bit kind of worried that er that usually in in these kind of projects er people just accept the bad sides but don't do anything [about them] </S31>
<S11> [yeah] yeah yeah and that's a ethical problem that's that's something i take for granted and ***that's why er what i talked about*** in terms of costs of these projects </S11>
<S13> ***i in fact go largely with*** <NAME S11>***'s*** <COUGH> ***position*** <COUGH> because . . . </S13>

The passage begins by S32 prefacing a question with discourse reflexive *can I ask*, to which S34 responds 'sure'. The exchange looks like something we hear at conferences all the time, but it is not quite like that, because S34 is neither the chairperson nor the presenter. But just before the extract begins, S34 had asked a question from the previous presenter (S11), so S32's apparent intention is to enquire whether S34 had finished, and S34's response suggests this is how he understood the question. In this brief exchange, the two speakers are *managing the situation* between them.

S32 then proceeds to his question and turns his attention to the presenter (S11), who acknowledges his role as the addressee by repeated back-channelling. S32 asks two things: (a) whether there's a difference between two scenarios, and (b) why this should be an ethical issue. Metadiscourse comes at the beginning of giving his reason for the question (*because I could ask the same question*). S11 starts by a discourse reflexive preface (*we could say*). A little later he addresses the second question, prefacing it with reflexivity again (*I'm not saying* . . .) and finally making a concession to S32's point (*I agree that* . . .). In this exchange, the speakers use discourse reflexivity to *manage the discourse*. Both apparently refer to their own speech, but in effect they are responding to each other – S32 to S11's talk, S11 to S32's question.

After S11 has finished his response, the chairperson (S18) takes over situation management and gives the floor to S31. There is a brief confusion when another speaker first takes the floor but immediately concedes it to S31 (*okay I'll be very brief er I mean <NAME S31> go ahead*), thus continuing to negotiate the situation. S31 first contextualises his question in relation to the previous one (*I think this connected with to your question also)*, then to his intended topic (***let's keep talking about** mobile phones*), and finally to S11's presentation (*you spoke about*). All his reflexive metadiscourse in this turn manages the discourse. S11 continues to work towards a convergent position like he did in his previous answer, indicating with metadiscoursal inserts that he is on the same side with S31 (*that's what I mean; that's why er what I talked about* . . .).

At this point S13 deems the floor to be his without overtly consulting the chairperson (there may of course have been eye contact or nods to the same effect) and joins the discussion by positioning himself in it (*I in fact go largely with <NAME S11>'s position*) before even embarking on his own comment.

We can see in the comments, questions, and responses an ongoing *negotiation* of positions as well as the contingencies of the situation. It would seem, like in this case, that the underlying strand in these negotiations is to expand everyone's grasp of the issues by enhancing mutual understanding. This will be discussed more thoroughly in Chapter 6. Example 4.1 is part of a long discussion, and it is worth pointing out that at the point where our extract ends, its centre moves on to revolve around S13's comment, away from the presentation. The relationship between the duration of a discussion and its tendency to become self-regulating is elaborated below (Section 4.2.2). We also see in this extract how reflexive metadiscourse is employed to refer to speakers' own discourse (*I'm not saying*) as well as that of their interlocutors (*this connected with your question*), together with the future, i.e. the speaker's intentions (*I'll be very brief*) and the past, i.e. what has already been said in the discourse (*you spoke about*).

In brief, this extract illustrates how discourse reflexivity is woven into social interaction. It helps attune interlocutors to each other, whether they want to agree, argue, explore, or perhaps engage in power struggles. The principal means of dealing with these tasks can be divided into *contextualising* upcoming speech at the present state of the discourse and *negotiating* arguments and positions. This chapter is concerned with contextualising, and Chapter 5 will continue the same theme in written dialogues. Negotiation is the central topic in Chapter 6.

This chapter is, then, at the most general level, about contextualising utterances with reflexive metadiscourse. By contextualising I mean making explicit how the utterance relates on the one hand to the discourse ('managing discourse') and on the other to the speech situation ('managing situation'). Discourse reflexivity thus captures both kinds of context that Firth (1968) postulated: the context of text (co-text), and the context of situation. I will discuss both below, starting from managing discourse (Section 4.2), which is the major domain of reflexive metadiscourse in the present data, and managing situation will follow in Section 4.3. The analyses in this chapter are quite data-driven, and therefore may look more protracted and detailed than those in the subsequent chapters. They nevertheless lay the foundation for the chapters that follow.

4.2 Managing discourse

Multi-party discussions require complex activity simultaneously and in quick alternation. Speaker-hearer collaboration involves simultaneous processing from participating individuals (Pickering & Garrod 2021) and is crucially entwined with co-constructing interaction (Hari et al 2015). In essence, interacting individuals need to attend to the 'substance' of the discussion as well as the interaction and share in the joint construction of both simultaneously. Correspondingly, discourse reflexivity straddles both levels.

To start disentangling the complexities of multi-party discussion, let us begin with the two principal levels that participants must manage in dialogic interaction: the more linguistic facet of *managing the discourse*, and the more action-oriented *managing the situation*. In a comparatively regulated, substantially verbal activity like academic discussion, much management is concerned with the verbal aspects –

prefacing turns, specifying addressees, or referring to preceding discourse, while other managing activities relate to the 'outer' movement of the situation – opening and closing episodes, allocating turns, moving to new stages. We will attend to both in turn, starting with discourse management and returning to situation management next (Section 4.3).

Speakers in multi-party interaction (mostly discussed as *dialogic* interaction here) spend an appreciable amount of time and effort in relating their speech to the state of the discourse at hand. This can be conceptualised as the *contextualising* function of reflexive discourse: connecting the present state of the discourse to where the current speaker is taking it. Contextualising essentially implies 'fitting in', making the upcoming discourse relevant to the moment of speaking, and showing this with reflexive metadiscourse. This takes place in two principal ways: either by *orienting*, indicating the function and character of what is going to be said next, or by *retrieving*, adopting something in the preceding discourse up to the moment of speaking and making it relevant to the present. The more recently updated and the more obvious the continuity is, the less explicit indication of the relevance of the next contribution to the present stage should be necessary.

4.2.1 Orienting

Orienting discourse reflexivity sets the scene, suggesting how the current speaker means their upcoming speech to be taken (*just a comment*), or not to be taken (*this is not criticism*). It can indicate how the discourse continues (*well maybe I should add*) or challenges the present state (*does it then make sense at all to talk about . . .*). Such acts steer the hearers' predictive processing, that is, generating hypotheses about which way the discourse is moving. Much of processing consists in confirming hypotheses – or discarding them, in which case we must update our situation models (e.g., Radvansky & Zacks 2014). Discourse reflexivity may support fluent hypothesis formation and serve to maintain apposite situation models.

Looking ahead

Discourse reflexivity of the orienting kind sustains interactants' efforts to adjust their situation models to each other. It builds on the speaker's express intentions, which for many is the prototypical case of metadiscourse: helping others anticipate what the speaker is likely to say next. For the speaker, orienting discourse reflexivity confers opportunities of sharing their thinking as well as manoeuvring the discourse towards their purposes. A typical case would simply be indicating the function of the upcoming speech act (*I just like to make a brief comment on this*). Many such instances are quite similar in monologic and dialogic discourse, and therefore likely to be familiar from the bulk of metadiscourse research. Below, some of the expressions (4.3–4.5) could perhaps equally well occur in an academic presentation, while others (like 4.2) show signs of people thinking on their feet rather than delivering a prepared talk.

(4.2) <S9> w- w- well i thi- i think if *if we talk about* knowledge mhm power in various ways is also linked with this thinking . . .

The speaker here names the topic she is going to elaborate. Although the example is from a dialogue, in principle the metadiscoursal expression itself could occur in a presentation. Yet in a presentation we might be more likely to give it a generic interpretation, even see it as a delexicalized statement (Chapter 2, section 2.7), but in its dialogic context the interpretation is more concrete ('since we are talking about . . .') – they are indeed talking about knowledge in this discussion.

Alerting others about the speaker's intention of expressing their stand on an issue (4.3) is also familiar from much metadiscourse research. It is not unusual for such discourse reflexivity, in this case itself tentative, to be accompanied by mitigating hedges (*at least in my thoughts*) in *discourse collocation* (cf. Mauranen 2001, 2003).

(4.3) <S3> er well basically i think that almost everything is tied to EU nowadays and all the peoples are just talking about European identity and things like that but *i would also say* that <u>at least in my thoughts</u> people can still feel that they . . .

Even though metadiscourse is usually seen as facilitating the listener's or reader's job, an act of helpful recipient design on the part of the speaker or writer (see, Chapter 2, section 2.5), there is also a competitive side to it: it is a way of imposing the current speaker's interpretation on the discourse (Mauranen 2001). As the speaker indicates how their speech is to be taken, their viewpoint assumes more space, while the hearers' scope of interpretation narrows down. Reflexivity reinforces the speaker's perspective on the discourse by directing it towards a given perception to the exclusion of others. Consequently, it takes more effort from listeners to contest the suggested viewpoint or the status of the locution. Imposing an individual's order on the discourse is an act of power, even dominance. Discourse reflexivity thus advances not only cooperation but also competition.

Speakers can likewise use discourse reflexivity for tactical purposes, such as shelving matters they will *not* be talking about (4.4) but mentioning them all the same. This is a way of simultaneously saying something and as it were not saying it. Writers have other possibilities for such tactics, in the form of notes for example, or parentheses, while speakers can alter their pitch or loudness or, like here, by using laughter for marking digressive remarks.

(4.4) . . . large countries somehow (which create) problems what well *i don't want to go @into it* i i@ there's no activity on Mediterranean countries . . .

Another tactical deployment of reflexive discourse is seen in (4.5), where the speaker offers his interlocutors the interpretation that his argument has persuaded them. His turn has been very long, and the comment is made in a jocular manner, which elicits laughter from other participants in recognition of the reference. Ad hoc humour is eminently interactional and quite common in academic discussions, frequently resulting in collective laughter.

(4.5) . . . okay <SIGH> i think *i should stop* there <SS> @@ </SS> but of course you can see *from what i'm saying* democracy <WHISPERING> hierarchy we've created hierarchies </WHISPERING> how can you have democracy with hierarchies

A relatively common tactic for speakers to reassure their interlocutors that what they will be saying next is not going to take much time (4.6). This might be considered a politeness strategy. Such comments may also notify listeners or readers that the issue is not very important or that it is a digression. In this context *shortly* seems primarily to indicate an intention to speak briefly:

(4.6) <S2> mhm . sh- *shortly* nunavut has created both cause of these problems, er er but it doesn't really . . .

Some kinds of anticipatory reflexive metadiscourse characterise only dialogic speech, a case in point being self-commentaries on speaker's ongoing thought processes (4.7), as if explanatory digressions while thinking aloud.

(4.7) more and more people acquiring that knowledge, i'm just *i'm just trying to, er try trying to sort of find a language for talking about these things* s- many that s- the we start talking of this body of knowledge and how it grows

Underlying complexities may be embedded in situations even when the action would seem quite straightforward, as in the extract below (4.8). The speaker names a speech act (*I have a suggestion)*, which would naturally direct others to hear the next utterance as a suggestion. What happens here, however, is a longish delay between the reflexive framing of the turn and the actual suggestion made (underlined). The suggestion, when it comes, consists of a possible solution to a problem under discussion. Before the speaker comes to the suggestion, he goes through several preliminary phases, indicating problems with alternative paths along the way. The articulation of the suggestion is further delayed by typical speech features such as false starts, either left in the air (*now er of course you might not get er it's; a gram-negative cell would be supporting that er assembly process er that you but*) or repaired (*the chances that you know that there's a small chance that; and it but it makes bam-35*). However, going through these preliminary steps does not seem to detract from listeners' willingness to wait till the predicted suggestion comes. Backchannelling shows the chain is followed by other participants. The underlying complication in this case is that S2, who makes the suggestion, is a senior academic and this is a seminar session that he is teaching. These situational factors may help sustain listener interest despite his embarking on a lengthy explanation of solution alternatives; he has a captive audience.

(4.8) <S2> *i have a suggestion* <SS> @@ </SS> now er of course you might not get er it's like the second cycle so if PRD1 would deliver this DNA into the cytosol the chances that you know that there's a small chance that it replicates <S5> yes </S5> and it but it makes bam-35 and [maybe] <S5> [yes] </S5> a gram-negative cell would be supporting that er assembly process er that you but the first thing of the system wouldn't the lysis system wouldn't work because it's a gram-positive but <u>if you open up the cells and plate them on the host on on the bam-35 host you might get a plaque</u> remember plaque is a single molecule er device system so y- you you might be able to see a a few plaques </S2> . . .

The example also illustrates shared humour indicated by collective laughter. In this case the laughter may arise from the awareness of the speech act being something of a misnomer: a "suggestion" offered by the seminar leader in effect implies explaining or clarifying the problem at hand and providing a solution. It is likely to be taken as the correct solution, which at the very least carries special authority. It will hardly be treated on a par with a suggestion from one of the students. Laughter is interesting in such cases, as it tends to accompany discourse reflexivity fairly frequently, and with its wide range of important functions in interaction (e.g. Glenn 2003) would be worth exploring further in connection with reflexive metadiscourse, although it is beyond the present scope.

All forward-oriented discourse reflexivity in this section has been about the speaker and their intentions. We can therefore call them *egocentric*. For the present it suffices to distinguish egocentric, or self-referring, speech from *altercentric*, or other-referring speech. The distinction becomes particularly relevant with retrieving discourse reflexivity in the next section (4.2.2) and will be discussed more thoroughly there.

Responding to others

The co-presence of speakers activates participants' awareness of others, and this affects the way the discourse takes shape. Even if speakers simply indicate the speech act they intend to perform, they tend to relate their turn to other participants, like *as you say* in (4.9).

(4.9) <S4> erm ***i have a question*** concerning these er rules which are b- @bound to be ignored@ *as you say* is it because of some conservative models in the society does this influence [the judgements] </S4>

The question (*is it because of*. . .) does not follow the reflexive expression immediately, much like *suggestion* in (4.8), even though in this case the delay is shorter. For how long a speaker can delay confirming the expectation they have set up, what factors can sustain it, and at which point will co-participants' expectation be revised if the prospection is not fulfilled is an open question. Clearly, distractions and interruptions happen in interactive speech situations, and it is possible that predictions will either be revised or simply fade away even if they have been strong to begin with. There may be ways of keeping predictions alive, but little is known about what the role of different means of prospection, specifically reflexive metadiscourse, might be in dialogic interaction.

Explicit prospection can flout implicit predictions of speech acts. S4 in (4.10) explains that instead of a question, she is going to give a *reminder*. In the situation there was, however, no explicit bid for questions. This is a graduate seminar where the presentation was followed by the chair's invitation to *reaction from the audience*. The first two people who took the floor did ask questions, then also challenged the responses, and argued back and forth with the presenter. S4's metadiscourse suggests an awareness of an underlying convention or default expectation that 'comments to the presenter' mean questions.

(4.10) <S1> <NAME S4> yep you first </S1>
<S4> *oh er no just a small reminder it's not meant a question* you mentioned that the turkey wasn't accepted because of they were religious </S4>

In conference discussions it is quite common to find reflexive references to other speech acts than questions. S25 in (4.11) presents a *challenge*. The example comes from a conference where the issue (*difference* referring to variable copyright practices) came up during discussion, not in a presentation.

(4.11) <S25> i don't know if there are experts in this room which might might might well address the difference but *one one more challenge i'd like to put* like like <NAME NS16> was speaking about the university practices that i'm i'm quite be- bewildered about . . .

Before representing his turn as a *challenge*, this speaker starts with an explicit call for collective construction of knowledge (. . . *if there are experts in this room which might . . . address . . .*) Hereby the speaker also steers the discussion towards his preferred direction, manifesting the competitive side of academic discussion.

A very common speech act following a presentation is a comment (see Section 4.2.2 for more discussion). In (4.12) the speaker is the chairperson and follows a tacit norm of allocating turns to others before himself. He again explicitly relates his turn to others, first to his fellow listeners who appear to have exhausted their comments (*if **you** don't have* [*more comments*]), then to the specific addressee (***your** presentation*). This is a typical case of discourse reflexivity contextualising turns with respect to discourse that is being jointly created.

(4.12) <S1> if you don't have then *i have couple of comments reactions* to this to your presentation . . .

Modifiers are used for a more nuanced idea of what is to be expected in a speech act. Example (4.13) gives a kind of forewarning that the addressee is going to be challenged by the question. At the same time the preparatory modifier *difficult* reduces a potential face-threat to the addressee in case he is not able to come up with a ready answer. Phrasing the reflexive move as a request (*can I ask*) further mitigates the presumed challenge.

(4.13) <S3> [mhm-hm okay] okay okay that's fine okay. *can i ask you a difficult question* <S2> yeah </S2> basically is this . . .

In regulated multi-party discussions speakers face the complex task of waiting for their turn while the conversation continues to directions that may or may not be relevant to what they had in mind when they made a bid to talk. Below (4.14) the current speaker (S24) returns to a previous topic, which had meanwhile been followed by a different topic with three turns between two speakers. The topic S24 revives is one that may have been particularly salient for her, because she had originally talked about it in her own presentation earlier in the same conference. Moreover, the speaker who first brought it up in the present discussion explicitly referred to S24's presentation. The chair (S23) offers the floor to (S24) when her turn comes.

(4.14) <S23> [mhm-hm] <NAME S24> please </S23>
<S24> uh-huh *just to continue a little bit* with regard to the UNESCO convention proposal . . .

Because the topic had been in the ongoing discussion in addition to the earlier presentation, it was presumably available in the representation that participants shared of the discussion at the time. In other words, it was likely to be in their shared situation models, and a reminding cue could probably help refresh the relevant long-term working memory representation. Using a verb like CONTINUE when the previous topic had been something quite different apparently requires some explicit contextualisation before the speaker can pursue it again. It is also interesting that when this speaker proceeds to what might be regarded as her 'own' topic, she mitigates the reflexive expression (*just . . . a little bit*) as if minimising the imposition on others. By elaborating the resumed topic at this stage, S24 contributes further to the collaborative incrementation of shared understanding, thus advancing the ongoing co-construction of knowledge.

In this section, many linguistically explicit signs of speakers' awareness of the presence of others in the situation are manifest. Our attention has nevertheless been on the orienting uses of their metadiscourse which refer to the speakers themselves, that is, are egocentric.

Involving others

So far, we have talked about discourse reflexivity preparing ground for what the speaker is about to say next. Metadiscourse need not of course precede the utterance it talks about but for instance in questions the grounds may come first, like in (4.15). Moreover, it then becomes relevant to address the person from whom the answer is sought, in an *altercentric* (other-centred) reference.

(4.15) <S1> . . . <NAME S6> already er touched this topic but is it somehow related to i would think about the tradition of Ostpolitik er er er in the first place but er *if you could ela- elaborate on that* er as well </S1>

Answer elicitations for assessment prompt an interlocutor to give their view of some topic matter either as an individual, as in (4.16), or as a representative of a group (4.17, 4.18). In (4.17) the addressee is positioned as a specialist, with the implication that collective expertise is behind her assessment rather than her personal view. The addressee has given a presentation in a graduate seminar, and a fellow student (S5) is trying to get to the bottom of the assessment of coffee quality. In (4.18), by contrast, the addressee is invited to adopt the viewpoint of a specified group.

(4.16) <S5> . . . Basque country or Northern Ireland so, *would you say* that in the Balkans they are more violent or they they are of a different importance or different significance </S5>

(4.17) <S5> [yeah] but still can you *can you say that* the c- coffee with l- less acid is better quality level (than) high acid </S5>

(4.18) . . . but anyhow it will take us somewhere better and and er *maybe you could comment from Indian Indian perception* but some (of the) at least in in s- in several aboriginal knowledge systems this kind of, notion . . .

An addressee can be pushed towards a very specific answer, as in (4.19), but sometimes questions can be vague, and not even identify an addressee (4.20).

(4.19) <S2> *can you say more precisely* who they are </S2

(4.20) . . . or whether, Sweden is too young a country to have er experienced this sort of wave of enthusiasm for a colonialisation *i don't know who would. could answer that question* </S10>

The last few examples have illustrated uses of metadiscourse other than advance orientation to the speaker's upcoming contribution or rhetorical addressing of their listeners. Speakers in these cases relate their turns to those of others and seek answers or new knowledge from other participants. They also tend to refer to previous stages in the discussion, which are scrutinised in more detail in the next section.

4.2.2 Retrieving

Participants in a discussion continuously make predictions and simultaneously keep track of the discourse as it evolves, adjusting their representations and models of it. As discussed in Chapter 2, it is a cognitively demanding task, because working memory is limited, short-lived, and verbatim memory lasts only a few seconds. Present discourse gets absorbed into what quickly becomes the past. Because retaining a verbatim record is virtually impossible beyond about ten seconds, representations of the discourse must be processed rapidly (Christiansen & Chater 2016), but they are also volatile.

As each participant processes the unfolding discourse, they generate their individual representations, which will not be identical but normally close enough to ensure a degree of coherence which enables the dialogue to continue. If not, or if different interpretations are experienced as conflicting in an important way, they can be contested and negotiated.

For something of past verbalisation to be re-introduced to present representations, its relevance needs to be restored, as anticipated in (4.14). What I call *retrieving* discourse reflexivity refers to something in a past state of the discourse which is brought into the present. Such segments of discourse may be retained in the current representations of all participants, or only some of them, at the very least the speaker who introduces them again. Often that past is very recent: previous turns and utterances, or things said just a moment ago. Discourse reflexivity cannot bring the past back. It picks an element from a past state, or more precisely, the speaker's representation of it, paraphrasing or otherwise transforming it, since the element is no longer available in unprocessed form. It is also devoid of much, or all, of its previous context.

Retrieving is one way of contextualising a speaker's new contributions. This is evinced in retrieving elements rarely occurring at ends of turns, but commonly at initial phases.

In the light of numbers, retrieving is a much larger category than orienting (see Chapter 8). This sets dialogue apart from monologic speech, and by the same token from written monologue. Retrieving discourse reflexivity falls into two principal types: egocentric (self-referring) and altercentric (other-referring). These two types were already seen operating in the previous section, where 'looking ahead' was essentially egocentric and 'responding to others' and 'involving others' were primarily altercentric. These two types also basically correspond to what I earlier (Mauranen 2001) discussed under *targeting* as 'monologic' and 'dialogic' orientations, mentioned already in Chapter 1. The third type, 'interactive' orientation, is now discussed under 'managing the situation' in Section 4.3. Part of the reason for modifying the terminology was that altercentric references have two major subtypes, addressee-reference and third-party reference, which seem important to keep apart in dialogic situations. Egocentric and altercentric reference are discussed in the next two sections, beginning from egocentric references.

Egocentric reference

Speakers often return to points made at an earlies stage of their own ongoing speech with *egocentric references*. Egocentric references are different from Hyland's (2005) self-mentions, in that these limit speaker-references to those that are accompanied by references to the discourse. Discourse reflexive egocentric references thereby include the speaker only in the capacity of the current speaker.

In discussions following a presentation, many references relate to the talk just heard. This is true of presenters and their co-participants alike. Presenters typically refer to what they said in their talk (4.21).

(4.21) . . . at the in the beginning *somewhere in my lecture i said something about this* and . . .

Egocentric references typically expand on what speakers have already said. They may clarify what they meant (4.22) or add something they might have wanted to say but did not in an earlier turn or presentation (4.23).

(4.22) <S11> erm er there were s- many erm the main female activities in Finland those days . . . schooling in the household matters was emphasised and er yeah *i maybe was not very clear saying* that i think it is a kind of a similar phenomenon like erm that er the American black took . . .

(4.23) . . . i do think it's it has less to do with the curriculum itself but more with the kind of interaction you are prepared to take in regard to the curricula <S3> mhm-hm </S3>, and *that's why i was putting this stress on* agency as a mediation between adult and child . . .

The expression *as I said* (with its rarer variant *as I mentioned*) deserves some special attention. While it seemingly accompanies a repeat of what the speaker already said, which in a strict sense would appear quite redundant because it should have been incorporated into shared knowledge already, it usually introduces a rephrase, or even something new. This consists of the speaker's construal of what they previously said and an indication of its current relevance. Such a reference raises a strong prospection that a restatement of a previous position will follow. Even though this expectation is virtually invariably fulfilled, it will rarely reappear in an identical form to the first time. *As I said* has a strong tendency to precede the reformulation: in only one instance in this data did a speaker add it as if an afterthought to his turn. *As I said* is thus a Janus-faced indicator of retrieving and prospecting discourse reflexivity. However, even though *as I said* is very frequent in monologues (Chapter 7), it is much less common in dialogues (4.24).

(4.24) <S6> well *as i said* there were some there were this er three threats . . .

Even though 'retrieving' discourse reflexivity makes retrospective connections, it also points forward as we have seen: the important distinction between 'retrieving' and 'orienting' is not that one looks back and the other ahead, but that orienting reflexive discourse only looks ahead. In terms of discourse dynamism, forward is indeed the dominant direction, in harmony with speech processing.

A small number of egocentric references nevertheless actually seem to look only back to what the speaker just said. These follow immediately after the utterance they refer to, thus staying within the limits of the working memory. They seem to occur in two functions, one of which labels a speech act retrospectively (4.25, 4.26). These retrospective characterisations appear at turn completions, as if confirming the nature of the speech act just made.

(4.25) <S1> er i'm using the the books and writings of . . . so i'm not i haven't done very much of that kind of temporal work yet *that's very short answer* </S1>

(4.26) <S8> . . . along with certain models of democracy *that is er my own reflection on the point* </S8>

The second function of these immediate retrospections is to follow an expression of stance or evaluation. Unlike retrospective speech act labels, stance and evaluation are not always turn-final but may be followed by a reason (4.27) or further elaboration (4.28).

(4.27) <S4> well maybe @more violent@ *i would say* consider all these wars and fights and even that it caused an interference like the United States and the united . . .

(4.28) <S6> well alright you may say it's a religion but its nowadays appearance is very much protestant *i would say* erm even more Zwinglian issue of life or Calvinist because erm er religion is not an abstract.

More commonly, discourse reflexive indications of evaluation come early in a turn, if not right at the beginning, then at least before the evaluative statement itself. An orienting example was seen in (4.3), and monologues also show a similar tendency (Chapter 7).

Egocentric referring also seems to play a role in indicating the speaker's self-consistency, which is obviously central to debating a point, as in (4.29).

(4.29) <S4> [i agree with] you because what *what i am saying* is really based on practical project for example . . .

This supports R. Craig & Sanusi's (2000) analysis identifying expressions like *I'm just saying* as speakers' pragmatic devices for claiming they have held a consistent argumentative standpoint all along.

Speakers also refer to what was *not* their past discourse, that is, what they did not talk about but now appear to have second thoughts about. Both (4.30) and (4.31) recognise an omission in their talks, the first one putting it down to the focus chosen, the latter using the omission as a springboard to say more. Both go on to talk about the previously omitted topic, so the reference in effect assumes a forward-looking role, despite its retrospective character.

(4.30) <S6> yeah well yeah here i wanted to focus only on this so <S5> mhm </S5> *i didn't talk anything about* the economic cooperation but of course this is in the in the ASEAN declaration . . .

(4.31) <S2> yeah well er there is er one thing *i forgot to mention*, there is a difference in the conditions . . .

Occasionally presentations are distributed in writing in advance. In such cases, the written paper can be referred to in the discussion. It could well be argued such cases are not part of the current discourse, and they certainly border on intertextuality. In the present analysis they were taken to be part of the current discourse when speakers treated them as shared experience, like in (4.32).

(4.32) <S2> yeah that's true and again *i'm referring to my paper* because there is there's this larger, er sort of framing . . .

By merely looking at egocentric references, we can begin to discern certain more general differences between longer and shorter discussions. Longer discussions are less confined to a given topic and assume more of a life of their own than do the five-minute conference slots. They branch out into new directions and wander off the point of departure, and there are more self-references to speakers' earlier discussion turns (4.33) instead of only to their presentations. In brief, long discussions show signs of self-organising.

(4.33) <S10> . . . Sweden has er now been redefined itself as a sort of the north as well just like er other (xx) and *perhaps i already said that* i thought ah yeah you know the the myth of Sweden as the the north . . .

Most conference discussion sections tend to be short and focused on the preceding presentation, but sometimes they consist of longer sessions after a few consecutive papers. By contrast, graduate seminars divide their time in favour of discussion, keeping presentations short. It would be very interesting to see more comprehensive analyses into this phenomenon, which might have the potential for altering conventional practices in conferences. Longer discussions might lead to more fruitful exchanges and more new ideas.

Altercentric reference

Most of the time people do not talk about their own earlier talk but that of others. The overwhelming majority (about three quarters) of retrieving discourse reflexivity refers to other speakers' speech, mostly to a second person addressee. These *altercentric references* typically consist of a representation of what the addressee had said or talked about, followed by a question, objection, or a comment. The typical pattern has two parts: first a paraphrase of an earlier statement and then uttering something new, which follows the same pattern as seen in egocentric references like *as I said.* Altercentric references thus typically act as springboards for the current speaker's point, comment, or question. They tend to occur as turn-initial segments that precede questions or follow an orienting segment (*I would like to ask a question **you mentioned*** er many . . .). Altercentric references are especially central in negotiating and debating (Chapter 6). There are two principal kinds of altercentric references: second-person references to specific interlocutors, that is, *addressee-references,* and third-person references, or *third-party references.* I will discuss addressee-references first and look into third-party references next.

Speakers usually turn to a particular interlocutor even in multi-party discussions. The overwhelming majority of altercentric references, more than two thirds (71.3%) are directed at a specific addressee. Given that an equally large majority of all retrieving references are made to others than self, and with retrieving being the principal type of contextualising dialogue, we can conclude that this is prototypical discourse reflexivity in dialogic interaction: talking about what an interlocutor has said. This stands in a clear contrast to monologue and thus implies a necessary departure from traditional metadiscourse study.

Many academic discussions are structured to make a dyadic exchange the default mode: discussions typically follow presentations, turns are allocated to one member of the audience at a time by a chairperson, with the expectation that turns are oriented to the presentation and consist in questions or comments to the presenter. The default expectation seems to be that questions are asked, as was seen in example (4.10). As already noted, longer discussions follow the structure more loosely, which allows for more varied reference patterns.

Contrary to what seems to be the general expectation, comments on a presentation are more common than questions, and addressee-references typically employ what I have previously (Mauranen 2010, 2012) called the *springboard function*: a speaker latches on to another speaker's turn and goes on to develop their own point from there (4.34).

(4.34) <S23> . . . i'm just, thinking of this basic pattern *you have been describing and er want to point out that* er the multinational corporations er partly the same corporations that are very eager to press on er in intellectual pro- er property er and to tighten . . .

The springboard from which the current speaker leaps onto their own views after connecting to a previous turn can occasionally be slightly wobbly, and lead to a new focus as happens with S11 below (4.35).

(4.35) <S11> but *but the question you used* about is there an urban history at all a discipline where (xx) many years ago Castells started the discussion about is there an urban sociology because . . .

As participants develop each other's topics, they also develop each speaker's own thoughts. While they increment the discourse, they also increment shared, emerging new knowledge (see Chapter 6). In the process they seek backing from each other and acknowledge each other's parts in the collaborative intellectual effort, as the speaker does with his altercentric reference in (4.36).

(4.36) <S10> . . . in the 17th century who thought of the north as the not the periphery but the centre *i think you mentioned it something to that as well* but the north was the place where the goths came from and they were the ones who se- seeded Europe with culture and they had this bizarre dream of of Sweden as the centre of civilisation . . .

Sometimes a speaker provides a *construal* of the addressee's meaning, a 'candidate understanding' (e.g. Couper-Kuhlen & Selting 2018). In (4.37), S5 offers a conceptualisation of what he takes S2's presentation to imply (*you are talking about sort of bureaucratic repression er that kind of repression call it repression*) and seeks confirmation from S2 to his comment arising from this interpretation (*wouldn't you say*).

(4.37) <S5> just a comment *wouldn't you say* that is a situation that is quite prevalent in in a number of countries in Europe i mean that happens if you if

you only talking about er or let me correct myself not only but ***you are talking about sort of bureaucratic repression*** er that kind of repression call it repression it goes on for example in . . . so it is difficult to get a citizenship it is difficult to get social security and so on </S5>
<S2> yeah yeah [i agree] </S2>

Construals are sometimes made in a very tentative manner, as illustrated by the next extract (4.38), which comes from a lively seminar discussion which has branched out from a presentation, and the presenter has become just one among the participants. Neither is there much intervention from the chair, so the discussion has much of the air of an informal intellectual conversation. Speakers respond to each other's developments of the themes. S9 resorts to hedging (*I don't know if I followed your idea*) and vagueness (*something like*) before his tentative construal of what S10 has said (*I wonder if you meant something like*). She confirms his interpretation (*yes I think*), and goes on to expand on it (*because in science* . . .).

(4.38) <S9> . . . in that sense i i i think knowledge is not value-free the values come come in and and i i *i don't know if i followed* your [idea] <SU-10> [mhm-hm] </SU-10> clearly i ***i wonder if you meant something like*** having for instance er modern science as a religion in place of religion or believing in myths and letting it explain the world or (xx) </S9>
<S10> *yes i think*, because in science we love this knowledge term especially </S10>

Altercentric references are good indicators of the collective nature of sharing understanding. By acknowledging each other's contributions, participants engage in mutual scaffolding of the understanding that emerges from the discussion (4.39).

(4.39) </S1> this case er obviously er aid in 96 was cut but not all aid so *like you said* it's very difficult to cut all aid it it er raises a question now in Tanzan- in Tanzania the the parties er supposedly reformed before they were told to . . .

Acknowledging other speakers also demonstrates positive evaluation, like above, even without overtly evaluative words like *good, important*, or *appreciate*.

Negative evaluation is harder to find, which is probably linked to the general *linguistic positivity bias* (aka *the Pollyanna principle*, cf. Matlin 2016) detected in several studies (e.g., Dodds et al. 2015). Dodds et al. assume that it is universal in human language. It is also found in academic writing (Wen & Lei 2022) as well as academic face-to-face conversations (Mauranen 2002). Negative evaluations tend to be more veiled and mitigated than positive ones. In (4.40), *I see what you mean* could in principle be regarded as positive evaluation, but the context gives it away as a small concession before a contrary view. *But* follows without a pause, immediately indicating the position the speaker is about to take. The verb MEAN is of course somewhat marginally discourse reflexive, but in this exchange, it refers to what the previous speaker had just said, motivating a discourse reflexive interpretation.

(4.40) . . . the argument for you know for argument for patent protection doesn't apply </S17>
<S22> erm well yes and no *@i@ see what you mean* but erm there's still a lot to be gained a lot of new knowledge i i imagine to be gained from traditional knowledge so giving no . . .

Other means for expressing negative evaluations than preceding concessions are indirectness (*struck me as being very national*) and using hedging (*struck me as **a little** odd*). In (4.41) the speaker employs both in turn. Ahead of the latter, more negative evaluation S4 makes a confirmation check on his construal (*right*). The reflexive elements highlight the way in which the speaker contrasts two perspectives on the topic: *you're talking about; your discussion* vs. *as we heard this morning*. S4 thus calls up support for his view from a previous talk, which also suggests his own representation of the issues may have moved on in the course of the macro-event.

(4.41) <S4> er i would just er wanted to ask you a question about the kind of framing of your paper which struck me as being very national and *you're talking about* diasporic commu- communities which probably as we heard this morning er all sorts of connections er telephoning and media and financial connections er with other parts of the world and yet er you *your discussion* on immigration was entirely in terms of the Finnish nation <SS> @@ </SS> <S2> yeah </S2> right <S2> that's true </S2> that struck me as a as a little o- odd

Even though comments are more frequent than questions in altercentric references, questions are of course also asked. Questions to presenters tend to be prefaced by identifying the topic. In (4.42) the speaker first refers to the talk (*two points you raised in the presentation you said . . . and you said*), which demarcate his interest area before actually asking the question (*now how come Zambia is not . . .*).

(4.42) <S1> okay more concrete perhaps er *two points you raised in the presentation you said* that voters for or or opposition party people er also critical people like journalists have been intimidated in Zambia and *you said* that there is a very weak democratic culture in the country er those two things would definitely be attributed to Zimbabwe now how come Zambia is not in the news all the time and how come Zimbabwe is </S1>

Unlike presentations, discussion turns are not prepared in advance, which shows in their occasionally complicated structuring. In the following instance (4.43), questions and altercentric references become interleaved in the framing and structuring of the questions. First a reference to the addressee prefaces a yes-no question (*are you referring only to . . . or are you referring to*), but the speaker does not pause for an answer before moving on to a second, more specific question of the wh- type (*what about Bulgaria*). Finally, the second question is followed by another reference to the talk (*because you mentioned that*) as if motivating the question. We get the impression that the speaker is thinking on his feet.

(4.43) <S5> *when you are talking about* the ethnic groups different ethnic groups *are you referring only to* former Yugoslavia or *are you referring to* some other countries in the region, what about Bulgaria because *you mentioned [that* these] <S4> [yeah well] </S4> ethnic that there are ethnic boundaries which prevent cooperation among [among the peoples] </S5>

Questions can be contextualised in multiple ways by clusters of different kinds of reflexive metadiscourse like below (4.44), where S9 goes through the phases of question flagging (*one more . . . actually I have the same question as* <NAME S8> *but I have another one for you too*), referring to the addressee's talk (*you told us about. . .*) and only after that proceeding to the question (*have you detected. . .*).

(4.44) <S9> *one more* <S2> yes </S2> actually *i have the same question as <NAME S8> but i have another one for you too,* er ***you told us about*** the general model of education have you detected any kind of regional interests or unease of technological teaching in Finland by the professors who first went to Germany and then came back to Finland, or *is it hard to say* if there are any </S9>

In all, altercentric discourse reflexivity referring to addressees makes explicit what speakers find relevant or interesting in other speakers' contributions, how pieces fit together as shared understanding is being incremented (or situation models aligned) by different participants and helps structure questions and comments in complex communication.

To move on to the second kind of altercentric discourse reflexivity, let us see how third-person references come into it. Apart from ourselves and second-person addressees, we can obviously also talk about what third parties have said in the ongoing discourse. When speakers invoke preceding discourse, they can attribute it to an identifiable individual (*the previous speaker talked about*) or to nobody specifically (*as I learned from earlier presentations*). However, although third-party references occur, they are not very frequent. While they are almost as common as egocentric references, neither of these occur nearly as often as addressee-references.

Third-person references resemble addressee-references in that they identify a relevant contribution by another speaker and bring this into the discussion. This focuses and contextualises the speaker's own utterance and serves as a springboard for developing their own point (4.45).

(4.45) <S24> yeah *i would just like to push a little bit further* ***his suggestion*** *because i think that* ***what he was suggesting*** (xx) with I-Ps you have this er incentive er objective but in traditional knowledge you don't have it ***as he said*** and maybe maybe the I-P type of protection is not at all the right kind of protection for traditional knowledge </S24>
<S22> yeah you're [probably right] </S22>

Academic (micro-)events can be embedded within larger macro-events, as discussed in Chapter 3. Cross-references to other micro-events in the larger whole or the macro-event are characteristic of conferences and university courses like graduate seminars. The next two examples illustrate both these event types and how metadiscoursal connections are made between the discussion at hand and a previous talk within the same macro-event. In both cases it is the chairperson who makes the connections. The first (4.46) comes from a conference where a section chair is linking threads from different presentations, and the second (4.47) from a graduate seminar where the leader is relating the present discussion to a previous presentation in the same course. Both instances show how new connections between concepts and ideas get stimulated and forged in these events. It is also interesting to note and supportive of the macro-event notion that the seminar leader in (4.48) refers to someone's presentation a month earlier as having taken place *in this discussion*.

(4.46) <S18> yeah i agree and er and there's yeah er i think *there's a very nice link between <NAME S8>'s presentation to to that what er <NAME NS16> said in his keynote in the very beginning of this conference* and <NAME NS16> is here so if he's got something to say, you can do that but here's another comment before that </S18>

(4.47) . . . these things like inference and arguments and and *what <NAME> was was explaining er a month ago here in in this er discussion* that that there's er something about this this er argument er *he was talking about* Socrates . . .

References to earlier talks can be specific without directly naming the person who presented the ideas reformulated by the current speaker (4.48):

(4.48) <S2> mhm *the last presentation on on on Tuesday er we heard* that there's still a very strong fixation in the region on on the nation state and not so much talk not so much practise in regional cooperation and *the person who made the presentation* recommended very much that there should be . . .

In addition to third party references to persons, presentations, or points made, collective references to all those present, a 'collective *we*' also appears in similar functions. This resembles an 'inclusive *we*', with the difference that the speaker may not have been involved in the discussion referred to (4.49). In some sense this is an imagined *we*, the group that comprises present participants communally. These collective references tend to prioritise a general topic, as in (4.49), where the speaker presents an interpretation of what is going on in this discussion. Before him, one other speaker has asked a question on the preceding presentation, but S20 has not spoken during this conference section before this point. *We*, therefore, does not strictly speaking include him. The next instance (4.51) also shows a speaker construing collective discussion with the group as the discussing subject, as it were. He also weaves distinct vagueness into his résumé of topics (*all these . . . and things like that*), which prepares ground for the fairly open question he then puts to the presenter.

(4.49) <S20> er thank you very much for the the interesting presentation er *some comments and then a question* from the UN perspective erm *i think here we are discussing* a missing link between er information technology and and er poverty reduction . . .

(4.50) <S7> yes er now that we've been *the last two days we've been discussing* <u>all these</u> open source software issues <u>and things like that</u> . . .

References to previous talk can be even less personal than collective *we*. The referent can be a presentation, or a point made, without any person-reference. Such references characteristically involve evaluation:

(4.51) <S1> [@*that's that's a very interesting*] [*question@*] </S1

(4.52) <S1> okay <COUGH> *this was* <COUGH> *more or less the first presentation which had a very strong theoretical* in in this (xx) so in that respective *it was a good presentation,*

In all these unattributed, apparently impersonal references, the implied addressee or referent tends to be present, or if not, is usually recognisable to the participants. Altogether third-party references are relatively infrequent, which would seem to reflect participants' predominant orientation to those present. The largest type of all contextualising references is the second person altercentric reference, which certainly seems to support the prevalence of orientation to co-present others.

This section has discussed altercentric references, highlighting the role of discourse reflexivity in navigating dialogue in interactional discourse. What has emerged as the core has been speakers' engagement with each other's talk and the many ways in which they weave their talk together. Different speakers' contributions get entwined into the common thread of the discourse, which progresses from its initial settings towards unforeseen outcomes through constant co-construction by the participants.

4.3 Managing situation

Discussion needs managing. Even casual conversations require ways of opening and closing, ways for people to join or leave the conversation, to move to a new phase or change physical location, and many other managing acts that may not appear prominent or important, but which ensure the smooth progression of talk. Institutional settings tend to impose more order on discussions which perform institutional functions. Meetings, formal procedures, and ceremonies are closely regulated, with clearly outlined role slots in institutional settings. This holds for relatively permanent institutions, such as universities, but also temporary academic event types like conferences, whose close adherence to traditions and disciplinary specificities is noteworthy. Even relatively free-flowing institutional discussions have their duration scheduled and their management assigned to select individuals. In our data, events usually also include at least chairperson roles. Some graduate seminars rotate the chair role among students, but most are chaired by the senior academic whose task is to run the seminar. Thesis defences have their additional set roles and procedures. Interestingly, even student work groups seem to get self-organised along the lines of institutional practices, appointing a secretary and a chairperson, although there is no formal requirement to do so.

Situation management in the present data is, unsurprisingly, far more common in dialogic than monologic discourse, but even in dialogues it accounts for just over a fifth of all discourse reflexivity, which suggests that it plays a relatively small though persistent role compared to discourse management, at least in terms of metadiscourse. It is possible that the situation management talk captured in our recordings is an underestimate of its amount because such talk easily gets cut off from event beginnings and endings. From time to time, practical talk around moving equipment, booting laptops, opening or closing windows and the like were recorded, but although these manage the situation in some sense, they rarely make reference to talk and were therefore excluded as irrelevant. Situation management corresponds roughly to the third type of discourse reflexivity in my previous classification of targeting in dialogues (Mauranen 2001) and is very similar to what at that point I called the 'interactive' orientation (clearly, not a felicitous term!).

Many practices of situation management are highly conventionalised and routine- like, though not all. At the most conventionalised end, chairpersons carry out situation management in discussions, usually with brief formulaic turns. Apart from routine openings (*questions comments arguments please*) and closings of discussion sections (okay *there aren't any other comments*), chairperson duties often include introducing presenters (4.53) and sequencing and ordering the events (4.54)

(4.53) <S4> everyone is now satisfied with coffee so *let's continue i have er i have a great honour and pleasure introduce*, professor <NAME NS13> er who already yesterday *gave us excellent lecture* . . .

(4.54) <S2> thank you er docent <NAME S1> . . . it's time to introduce doctor <NAME S3> er *we probably have these two presentations first and after that we will have a joint discussion* . . .

Situation management is not, however, limited to routine exchanges. It also happens that managing discourse and managing situation get interleaved when participants other than the chair make a move to alter the flow of the discussion. If a speaker adopts an 'external' perspective of the ongoing discussion instead of engaging with the issues being talked about, we can talk about a *plane-shift* and regard the instance as managing the situation rather than managing the discourse, as we can see in (4.55) and (4.56).

(4.55) . . . *I better be @be quiet now@ otherwise we* ***this would be di- dialogue between us professors*** *and and it's not the purpose of the course;*

(4.56) <S3> *no actually* ***it was a very very nice discussion*** *I really enjoyed it I really liked it* </S3>

A plane-shift can be a competitive move, or an act of power, where a discussion participant seeks a leader position, trying to steer the discussion towards or away from topics, as if a self-appointed chairperson (see also Chapter 6). To look first at a case (4.57) where a chairperson suggests where the discussion could go next, and a participant taking this up, the chair (S23) prompts participants to move towards a certain direction (*I would . . . encourage er you to carry on with the discussion . . . so let's talk er more generally of . . .*). A participant (S24) is quick to act upon the suggestion. He refers to a third participant's earlier point as a springboard for his own (*I would just like to push a little bit further his suggestion*). Here the new direction came from the chair and there is no evident issue with power.

(4.57) <S23> mhm *i would* <COUGH>, *encourage y- er encourage er you to* ***carry on with the discussion*** *er er suggesting that* that we forget a- about patents here because . . . and in traditional er kna- knowledge er er that is a er non sequitur <S22> mhm-hm </S22> *so* ***let's talk er more generally*** *of* erm I-P protection, please </S23>
<S24> yeah *i would just like to push a little bit further his suggestion because i think that what he was suggesting* (xx) with I-Ps you have this . . . but in traditional knowledge you don't have it *as he said* and maybe maybe the I-P type of protection is not at all the right kind of protection for traditional knowledge </S24>

Even though it is the chairperson's prerogative to act on the situational plane, conference chairpersons do not usually attempt to dominate the discussion. They tend to act more like moderators – there to run the discussion. Chairs and moderators can direct co-participants' attention towards topics and foci and away from others but this is not a duty following from the position. By contrast, plane-shifts by other participants come across as deliberate moves to alter the course of the discussion. This implies challenging the way the discourse is moving. These interventions are power-related more than those by a chairperson precisely because situation management is allocated elsewhere.

Participants' spontaneous plane-shifts fall into two types in our data: speakers either try to instigate a topic change, or they seek to alter turn allocation. The first kind concerns the choice of topic. Example (4.58) comes from a discussion which started after a presentation but has moved on to less structured talking about more general issues. S2 and S4 debate the value of a given topic for the discussion. S2 makes a plane-shift and challenges a topic S4 started earlier (*we have to try to, you know* ***go away from this these talks about*** *. . .*), upon which S4, also assuming the management plane, comments on S2's topic choice (*now you're talking about*), and after a concession towards it (*it's essential what you say*) moves back to his own position. S2 will not give up (*i would ask if you say that*), but S4 now completely dismisses S2's proposal (***it's one of those general questions we can talk over and over again***). The two speakers thus debate the terms of the discussion, and their arguments defend their respective preferences concerning the situation, rather than issues within a discussion.

(4.58) <S2> no but i think we have to ***we have to try to***, you know ***go away from this these talks about*** content here and process there <SU> yes </SU> <S4> mhm </S4> but look at at concrete examples . . . what does it mean to be a citizen [within] <SU> [yes] </SU> a classroom and things like that which is very much process isn't it </S2>
<S4> well it all depends on the content i mean ***now you are <SS> [@@] </SS> [talking about], now you're talking about*** i can understand why *you argue this way* and *i agree* with you but but sometimes and apart from that other it's very *it's essential what you say* i have to train teachers who have to teach history . . . at a certain time they start teaching history you start teaching literature you start film, er art history and then there's a different er content of content </S4>
<S2> okay *i would i would ask if you say that* you know i have to teach history so, what what is history why is history for me important in that that moment in time er it [it it means if you are] </S2>
<S4> ***[it's one of those general questions] we can talk over and over again*** [(xx)] </S4>

Topic challenges can be successful. In (4.59) a speaker (S4, not the chair) instigates a plane-shift by suggesting a change of topic (***I would like to suggest not to go on about this term . . . . let's stop about it***). It provokes a self-justification from the person (S1, the chair) who originated the topic (*my kind of argument is*) and now repeats her initial argument, but then backs down on her previous position, and underscores her agreement with S4 on the appropriate topic (*but of course* ***I agree with you*** *. . . I was just trying to account for my reluctance* ***to use this***

kind of words *but it's you're quite right* ***I quite agree with you***). S4 then takes the floor and, shifting back to discourse management, puts a question to the previous presenter, in effect steering the discussion away from what he found an objectionable topic.

(4.59) <S4> **i *would like to suggest not to go on about this term*** but anyway i would like to defend some philosophers of postmodernism . . . doesn't exist but ***let's stop about it*** but <SS> [@@] </SS> [there are] there are some intelligent postmodernists who can [(xx)] </S4>
<SS> [@@] </SS>
<S1> sure now it's just you know it th- ***my kind of argument is er was*** along the line that in fact we tend very easily . . . we tended to forget the child *but of course i agree with you* it's er if you go down to it it's not it *okay* ***i was just trying to account for my reluctance to use this kind of er words*** *but it's you're quite right i quite agree with you (it's)* </S1>
<S4> <u>can i ask one question to the speaker</u> er i also agree with . . .

The second kind of plane-shift concerns turn-taking. When speakers initiate a change to this, they often admit to deviating from the standard practice, for example by seeking corroboration from the chair, as in (4.60). S34 takes the chair's (S18) *mhm-hm* as a permission to take over answering a question.

(4.60) <S34> [i think] i think e- e- everything is changing *can i answer* <S18> mhm-hm </S18> *this* i think it's changing because . . .

Speakers also occasionally use plane-shifts as deflection tactics (4.61) by passing on a question to someone else, likewise assuming a role in running the situation.

(4.61) <S6> *could you* <NAME S3> *specify* the difference between the German and the Swiss system here during the late 19th century *i didn't get really the er point* how change . . .
<S3> *i can't answer that maybe er* <NAME S7> *can answer to that* </S3>
<S7> *i mean i think the a- answer to this is* is er very easy i don't i don't think that there was anything different . . .

This section has illustrated situation management as manifest in discourse reflexivity. Although the same functions were found in conferences and graduate seminars, there were differences in their relative proportions. Instances of situation management were somewhat more frequent in seminars than in conferences (21.2% vs. 15.2%), but a striking difference appeared in the relative numbers of who was doing the managing, the chairperson or a participant: while most management acts (87.6%) were by the chair in graduate seminars, in conference discussions close to a half (43.3%) were initiated by participants. This might reflect the unequal power balance in graduate seminars where the seminar leader represents academic staff and thus holds a higher institutional position. A fair number of seminars were student-chaired, though, thus ostensibly based on power equality, but the practice remained the same. Conference discussions take place between peers; although participants vary in status and seniority, discussion chairs may not be academically the most senior. Participant-instigated plane shifts should by this reasoning be easier at a conference than in a graduate seminar, where authority is more invested with one person.

4.4 Conclusion

This chapter has elaborated ways in which discourse reflexivity functions in dialogic academic discussions. At the outset, the discussion was limited to the *contextualising* function of reflexive metadiscourse, and the *negotiating* function postponed to a later chapter (Chapter 6). An initial distinction within contextualising metadiscourse was drawn between managing the discourse and managing the situation. *Discourse management* was easily the larger and more varied category, but *situation management* especially in its less obvious uses revealed certain interesting phenomena that have a bearing on how the interaction develops and how power may be involved in this and is therefore also worth taking on board.

The categories arrived at with the analysis are summarised in Figure 4.1 Reflexive discourse management serves a contextualising function, which makes the upcoming discourse relevant to the moment of speaking. There are two main ways of doing this: either a speaker can focus on what they are going to say next and provide advance orientation for listeners to expect it (the *orienting* function), or they can contextualise their speech by relating it to a topic that has been in the discussion previously and take that as their point of departure (the *retrieving* function). In effect, listeners use all available cues for anticipating what is to come, and both orienting and retrieving discourse reflexivity support their predictions; the difference is that orienting reflexivity only looks forward from the present, while retrieving reflexivity looks both ways and thus straddles past, present, and future states of the discourse. In some cases, there was a distinct delay between an explicit prospection and the prospected speech act, and the question arose as to how long it takes for hearers' predictions to be either revised or otherwise disappear after an explicit discourse reflexive prospection. This would warrant further research.

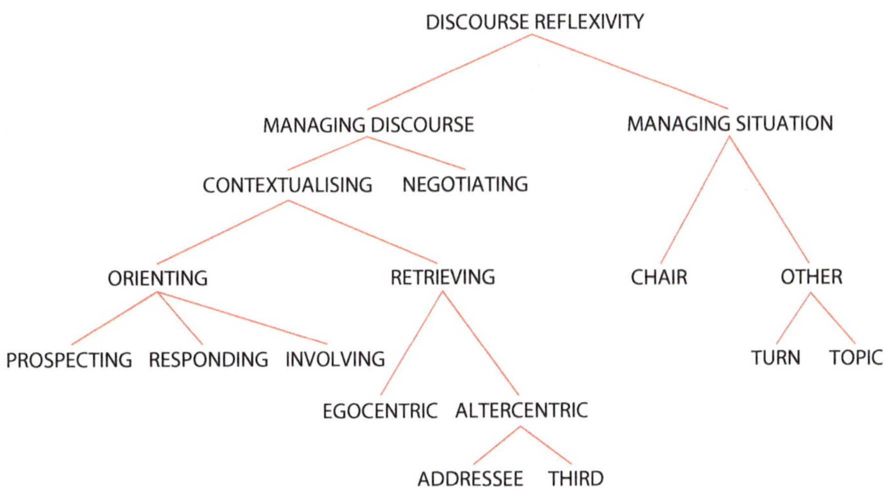

Figure 4.1: Discourse reflexivity in spoken dialogue.

Orienting reflexivity is not limited to prospecting (*pointing ahead*) and structuring the speaker's turn rhetorically, but a dialogic situation means that speakers also take steps to fit their turns to those of others (*responding to others*) and seek to bring others into the discourse (*involving others*). An important distinction cuts across these categories: referring to self, or *egocentric* discourse reflexivity, and referring to others, or *altercentric* discourse reflexivity. Egocentric reflexivity was by far the larger type in orienting discourse and accounted for over 70% of it in both conference (72.2%) and seminar (80.8%) dialogues. Attuning to other participants was evinced more clearly in retrieving discourse reflexivity. Reflecting this, the category divided into egocentric and altercentric types from the start. Egocentric discourse reflexivity refers to the speaker's own previous discourse, typically expanding on their earlier points, and if the retrospection is immediate, it tends to be evaluative. Egocentric references are also found to indicate the speaker's self-consistency. Perhaps somewhat unexpectedly, speakers occasionally employ retrieving egocentric references to talk about matters they have not in fact discussed but present them as if they had. Yet, often the previous occasions were way beyond working memory capacity, therefore presumably only available in processed form rather than verbatim.

The more common type of retrieving references is altercentric. These are typically second-person references (*addressee-references*), which were more frequent than first- and third-person references put together. Typical uses of altercentric references were identified as *springboard*, the current speaker contextualising their own upcoming contribution in something the addressee had said, and *construal*, where the current speaker offers their interpretation of what the addressee had said. In addition to an addressee, speakers also make retrieving references to third parties, either specified or unspecified others (*third-party references*).

An interesting difference was detected between longer and shorter discussions. Conference discussions tend to be short and structured for exchanges between listeners and presenters, with the default expectation that hearers mostly ask questions from the presenter. This was not borne out by the data: comments were more common than questions. Moreover, it is interesting to note that longer discussions, be they conference sessions or graduate seminars, drifted off the confines of the five-minute slot not only in talking points but also in their more varied reference patterns. It would seem that although certain constraints apply to academic discussions, such as a generally strong topic-orientation, others may start loosening if restrictions like tight scheduling are removed; less temporally constrained discussions seemed to acquire characteristics more associated with ordinary conversation. This is certainly an issue worth further investigation, which could influence the ways conferences are typically shaped.

Discourse reflexivity is much less involved in managing the situation than in managing the discourse. Most of the time it is, predictably, chairpersons who perform situation managing acts, and much of it consists of routine speech acts, such as inviting questions, introducing speakers, allocating turns, and monitoring the schedule. More interestingly, other participants than the chair also take part in situation management. Such spontaneous management is typically performed as *plane-shifts*. Spontaneous plane-shifts are of two kinds: those seeking to set off a topic change and those trying to alter turn allocation. The former tend to occur without consulting the chair, the latter typically seek confirmation from the chair. A slightly surprising finding with regard to situation management was that graduate seminars and conference discussions were quite dissimilar with regard to who performed management acts: in graduate seminars 87.6% of management was run by the chair, whereas in conferences close to a half (43.3%) were participant-initiated, that is, spontaneous plane-shifts. This would seem to reflect the social parameter of status. A more equal power structure appears to give rise to a more equally distributed structure of situation management.

In all, a thread that runs across this chapter is a perceptible altercentric orientation among interacting participants. Discourse reflexivity serves to make explicit what participants see as relevant or interesting in other speakers' contributions and what it sparks off in their own thinking. Shared understanding is being incremented by co-present participants jointly, potentially leading to new ideas. Social parameters come into dialogic interaction in various ways, especially in self-organising tendencies, which seem to increase along with discussion length and power equality.

Chapter 5
Discourse reflexivity in dialogic writing

> I think that conferences have become a rather sterile ground lately: people are afraid to speak up, lively discussions never arise because the agendas are too tight, and moderators cut out anything that seems controversial. Fortunately, there is the web :)

This quote from a science blog comment thread reflects some of the tensions that perhaps inevitably whirl around established high-stakes genres: some people feel standard formats are holding things back, and that there is a real need for new forms and new arenas for research to flourish freely. Hopes have also been pinned on the potential of digital science communication to democratize science. As digital media affords a whole new universe of discourses with a potentially global reach and an interactive disposition, it has also added a *terra incognita* to the quest for uses of discourse reflexivity: the usual gatekeeping practices of academia break down in this huge public arena where anyone can participate in discussions around scientific matters. How do these web-based communities work, where do they adopt linguistic norms and practices from, what practices do they develop independently – and for the present study specifically – how do they use discourse reflexivity? Research into digital genres has begun to take metadiscourse on board only relatively recently (e.g. Smart 2016; Bondi 2018; Mauranen 2013a; Zou & Hyland 2020; Papers in D'Angelo, Mauranen & Maci 2021), but the interest is rapidly expanding.

The digital age has meant a massive expansion in dialogic, multi-party writing, and digital communication in its various forms has attracted enormous research interest. Blog communication, for example, has been approached through its technical properties (e.g., Herring 2007), or investigated by content analysis (e.g., Gunawardena, Lowe & Anderson 1997; Ng, Cheung & Hew 2012), and a variety of other perspectives on specifically academic blogs have also been put forward, for example in Myers (2010), papers in Kuteeva & Mauranen (2018) and Luzón in several studies (e.g. Luzón 2011, 2012, 2013a,b, 2018).

This chapter continues to investigate dialogue in metadiscourse by changing the medium (speech to writing) but keeping the mode (dialogue) intact. It explores discourse reflexivity in dialogic writing in discussion threads on research blog sites. There is little previous research into discourse reflexivity in web-based written dialogue that I am aware of (but see Smart 2016; Biri 2021. Smart's (2016) study in online message board discourse was pioneering. His approach to discourse reflexivity is very similar to the current one, which makes his results sufficiently compatible with mine to warrant comparisons despite his somewhat

https://doi.org/10.1515/9783110295498-005

different data and minor differences in the model. Smart principally investigated discourse reflexivity in linear units of meaning, following the Linear Unit Grammar (LUG, Sinclair & Mauranen 2006). He looked at discourse reflexivity dynamically in entities at two different levels, one of 'elements' resulting from linear chunking, and a higher one, his own extension of LUG, comprising larger 'linear units of meaning' that the elements were part of. His data was compiled from a non-academic discussion – a film-related message board, the *Internet Movie Database* website. Recently, Biri (2021) has also analysed metadiscourse in a few online discussion platforms. Even though she uses a model broader than mine, some of her observations are relevant here, for instance regarding evaluative comments.

Multi-party discussions in the written medium reflect developments of the digital age, but at the same time they have their precedents in the print medium in research-related media like academic journals in their discussion sections, popular science magazines, newspapers' science pages and outside the academic world in letters to the editor sections and variants thereof, which have been a stable feature in the printed press for two-three centuries. Public, written discussion is therefore not without its ancestry, any more than blogs are as a genre (for more discussion see, e.g., Miller & Shepherd 2009; Mauranen 2013a). Digital communication has nevertheless meant radical changes to many old conventions and practices.

5.1 The research blog as a concept and a genre

We can talk about *digital genres* as an umbrella term for a large and variable group of genres. Hafner and Pun (2020) define them by the technological media they all depend upon as genres mediated in the communication process by digital tools like computers, smart phones, or other similar devices. The resulting genres tend to be multimodal, intertextual and reach out to diverse audiences.

When academia entered the blogosphere, the science blog began to interest many researchers of science communication, but the research area has remained small compared to the enormous overall activity in blog research. Science blogs did not expand into a significant research communication territory on the scale perhaps initially expected, and they soon faced competition from several other digital channels; a range of opportunities are currently available for talking about or publishing research online, fast, and with open access. Blogs nevertheless maintain their special character as a channel for active researchers and research groups for talking about their own and related research with anyone interested. For the present research, blog comment threads are useful because they can help deepen our understanding of dialogue at the intersection of two-way communication and the written medium. Moreover, they can shake up some of our established notions of genre. We can expect both the medium and the overall genre practices of the blogosphere to affect the kind and amount of discourse reflexivity used in comparison to spoken dialogue: online dialogue operates on a slower timescale than speech because writing takes time, and asynchronous communication is likely to alter the terms of interaction. On the other hand, online comment threads seem to be associated with for instance enhanced explicitness (Bolander 2012), which could mean a relatively high level of discourse reflexivity. We might also assume that generic complexity and the uncertain position of research blogging between academia and an open online forum work as discourse-shaping social factors.

Science blogging can of course mean different things for bloggers as well as researchers and as Mahrt & Puschmann (2014) note, there are many different coexisting conceptualizations of academic blogging. One major line of science blog research is specifically concerned with science communication, that is, recontextualisation of scientific discourses for knowledge dissemination, that is, the public understanding of science (e.g., Luzón 2013a; Mahrt & Puschmann 2014; Myers 2003; Puschmann 2013), or what was in earlier days construed as the 'popularisation of science'. Such research investigates and estimates success in actually engaging the wider public in scientific discussion and is thus concerned with outreach from the ivory tower as it were, or the democratisation of science (for an overview, see Mahrt & Puschmann 2014). As opposed to a simplistic dichotomy between the communicating scientist and the receiving general public, this line of research emphasises the plurality of publics interested in scientific discourses, from research papers through conference presentations and textbooks to science news (e.g., Myers 2003; Luzón 2013a). Scientists and scholars are not outside the target audience. As soon as they step outside their narrowest specialist area, they need to engage with colleagues in neighbouring specialisms, other disciplines, and different kinds of interested public, adapting their discourses accordingly – both for imparting and receiving new information. It is in this multifaceted environment that science blogs find themselves in.

Another line of research stems from an interest in blog discourses themselves, in the ways in which bloggers respond to the heterogeneity of audiences and the affordances of the channel, and how their choices affect the potential readership and the responses they receive (for example Luzón 2013a, Myers 2010). An intriguing new departure in this line of research was made by McGrath (2015), who analysed collaborative research writing on a blog site among pure mathematicians. This cooperation takes place via blog posts, through which mathematicians collaboratively write up publishable research articles out of preliminary drafts. Such activity makes writing for publication more transparent through the affordances of digital media (cf. Myers 2010), and above all it shows active co-construction of knowledge in action through open online cooperation.

With different conceptualisations of the research blog, is it motivated to regard the research blog as a genre, and does it conform to our previous notions of genre? Bloggers and their commenters on the blog websites seem to be sensitive to its generic nature as well as its value (cf. Mauranen 2013a). Evaluative comments reflect the somewhat unsettled status of blogs, and consequently divergent conceptualisations. Participants are divided about the value of the blog as a channel for presenting research: while for some it is a welcome, long-awaited opportunity to present new findings and ideas without conventional restrictions, others dismiss it as an improper forum for either presenting or discussing serious research. This chapter started out with a quote from the former view, and examples in 5.1 illustrate the latter.

(5.1) (a) A blog is not worthy of that post. That should be a paper published in a medical journal

(b) . . . the amount of research that goes into each blog post is astounding. *you really should figure out a better medium for this* . . . something more formal, where people will take notice of all the hard work that's gone into the article.

Genre researchers are not in unison about the nature of genres any more than blog researchers about blogs, though relatively few have addressed the blog genre specifically. Luzón (2013a) mentions in passing that she does not consider science blog postings a genre but does not elaborate her view further. In genre analysis, we can distinguish two lines of thinking. One has seen genre as an essentially coextensive with the Hallidayan concept of register (notably Stubbs 1996; Biber 1988; Biber & Egbert 2018). This can be called a 'integrationist' position, which regards register as primary to genre or genre not of much interest and seems to imply that if we can efficaciously categorise register features in blogs, that will take care of the genre, too. It appears unduly simple in the light of research showing that register features need not stay consistent throughout events representing a genre (e.g. Biber, Connor & Upton 2007; Ventola 1987). We cannot thus simply assume that genres and registers are coextensive. On the contrary, registers seem not only vary within genres but show similarities across them, so that, say, formal ceremonies like taking oaths share register features, but it does not follow that taking the oath in court and taking the Hippocratic oath are the same genre. They instantiate different social actions.

Keeping the social and the linguistic logically independent is a more fruitful point of departure for exploring their interrelations. The alternative position (e.g. Berkenkotter & Huckin 1995; Miller 1984; Swales 1990) to the integrationist could be termed 'dualist': it takes genres to be types of social action and allows linguistic description to proceed separately without a priori assumptions about their interconnectedness. Biber and Conrad (2009) suggest a mediating position where register features are conventionally associated with particular genres. This is arguably dualist because it does not posit a necessary connection between (social) genre and (linguistic) register, but a contingent relationship. It also paves the way to what I would like to see as the co-evolution of typified social action and the linguistic features that characteristically go with certain social situations. Registers would seem to reflect speakers' linguistic sensitivity to social situations, while genres constitute social action, which of course includes using language.

Discussion around blogs can contribute to genre analysis via the concept of *discourse community*, particularly salient in dualist theories of genre. The term and concept come from Swales (1990), who drew on Miller's (1984) early definition of genre as a type of social action recognised in a speech community or context. Swales understands genres as discourses that belong to, or are possessions of, their discourse communities. Communities recognise and name genres, as Miller suggested. 'Blog' fits into this well, as a generally recognised label for a type of communicative action even among people who do not blog. But what would be the community in the case of blogs is harder to resolve, the community that the label originates in and that possesses the genre? The blog is a global concept, but the relevant community cannot be 'people in general'. The web environment is clearly not a community – it is a communicative context. This interpretation is also compatible with Miller's (1984) formulation ". . . recognised in a speech community *or context*[1]".

If we accept that a group of regular followers of a given blog constitute a community of a kind, a "self-organized community that support blogging" as Miller and Shepherd (2009) describe it, then the relationship must be seen the other way around: it is the genre that determines the community (as suggested in Mauranen 1993a), not the community that gives rise to the genre. In this way, the intuitively satisfying notion that the blog is a genre is supported. Moreover, this conceptualisation fits the more general notion that communicative contexts, like in this case the web, spawn genres and communities around them instead of being necessarily embedded in the activities of pre-existing communities (Mauranen 2013a).

Assuming the blog is a genre, a basic level category (Rosch 1978), the research blog would most naturally find its place as a subgenre. As already noted, register variation is found within genres and similarities are found across them. This would seem to hold for research blogs as well, where actual blog postings tend to

1 Italics mine.

be carefully crafted texts much like poster or other conference presentations, but discussion threads look far more spontaneous, ranging from colloquial to relatively formal contributions. Large-scale register analyses of blog discourse place it among other online forms of communication as a hybrid between more traditional spoken and written registers (e.g. Grieve et al. 2011). It is nevertheless important to bear in mind that counts of register features, even large ones, are aggregate comparisons of data masses in a stable state, and do not show internal variation or real-time temporal dynamics of change.

A small illustration of register variability drawn from the present data shows simply how thanks are expressed in blog discussions as compared to conference and graduate seminar discussions (Table 5.1).

Table 5.1: Thanks in different discussions.

Conference discussions (all; 74,057w)		
Thank you	130	81.4%
Thanks	18	11.2%
Other	13	8.1%
Total	161	
Seminar discussions (sample of 10; 51,837w)		
Thank you	31	72.1%
Thanks	12	27.9%
Other	–	–
Total	43	
Blog discussion threads (all; 129,924w)		
Thank you	65	24.8%
Thanks	195	74.4%
Other	2	0.8%
Total	262	

Blog discussions in view of this little example would seem to be more colloquial than conference or seminar discussions. Conferences appear the most formal of the three, and the verbal form (*I should thank* NAME *for . . .*) was also used more than in the other event types.

It has been shown that the internet context has consequences to language features. Multivariate register analyses including a variety of online sites along with more traditional spoken and written texts (e.g. Biber & Egbert 2018; Grieve et al 2011; Ehret & Taboada 2020) show that online communication mixes features from both spoken dialogue and written text. This has led authors to talk about register 'hybridity' (Biber & Egbert 2018). It would rather seem motivated to regard the genres along with the accompanying register features of online communication as emerging ways of communicating, which is establishing itself as something 'third' besides speech and traditional writing. The web has become an everyday communication channel that generates its distinctive behaviours and uses of language.

Research blogs vary considerably in how much commentary they attract, as already noted (Chapter 3), as they do in how much of the commentary consists merely of thanks, how much of questions to the blogger, or how much engagement there is with other commenters along with the blogger. This variability has further implications on the notion of genre. The blog genre develops in 'local' interactions (the locus in this case consisting of a site on the web). The genre emerges in the self-organised activity of bloggers and groups that gather around them, with each blog site developing some conventions or habits of their own but resembling kindred communities in similar environments. This process is shaped top-down by the internet environment, but it is also a bottom-up process, which affects and shapes its environment in turn. The web has no authority structures that would regulate its genres in the way for example traditional publishing channels do. There would thus seem to be a co-evolution of genre and community in local interactions that take shape in and around blogs. The bulk of established genre analyses have based their models on 'mature' genres with a relatively stable existence, although less prominent genres and especially the historical development of genres have likewise attracted a few researchers.

For a better understanding of genres, blogs as genres in the making offer a good case. In the same way, register developments in blog genres are intriguing because they reflect the linguistic sensitivity of bloggers and commenters, and in English-using sites they represent in principle anyone in the world, thus in essence ELF. In all this, there is no single national culture involved, which means that emerging shapes and variability within and across them must originate in something that remains outside traditional conceptualisations of 'lingua-cultures'.

5.2 Blogs as dialogue

Blog discussion threads consist of participants responding to each other's turns, which makes them unmistakably dialogic events. The disembodied character of technologically mediated writing nevertheless immediately sets them apart from spoken dialogue, with social, cognitive, and linguistic consequences. The most obvious consequence of disembodiment is the lack of paralinguistic and non-linguistic communication such as gestures, glances, voice, or prosody. Tools like emoji are commonly employed in blog discussions apparently to compensate for the missing indicators of emotional quality, but a myriad of features such as changes in speech rate, blinks, or exchanging glances can be much subtler than whatever is readily conveyed by emoji. The social or cognitive meanings of nonverbal and paralinguistic communication are not as well researched as verbal communication, but the main point is that they are an essential part of face-to-face speech missing from written digital dialogue.

An important social factor in blog dialogues is anonymity; commenters typically use pseudonyms, which help identify and follow messages from a given participant, although we do not normally know who they are. In this respect comment threads are also unlike most monologic writing, including actual blogs, whose authors normally use their own names. Other social parameters include the varying and changing communication patterns from one-to-many communication to one-to -one and many-to-many. Finally, the multiple potential audiences are heterogeneous, their members ranging from closely associated experts in the field to the interested novice or layman. Commenters sometimes self-identify as, say, students or science teachers, but from a linguist's point of view it is interesting that usually it is only their verbal output which reveals their level of expertise and engagement.

From a cognitive perspective, the crucial differences between digital dialogue and spoken interaction lie in their temporal properties: comment threads are not only asynchronous, but slowly paced compared to speech. Speaking progresses in milliseconds, commonly with speaker overlaps, whereas writing is a matter of seconds (Chapter 2); the verbatim representation of speech disappears within a few seconds, while the written record remains intact, and the response can be composed at leisure. Responses can also be edited before being submitted. Altogether, written blog dialogue can be likened to writing letters or exchanging text messages, and thereby we might want to call them *reactive* as Hari et al. (2015) termed computer-mediated talk between two speakers, meaning that the receiver reacts to an output of an interactant instead of forming a dynamically adapting dyad as they would in spoken interaction (see also Reagle 2015). Digital written interaction is thus in many important ways different from its spoken co-present counterpart, but it also differs vitally from monologic writing. It is real social interaction between participants who orient to each other and engage with each other, despite missing many speech elements and despite a pace more adapted to writing than to speaking. Written digital dialogue therefore occupies a territory of its own in cognitive as well as social terms and offers unique possibilities for making sense of how discourse reflexivity responds to changes in contextual parameters. This is important for understanding the context-sensitivity of digital communication through writing and language generally.

The rest of this chapter analyses blog discussion thread data. Online dialogues, then, occupy a separate territory from either spoken dialogue or written monologue, but bear affinities to both in terms of social action, i.e. genre, as well as register, and therefore can throw light on both. The primary task is to relate written dialogue to spoken, which was already analysed in the previous chapter. Thus, to render online dialogue comparable with spoken, the category framework developed in Chapter 4 is imposed on the discussion threads. This serves as a rough test of similarity between the two and at the same time leaves the door open to new categories and distinctions that might emerge from the data.

5.3 Discourse reflexivity in dialogic writing

A brief glance at discourse reflexivity in blogs suffices to show that many expressions are familiar from earlier metadiscourse research:

(5.2) (a) *I would argue that* this scenareo . . .
(b) *Just to be clear, I don't mean to imply* that string . . .
(c) *This is not to say* the van Kuppeveld isn't sick . . .
(d) *Just an example, here is a quoted definition* of their . . .
(e) *I am not proposing* a . . .

These are typically writer-oriented, forward-looking expressions, which could just as well appear in monologic writing. Others are not what we might expect to find in monologic text, but more like what we saw in Chapter 4:

(5.3) (a) *I absolutely agree with you that* a language is more than . . .
(b) *A quick reply to your comments:*
(c) Moreover, *could you please substantiate the following statement* . . .

In this batch, the orientation has shifted from the current writer to other writers' texts. These examples resemble those Smart (2016) found in an online message board.

Another similarity to spoken interaction is that we can observe a concentration of discourse reflexivity when writers are negotiating disagreement or other sensitive issues in much the same way as speakers do (Chapter 6). It takes a longish exchange to show how it works (5.4). In the example, the blogger's[2] first turn has been shortened a little, because the preceding part was outside the topic that got discussed, and some detailed explanation from C2's comment is similarly omitted.

2 Bloggers are identified as B, usually B1, but in some cases there are blogger pairs, so that we get B1 and B2. Commenters on the comment chains are identified as C (C1,C2, . . .).

(5.4) <COMMENT BY B1 ON 05.06.2011>
/. . ./
(by the way from a librarian standpoint I wonder whether mere retraction doesn't affect the retrieval of such a paper. One should always be able to access the erroneous data. So I would rather see a red stamp: retracted).
But my main point wasn't that the paper doesn't deserve retraction. It is more that I'm wary of Science real intentions.
Like @<NAME C5> explains so well: *Yes they [science] don't want to miss a groundbreaking study but it is better to miss 10 of them than publish one that is wrong.* So I found they had should have done a better job to peer review the paper and not just go for the glory. The same is true for PNAS that doesn't "accept several XMRV negative papers also of high calibre science", but only high sensationalist positive papers. (***your last post*** – & I agree).
My main point thus is that I find Science editors are chickening out of the situation, they have created thenselves. (approving sensationalist paper without appropriate peer review.)

<COMMENT BY C2 ON 05.06.2011>
Since when is this [authors behaviours] sufficient reason to retract a paper?
I dont mean their questionable recreational activities (as non-standard as they are). ***I mean*** their refusal to retract an unsalvageable paper is non-standard – the entirety of the data and the entirety of their conclusions are based on a contamination/. . ./This has happened before, and it will happen again. Could happen to me tomorrow *shrug*
But these authors *refuse* to retract.
I dont think that has ever happened before.

<COMMENT BY B1 ON 05.06.2011>
Ok. Thanks. Oh, yes it is quite extra-ordinary for authors to adhere to their data, that are crumbling day by day. I don't understand their attitude either. I even doubted myself when my data *were* right. I used to drive my supervisor mad with all my "buts" and "perhaps". It is so U-N-S-C-I-E-N-T-I-F-I-C not to doubt your data when no one can reproduce them and there is clear indication why you are wrong. It is so U-N-S-C-I-E-N-T-I-F-I-C NOT to take the doubts serious. ***Still I remain with my point of view, that*** the attitude of Science is not of a very high standard. They're taking the easy way out.

<COMMENT BY C6 ON 10.06.2011>
I think it is different in that the Lombardi et al. authors are implicitly using ScienceMag's reputability to keep advancing their views. Even in her

reply to Bruce Alberts, Mikovits only really centred on the original study and its seemingly infallible methodology.

This extract involves three parties: B1, C2, and C6, in addition to which an earlier comment by C5 is referred to and partly reproduced. The parties do not so much disagree with each other than discuss a sensitive issue, which clearly arouses emotions: whether a particular paper should be retracted, and related ethical issues in scientific publication. Our example also illustrates a fairly typical discussion with a propensity to move to general issues of doing science in addition to the specific topics of blog postings.

In addition to similarities to and divergences from traditional writing and speech, the communication channel also makes its presence felt. References to writers' mobiles or seeing that comments are "up" are reminders of the tangible differences from print or face-to-face discussions.

(5.5) @<NAME C2> *Just a quick response from my mobile*: . . .
I see that your comment is up <NAME C3>! I wonder how she would reply . . .

Beyond the technological environment, social behaviour also manifests features we do not expect to see in public spoken discussions (or in print).

(5.6) (a) Dear <NAME C11>, *I would love to see something else than vacuous post-modern babbling in the text above, but I simply can't.*
(b) *Do we really have to discuss these elementary things?*

A high degree of emotionality and negativity, or their "argumentative, evaluative or opinionated nature" as Ehret & Taboada put it (2020:5) is a common finding in studies of social media and online commentaries, including Smart (2016) and Biri (2021). The linguistic positivity bias discussed in Chapter 4 is ceding ground to negativity and downright rudeness. This is noteworthy, because it implies different social norms from comparable contexts of speaking or traditional academic writing. We thus see special genre properties evolving, that is, a particular kind of social action, which is reflected in register features and also incorporates reflexive discourse.

Following the distinction drawn in spoken discourse in the previous chapter between managing the discourse and managing the situation, we tackle them in the same order here, and again discourse management is by far the more prevalent kind, covering over two thirds of the instances.

5.3.1 Managing the discourse in blog discussions

Discourse reflexivity in written dialogue follows the route of spoken dialogue in that managing the discourse serves an overall contextualising function and falls readily into two main types, orienting and retrieving, of which the latter is larger. As a shorthand, we can characterise the orienting kind as prospective and the retrieving as retrospective, although as already discussed in Chapter 4, both orienting and retrieving metadiscourse in effect prospect ahead, although only the retrieving kind looks both ways.

Orienting discourse reflexivity in blog discussions

Orienting discourse reflexivity basically indicates to hearers or readers how speakers or writers mean their discourse to proceed. Speaker–hearer collaboration depends on an adequate match between speaker's signalling and hearer's anticipation and confirming /discarding hypotheses as the discourse moves on. Signals that we have called orienting have been detected in written dialogue in previous research, too (Smart 2016). Reflexive signalling may therefore be a fundamental part of turn-taking, where new discourse increments need to be contextualised independently of processing speed. Alternatively, it is possible that dialogic writing has simply internalised orienting reflexivity from the model of speaking, or indeed from monologic writing, where orienting metadiscourse is common.

As noted in Chapter 4, orienting discourse reflexivity is the textbook example of metadiscourse, included in all commonly used analytical models under different names. In written dialogue it also follows the well-trodden path of indicating the function of the upcoming speech act, as in (5.7). Expressions with a personal pronoun are the most typical, but impersonal expressions to the same effect are not uncommon.

(5.7) (a) I have had a look at the model, and *I have a couple of remarks*. The first one is, you're using the same vision for people and cops.
(b) *However it is important to mention that* some information escapes from the hand of science.

Writers also use discourse reflexivity to indicate focus or emphasis (5.8) and stance (5.9).

(5.8) *But I can say* their paper makes novel claims (***to say the least***) and the burden of proof is certainly on them.

(5.9) *Well, I wouldn't say so.* They are just some quantities, . . .

These uses are familiar from metadiscourse research into written academic prose. Less familiar can be the style of self-presentation, or the speech acts used, which are not always what we conventionally expect in academic contexts:

(5.10) (a) *I assure you* that I am 100% honest.
(b) *Not to go on a rant any longer* . . . Yes, there does exist content on the internet worthy of citing in research paper
(c) *P.S. I earnestly promise to* (shall try as far as I can a Sly Creep) to not use an emoticon for any other expressive purpose than what it is conventionally meant for!!

More speech-like is anticipating questions and answers with speech act labels (5.11). Questions and answers work broadly in the same way as in spoken dialogue: questions expect answers and answers respond to questions that have been asked by another participant, unlike the rhetorical questions of written monologue that writers themselves answer. Reflexive metadiscourse frequently identifies the addressee of a question or specifies which question an answer is a response to. Such explicit identification seems to arise from the demands of the technical environment, since the discussion thread format is organised from newest to oldest. Therefore, other than immediate responses require more precise identification, and a commenter can never know if their message is the first to find its way to the site. In this, research blogs are like personal blogs where interlocutors have been found to make explicit who the message is meant for (Bolander 2012).

(5.11) *My answer to the blog post title question* is the definitive: it depends.

Commenters also design their turns in subtler ways. They may preface their message with the apparent purpose to excite the reader's interest (5.12) which may involve fine-tuning it with a specific angle or status (5.13). Studies of academic blogs have found bloggers using various means of seeking to engage their readers' interest (Luzón 2013a; Mahrt & Puschmann 2014). Clearly, commenters on threads use similar tactics.

(5.12) *And here's a little secret,* the IEC has suggested that Psych consult thing . . .

(5.13) (a) Hey, <NAME C12>, *my experimentalist view is* 1) Every particle/energy quantum state has a gravitational interaction . . .
(b) *On a personal note,* I can see the other side as well.

Commenters anticipate reader reactions by simply predicting them (5.14) or pre-empting their imagined objections or misconceptions (5.15). Pre-empting anticipated misconception differs from clarifying mismatches in interlocutors' interpretations, because prospected misunderstanding has no evidence of any having taken place and is based solely on the writer's theory of mind (Chapter 2), while clarification follows a perceived mismatch (this will be discussed in spoken interaction in Chapter 6).

(5.14) (a) *I'm sure this sounds like a conspiracy theory to you,* but imagine the players are all delusional so they realy do believe . . .
(b) *I know I have posted similar sentiments before but I want to get it off my chest once again:* To me, this quoted statement further "rubs in" a slightly frustrating predicament of mine.

(5.15a) (a) *Again, I am not proposing anything,* I am trying to understand.
(b) *Just to be clear, I don't mean to imply that* string theory has replaced all of spacetime with strings,

In principle, questions in online discussion can be wrapped in discourse reflexivity just like in speech. In practice, questions only occasionally used altercentric references. The few individual instances (like those in 5.16) did not even amount to one percent of orienting references, which indicates that orienting discourse reflexivity is even more egocentric in online than co-present discourse.

(5.16) (a) *Can you tell us more* about the platypus and echidna, which are . . .
(b) Moreover, *could you please substantiate the following statement* « I am *almost* sure that the average age of SNS users (especially FB) is decreasing »

Anticipation of reader reactions seems to blend elements of writing and speaking by echoing both an author's anticipation of the reactions of an imagined audience and conversational anticipation with co-present interlocutors who can respond.

Some properties in the comment threads, however, align more with previous findings on blogs than characteristics of speech or writing. This manifests itself for instance in more personal and less conventionally academic speech acts, and apparent tactics for engaging a reader's interest in ways that deviate from accustomed academic practices. There is also some evidence of specific ways of identifying addressees that suggests a channel-induced practice.

Retrieving discourse reflexivity in blog discussions

As already discussed in the previous chapter, the ephemeral nature of speech makes retrieving discourse reflexivity a natural strategy for speakers who wish to remind their interlocutors of something that has already passed in the discourse but which they wish to make relevant at this point again. By contrast, the written text stays available for consultation, and we might therefore expect fewer instances of explicit retrieving. Yet the retrieving use of discourse reflexivity is equally extensive in written and spoken dialogue. How this works in digital dialogues is explored next.

The predominant type of contextualising discourse reflexivity in both spoken and written dialogue is retrieving, which accounts for about 60% of all reflexive metadiscourse. Additionally, more than 70% of retrieving references are made to other speakers or writers, not the writers themselves. The overall proportions in the samples are very similar (for more detail, see Chapter 8). But when we zoom more closely into the altercentric references, we observe a bifurcation of speech and writing: overwhelmingly, most references to others (71.3%) in speech are to identified addressees (the 'you' of the conversation), while in blog discussions these account for 40.1%, and 59.0% references are made to third parties – often impersonally to texts. Before going to these differences in detail, let us look more closely at the categories where the distributions were similar to speech and examine egocentric references first.

Some retrieving self-references are familiar from speaking:

(5.17) (a) *As I said,* I only scanned their paper.
(b) *I did mention,* that there are APA publications guidelines . . .
(c) *I was just saying* that your alignments nicely visualised the homogeneity of the sequencing products . . .

Others can be instantly identified as originating in blog discussions by their blog-specific lexis like *post, blog,* or *blogger,* but could *mutatis mutandis* appear in speech as well.

(5.18) (a) Btw I thought that homogeneity was established earlier. *It is already mentioned it in my first post about* XMRV and M/CFS . . .
(b) *Of course bloggers like me who blog about all kinds of topics will not cover* anything that appears about CFS, but only really pioneering work, which looks very promising or which is controversial . . .
(c) *As said at the very beginning of the post,* this is just a summary of a PEW survey.

There is also reflexive metadiscourse that is characteristic of the channel, that is, digital communication. One egocentric reference type can be called *self-reporting*, where we find a writer describing their recent discourse-relevant actions (5.19). Academic bloggers have been observed to talk about their activities (Luzón 2013a) that are unrelated to their current writing or reading, somewhat like self-narrative in conference presentations (Mauranen 2013b). Likewise, commenters report their activities around blogs, including discourse reflexive ones.

(5.19) (a) *Well, left a comment on the blog.* RIDICULOUS premises man.
(b) *I've read your 3rd post* XMRV and chronic fatigue syndrome: So long, and thanks for all the lulz, Part III.
(c) Not my best work, admittedly, but *I was too furious to not write* just exactly what I felt!
(d) *I think I have to read it again,* because I still have to recover from the first paragraph . . .

Luzón (2013a) talks about 'self-disclosure' in academic blog postings. Self-disclosure encompasses more than self-reporting, since the latter is limited to discourse about the ongoing discourse, but both are types of self-presentation beyond the demands of the progression of the discourse. Luzón suggests this is a blogger's "strategy to engage the reader". Self-disclosure has been commonly observed in personal blogs, too, and personal presence is found to characterise the blogosphere generally (e.g., Qian & Scott 2007). This suggests that it is a characteristic of the blog genre, rather than a speech-writing hybrid feature. It need not thus be chosen for special effect, because it seems conventional in the genre. Self-reporting is, however, clearly not limited to bloggers, but in the present data it is commenters who report on their activities.

Retrieving self-references (5.20) are also found in contexts of negotiating clarity or debate, as are addressee-references (5.21) These are discussed further in Chapter 6 for speech.

(5.20) *I just meant* they really want to hear the translation, the message to the public even if it isn't there (yet).

(5.21) @<NAME C10> . . . not sure *what you're referring to* regarding "Watch this space". I suspect there must be another <NAME C11>.

Clarifying and inviting clarifications about what was meant suggests that although writers anticipate reader responses (see examples 5.14 and 5.15 above), they do not necessarily predict them correctly. Instead, there is considerable individual variation in how texts are taken. Texts also abound in vagueness and can even be said to be inherently vague (Channell 1994; Cutting 2007). Dialogic negotiation about what was or is being meant is another indication of problems that arise from the assumption that writer-reader interaction can be reduced to unidirectional writer-to-reader communication, as discussed in Chapter 2.

The previous example already took us to the largest retrieving category, namely altercentric references. Many of these are made to addressees identified either by a pronoun or a name, mostly a pseudonym. Individuals are addressed in a very similar way in blogs (5.21, 5.22) as they were in speech.

(5.22) (a) Following *your suggestion*, we have looked at the model again and noticed that the number of . . .
(b) I understand *your point*, the difficulty of getting research done, the difficulty of getting research funded.
(c) I think *your mention* that different libraries do – and need – very different things is . . .

Commenters often give positive evaluations or pass compliments (5.23), while they can also make rather negative comments (5.24) that look much less inhibited and more direct than is customary in seminar or conference discourses. The latter are more common when directed at a third person or text.

(5.23) (a) @<NAME C3> *Nice to hear* the experience of a journalist (I didn't know you were one).
(b) Wow, you really work hard to make *your posts* perfect Keep up the good work.

(5.24) (a) Dear <NAME C11>, I would love to see something else than *vacuous post-modern babbling in the text above*, but I simply can't.
(b) If you mean something else by *your question*, then I don't know what it is.

Sometimes references in blog threads are made to another, identified participant.

(5.25) (a) I think *<NAME C5> put forward a good point*. Why haven't the magafauna adapted to the climate change?
(b) The goal of HIFA2015 is ambitious, but not quite as ambitious *as Dr Skeptic suggests above*. The HIFA members define . . .

Most typically, however, references are made to an unidentified or impersonal 'other'. These can just refer to the content of a previous post in a neutral way, as in (5.26), but far more often they are evaluative. That is, strong evaluations of earlier postings abound in comment threads, either positive (5.27) or negative (5.28).

(5.26) (a) *Third sentence*, an "Editorial Expression of Concern" is normally only used when there has been evidence of outright . . .
(b) *This* is also one of the points made by the journalist I listened to the other day. She said that we should be able to see Barroso . . .

(5.27) (a) *Great conversation*!
(b) *Interesting argument!* I wanted to do that, but was worried of the patient confidentiality issues.
(c) *Lovely post!* (I'm busy catching up on all the ones I missed over the last few hectic weeks)

(5.28) (a) Well, i may be a wee bit responsible for trolling things up a bit, but *the whole post is littered with so many insinuations that gets under the skin is very irritating.*
(b) And what is this question supposed to mean? *It is just a meaningless combination of words.*
(c) I find this an *unnecessary hostile comment* towards @<NAME C3>.

Evaluative comments, whether admiring, balanced, hostile, or something else, flourish in blog discussions. Similar observations have been made on non-academic online commentaries (Smart 2016; Ehret & Taboada 2020; Biri 2021) as well as on academic blog postings (Luzón 2013b). Negative evaluations, moreover, seem to dominate. The negative instances would seem to suggest that the linguistic positivity bias (Dodds et al. 2015; Chapter 4, 4.2.2) is not maintained to an equal degree in digital discourses. This may not come as a surprise in a world inundated with the web, but it is interesting to note that this propensity for strong evaluations has percolated into academic blogs and commentaries. Like the heightened personal presence discussed above, it would seem to be a characteristic of the digital channel (thus digital genres), not possible to trace back to either speaking or writing or their mixture. Traditional academic discourses, moreover, tend to be comparatively toned down. There is nevertheless wide variability among blog sites and comment threads in this respect and their debates vary considerably in tone. This point is made explicitly by a commenter (5.29) comparing two blogsites.

(5.29) Actually, I don't have the technical background to argue too much; it's me who's learned some things from this and another column, but I'm grateful for *the less inflamed discussion here.*

Retrieving discourse reflexivity in blog discussions supports a central finding from spoken dialogues: like speakers, writers chiefly refer to texts written by others rather than to those they themselves are writing or have written during the discussion. This stands in sharp contrast to findings from metadiscourse research of written monologue, which repeatedly show that the writer's references primarily concern their own current text.

However, retrieving discourse reflexivity also shows a marked difference in spoken and written dialogue: interlocutors' written comments are mostly made to third persons' texts, while in speech, altercentric references are made to a particular addressee. Blog commenters thus refer more to texts than to writers.

Retrieving discourse reflexivity also shows channel-specificity which is not reducible to mixing features from spoken and written registers but characterises blog genres more generally: self-reporting is a facet of the wider personal involvement and self-disclosure that has been commonly found in online discourses.

From a quantitative perspective, the proportional shares of orienting and retrieving discourse reflexivity are strikingly similar in spoken and written dialogue in our sample. In each case, retrieving discourse reflexivity is the predominant kind, covering about 60% (60.1% in speech, 59.0% in writing) in the current data, while the orienting type accounts for about 40% (39,1% in speech, 41.0% in writing) of discourse reflexive expressions in discourse management. The overall dominance of a retrospective, that is, retrieving, orientation in dialogic online discourse reflexivity is supported by Smart's (2016) results from an online message board.

5.3.2 Managing the situation in blog discussions

For spoken dialogues, we distinguished managing the situation from managing the discourse and noted that situation management orients to the 'outer' movement of the speech event, such as opening and closing episodes, allocating turns, or changing direction. While it was normally an appointed chairperson's prerogative to handle such discourse, we also saw participants from the floor instigating plane-shifts and thereby taking hold of situation management for a while. Unlike the spoken discourses, our written online dialogue is obviously not bound by similar institutional norms, which means they could show quite different tendencies. However, even self-organised groups develop rules and conventions of their own. For example, blog sites can have moderators in place of chairpersons, usually bloggers themselves. On the other hand, institutionally framed groups can adopt self-organised practices when the discussion lasts longer and tends to drift away from the initial point of departure (Chapter 4). On this basis, it looks like there is no entirely sharp division between self-organising and institutional regulation.

By extension, situation management can be expected to take place in blog threads simply because it is a facet of dialogic interaction and features in spoken dialogues. Indeed, it turns out that situation management occurs in proportional terms similarly to spoken dialogue, just under a quarter of reflexive metadiscourse in each medium (23.0% in speech, 22.6% in writing).

Commenters also effect plane-shifts in much the same way that speakers do. Bloggers participate in the discussion among commenters, without assuming a conventional chairperson role. That is, they do not allocate turns or initiate or conclude discussions, but in a moderator role they may take down what they deem irrelevant or excessively offensive comments. These will not make their way into the data, of course, but can leave traces (see, example 5.39 further below). Without externally appointed regulators, plane-shifting does not mean snatching a chair's role but adopting a bird's eye view on the discussion and assuming a regulator role in it. Plane-shifts are the principal type of situation management in comment threads. Like speakers, commenters as it were step back from the discussion to give their interpretation of what the discussion is about (5.30), openly challenge the discussion (5.31), or defend it (5.32).

(5.30) (a) *This is really a debate* what is science and what is not science
(b) *This discussion was* surrounding the reasons for the asked for retraction, and those surrounding retraction in general.
(c) But anyway, *we were only discussing to which extent* I would find new ME/CFS findings interesting enough to BLOG about.

(5.31) *Do we really have to discuss these elementary things?*

(5.32) (a) We could talk about the WPI and its' 'failings' in my eyes, but *this was and should be about* Lombardi – and more particularly, here, the asked for retraction.
(b) *That is the way we are communicating now on this board.*

By plane-shifting individuals refrain from participating in the discussion on its current terms and switch the focus from the topic matter to the terms of the discussion. Plane-shifts thereby constitute acts of power, seeking to regulate interpretations of the situation and thus making a wholesale bid for control.

Despite many similarities between spoken and written dialogue, certain phenomena in blog threads can be related to the online channel. Negative evaluative comments already evinced in discourse managing are also part of the situational plane-shift discourse in adverse reactions to the quality of the discussion as a whole (5.31, 5.33).

(5.33) *I don't enjoy discussions about* crackpot theories all the time.

Some comments that are essentially *ad hominem* attacks can be analysed as plane-shifts, like those in (5.34), because they are generalisations about the objects of attack, not responding to a particular point or argument.

(5.34) (a) I respect your comments from a scientific standpoint for the most part, but *your consistent inability to express* your differences with others *without stooping to defamation and curse words* is highly unprofessional.
(b) *It's this totally unlimited mixing of words* from totally different worlds and disciplines, from all conceivable levels, [. . .] *words that have no scientific relationships of a well-defined kind,* that totally drives me up the wall.

Such emotional reactions were a small category, making up only 11% of situation management. It is nevertheless more than in face-to-face interaction, where openly emotional responses were very rare, with only a few positive and none that were negative. Instead, the finding is very much in keeping with previous findings from online discourses.

Some kinds of situation management talk indicate some engagement with the topic, even though indirectly. One type is an utterance of intention, which refer to envisaged future texts or discussions. These again reflect the flavour of personal presence seen in self-reporting above, which appears to be shared across blog genres.

(5.35) (a) *Gonna write about it on my blog too* though! Thanks for bringing this to our views!
(b) Thus no, *I don't think I will blog a lot about CFS anymore.*
(c) *nod* *Im working on a similar summary post*
(d) *I'll definitely be including this blog carnival in my upcoming report* on state of biology blogs

Utterances of intention occasionally mediate between the blog and other means of communication like the next two (5.36), which also show how anonymity is not watertight in web discussions.

(5.36) (a) *We can talk about this person very soon!!!* See you in a few days Umberto!
(b) *Let's discuss* more details via email.

The remaining types of situation management consist of comments of a technical kind and thanking. A good proportion of management talk is concerned with technical management. Half of these are what might perhaps best be described as *metacommentary*. In other words, they comment on their commenting activities. This is not far from self-reporting but orients to a specific blogging action rather than to themselves as persons or the writing process. In these examples (5.37) we can again see how anonymity can leak in the blogosphere, with some contributors apparently aware of each other's offline identities, whether they use pseudonyms or proper names.

(5.37) (a) @<NAME C4> (*sorry for not being able to respond at Facebook*). I have had similar experiences.
(b) @<NAME C3> (*bit of a late reply*) this was the last question in a short telephone interview after a press conference.
(c) Hi Lucas, *I know this is the comment section*, BUT, I really try to get in contact to you.
(d) *I have minimal time to respond to this blog* so you can all have fun stating whatever you want.

Apart from literally technical comments (5.38), there are those that are best regarded as more broadly technical attempts to manage the situation. They concern blog monitoring, typically allegations or denials of censorship (5.39).

(5.38) (a) *Tried accessing your blog*, but your user name isn't linked.
(b) Thanks <NAME C3>. Last time I looked, *your comment was still not up*.
(c) *NOTE: Sorry for late publication. Comment was in my spamfilter*
(d) *I see that your comment is up* <NAME C3>! I wonder how she would reply, if she does at all.

(5.39) (a) Oh *well, comments posted after me have been allowed through but not mine!* P
Guess that means I WAS caustic enough. Aaah! The pleasure.
(b) *I have definitely allowed both your comments to be published* . . . and thanks for the remark – 'discriminatory bigot'. That you call me this by itself the success of my post!
(c) *I don't see any of my comments being allowed through!* I wrote in some 3-4 comments (none of them complimentary, as you might imagine without any difficulty) since last night including one inviting her to comment on my post, but she has not allowed them through.

The final class of situational management is simply thanking. Thanks often include reflexive metadiscourse in connection with the reason for thanking. They come from both commenters (5.40) and bloggers (5.41).

(5.40) (a) *Thanks for the interesting post.*
(b) This is a very important point so *thank you for posting.*
(c) *Just wanted to say thanks for taking the time to answer my questions.:)*

(5.41) (a) *Thanks all for your comments.*
(b) Hi <NAME C2>. *Thanks for commenting.*
(c) *Thanks for taking out time to read and comment on the post!*

Commenters' thanks usually go to the blogger, and vice versa. Bloggers tend to be thanked for a blog, for taking the discussion forward, or for their feedback or observations. In a study of blog posts and reader responses Mahrt & Puschmann (2014) noted that posts that aim at explaining events to laypersons receive more thankful comments than those presenting a blogger's academic or political views. In our data thanks also go to the other direction, from bloggers to those who have given comments.

It seems that situation management in blog discussion threads is affected by social parameters like self-organising not only the discourse but the community, and anonymity, which also set blogs off from spoken dialogue. Comment threads organise themselves on their own terms, limited only by bloggers possibly monitoring and removing irrelevant or offensive contents. Anonymity, in turn, is likely to give space to open expression of negative, even hostile reactions. Both these properties are apparently shared in digital genres, with their communities that form around blog sites and regulate themselves.

5.4 Conclusion

This chapter has explored discourse reflexivity in online comment threads on research blog sites. It has begun to tease apart effects of medium (speech vs writing), channel, (online vs co-present) and genre on dialogical reflexive metadiscourse, and as a result, what could be specific to the dialogic mode, whether spoken or written. The analytical framework for categorising the data was initially borrowed from spoken dialogues (for a snapshot, see Figure 4.1) to find out how far it could be applied to writing. The approach was thus the reverse from Chapter 4, where the framework was built from the bottom up. The aim was to test how far categories based on the dialogic mode would hold despite the change of medium, channel, and the genre context. In Figure 5.1 we can see that for managing discourse, all major categories were a good fit with spoken dialogue, but managing situation was somewhat different. This would seem to suggest that when we are concerned with organising discourse, dialogue has some distinct properties independent of medium, but when we move from this core towards the outer edges, parameters of the social situation gain more ground.

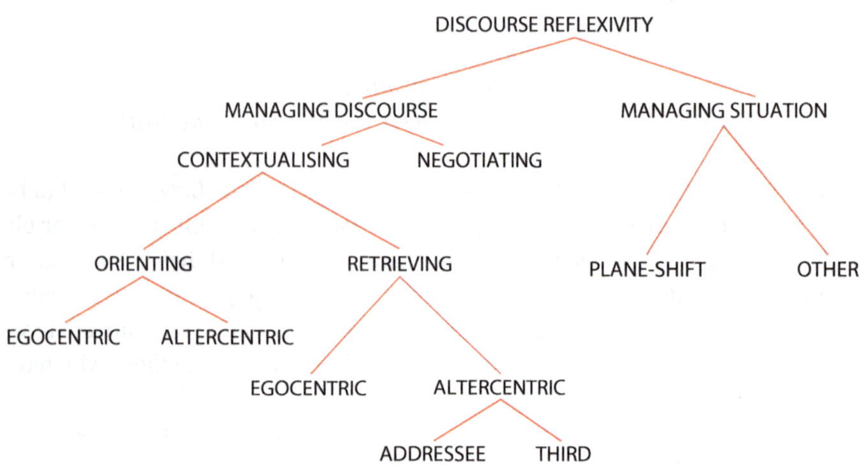

Figure 5.1: Discourse reflexivity in written dialogue.

Figure 5.1 gives us a skeletal overview of the main categories, like Figure 4.1, skipping over many subtleties. This is deliberate, because overall comparisons do not benefit from fine-grained minor category divisions, which in any case tend to become more uncertain as numbers get smaller. The closer we get to individual cases, the greater the danger of over-categorising language use with all its fluidity and ad hoc creativity.

Overall, discourse reflexivity is as important in online dialogue as it is in spoken dialogue. This is in line with research that indicates enhanced explicitness in online comment threads, which suggests a potentially high incidence of reflexive metadiscourse. In fact, there is proportionally even more reflexive discourse in blog threads than in spoken discourse in the data. Two points seem to emerge from this: first, that reflexive signalling is a fundamental part of dialogic interaction, which requires new discourse increments to be contextualised in the discourse whatever the medium. Secondly, there is also a medium-dependent effect, that is, online discourse may require more verbal explicitness around turns than physical co-presence because there are fewer resources for paralinguistic and nonverbal communication. If this is so, we should indeed expect a higher degree of explicit verbalisation in online than co-present dialogues.

The domain of managing discourse lends itself without difficulty to the same categorisation as it did in speaking, in addition to which the proportions are similar in important ways. The shares of orienting and retrieving discourse reflexivity are virtually identical at roughly 40% vs 60%. Dialogic reflexive metadiscourse thus consistently appears to refer to others' text and talk more than those of the current speaker or writer, and to preceding discourse more than to anticipated discourse. The predominance of retrieving altercentric references therefore seems to be a property of the dialogic mode, not of the medium or channel.

Further, the proportions of egocentric vs altercentric references within orienting and retrieving reflexivity show a parallel trend in speech and writing, orienting discourse reflexivity being mainly egocentric and retrieving mainly altercentric. The tendency is even stronger in blog commentaries, where egocentric references cover 94.5% of orienting discourse reflexivity, while in spoken discussions they account for 'merely' 70–80% of the same (72.2% in conferences, 80,8% in graduate seminars). The numbers suggest an effect of the medium: participants in written dialogue talk about their own upcoming discourse proportionally more than participants in spoken dialogue. Secondly, blog discussions diverge from spoken discourses in how they refer to others: the share of third parties (57.5%) clearly exceeds that of identified addressees (42.5%) in retrieving references, whereas the proportions are the reverse in speech (71.3% to identified addressees). Thirdly, the third-party references in blog commentaries are nearly exclusively (92.2%) impersonal: made to texts, not to individuals. The propensity to refer to texts or third parties instead of identified addressees would again seem to relate to a difference of the medium of communication in a way that ultimately derives from the social context of interaction: whether it is co-present and embodied or asynchronous and disembodied. The absence of addressees in the same physical space is likely to reduce the motive to address them directly, and the object of address becomes more often the traces that interactants have left, that is, their texts. In addition, as the interaction is devoid of paraverbal and nonverbal cues like tone of voice, prosody, eye contact, or gestures, linguistic means must adopt a larger share of the communication. Blog comment threads for instance often display intended humour with signs like emoticons, but of course typical co-present markers of humour like laughter are missing, and with them, the synchronous feedback they give to the presenter.

Even though discourse management in digital dialogue shows similarities to spoken dialogue, situation management online diverges clearly from corresponding face-to-face discussions. In quantitative terms, no overall medium effect is seen since situation management accounts for around 23% of discourse reflexivity for both speech and writing. But within the category, plane-shifts dominate in both conference and online dialogues, covering over 40% of both (43.3% in conferences, 40.7 in blogs), vs 12.4% in graduate seminars. This could most likely originate in the social characteristics of the situations. Blog threads stem from a comparative lack of external control, the absence of chairpersons, and the ensuing self-organising nature of online comment threads. In this respect comment threads resemble spontaneous conversation more than organised academic discussions, but as already transpired in Chapter 4, longer co-present discussions, even if in principle regulated, also appear to take on a more self-organised character. Why the plane-shifts differ so radically between conferences and graduate seminars was discussed in Chapter 4 (Section 4.4) already and attributed to social power structure. It would seem that the more egalitarian power structure of academic conferences applies to blogs at least equally.

To tease apart some of the factors behind the findings in this chapter, it is useful to consider the likely effects of mode, medium, and genre on discourse reflexivity. To begin with mode, the influence of dialogicity seems strong and consistent, especially as regards discourse management, as can be seen in the synopses of this and the previous chapter (Figures 4.1 and 5.1). However, we also notice differences, some of which seem to derive from the medium. Compared to spoken interaction, the mismatch in temporality, i.e., the asynchrony and the overall slower pace and greater permanence of writing can give rise to rhetorical tactics like those that seem intended to pique the reader's interest. Action that requires such deliberation implies more time spent on constructing a message than is possible in real-time interaction. Written dialogue is nevertheless genuine dialogue, even though produced in solitude like written monologue. In online commentary, the imaginary reader can turn into an actual, active reader and assume the writer position in their turn. The alteration in producer-receiver roles differs from monologic writing by for example asking and answering real questions instead of rhetorical ones. Written dialogue is disembodied and reactive, thus in important ways different from its embodied spoken counterpart, but it also differs vitally from monologic writing. With respect to both, then, written dialogue is a 'third'. Online communication in its dialogic as well as monologic forms has become an everyday channel of communication that generates distinct, novel behaviours and uses of language, and deserves to be studied in its own right. Research seems to be moving increasingly towards multimodality in the field, and this already includes studies of metadiscourse (e.g. Ädel 2021; Liu 2021; Delibekovic Dzanic & Berberovic 2021; Sancho-Guinda 2021).

One social parameter that is related to the online channel rather than mode or medium is anonymity, which is both selective and asymmetrical in blog comment threads: some participants are known to each other offline, some use each other's proper names while most resort to pseudonyms. Bloggers normally use their proper names like any authors, while commenters mostly not. Anonymity is widespread in online discourses, and it has been suggested to encourage the expression of negative, even hostile reactions. Whether hostility originates in anonymity or not, openly negative evaluation and negative expressions of emotions are clearly more prevalent and pronounced in research blog commentaries than in academic face-to-face discussions, where they are virtually nonexistent or quite subdued. This does not hold across the board, though, and there is considerable variation among blog sites. Moreover, personal and emotional presence is not limited to negativity, but is above all polarised, which can be detected in metadiscourse, too (see also Biri 2021). Expressions of praise and enthusiasm also abound, and participants tend to talk about themselves in relation to the issues, including discourse reflexive self-reporting. The higher emotional loading and its open expression implies different social norms from traditional academic writing or speaking. This suggests different generic properties, that is, different social action.

It was argued earlier in this chapter that the research blog is a subtype of the basic-level category 'blog' which can be regarded as a genre in the context of the web. The blogosphere would seem to have given rise to a co-evolution of genre and community in 'local' interactions. We could thus characterise the blog as a specific kind of social action: written public discourse with little external regulation, open to dialogue in the context of disembodied communication. In this it aligns with other online genres. Like online genres generally, the blog is evolving fast compared to traditional written media and thus also continues to offer fresh material for genre theory.

Blog discourses also seem to have their own register characteristics. This is linguistically intriguing because registers reflect users' linguistic sensitivity, and in the global context of the web, users find themselves in a context of ELF. No national culture or local standard of English is therefore involved, which means that variability as well as emerging norms originate in practices that remain outside traditional conceptualisations of 'lingua-cultures'. The comment threads in the present data appear to comply with what large-scale register analyses have found about blog discourse, a hybrid between more traditional spoken and written registers. Nevertheless, the overall finding may conceal considerable variability because large-scale quantitative studies tend to come up with broad and complex categories, which are likely to ignore subtler internal divisions and sources of variability within data. For example, actual blog postings are likely to differ from comment threads. On the face of it, blogs appear more formal than commentaries, which supports the notion that register characteristics change as the interaction unfolds. The typical comment thread register also appears more colloquial than conference or seminar discussions in the light of the very small comparison in this chapter, which accords with an intuitive impression. To say anything definite would obviously require more research. It is also important to keep in mind that register hybridity, which has been reported as typical of online discourses, is a consequence of a specific social context which has many hybrid features. Register hybridity, if any, is therefore a reflection of the context, a description of its linguistic features rather than an explanation.

Some discourse reflexive comment practices support the notion of online discourses being hybrids of spoken and written features, as suggested in some register studies (e.g. Grieve et al. 2011), though not all (Zhang 2022). Anticipation of reader reactions seems to echo an author's normal anticipation as found in many written metadiscourse studies, but simultaneously show signs of conversational anticipation where interlocutors are in fact able to respond. At the same time, there are indications of practices that resemble those discovered more generally in blogs and other online discourses, which would suggest channel-related and probably generic influences.

Many traits in comment threads thus cannot be traced back to either speaking or writing or their mixture, and they do not seem to originate in the dialogic mode either. Instead, they seem to have much in common with blog discourses and other online discourses and could therefore be best attributed to effects of the online channel and to the blog genre. Blog followers seem to be sensitive to genre and the apparently unsettled status of blogs bothers some commenters.

Written digital dialogue resembles both spoken dialogue and monologic writing but cannot be reduced to a mixture of the two. Blog discourse constitutes a genre of its own, and as we have seen has cognitive and social determinants and consequences. Earlier findings from discourse reflexivity in online discussions are supported in the present sample on two accounts: the prevalence of retrospective orientation and negative evaluation (Smart 2016). More general blog-related observations like the tendency to self-disclosure (Luzon 2018) and enhanced explicitness (Bolander 2012) were also supported. These and other characteristics shared with online discourses, including ways of overcoming the lack of expressive resources available in co-present interaction might lead to interesting research at the intersection of academic and online environments, such as research tweets or 3-minute thesis presentations, not to speak of the affordances of multimodal presentations of research, including video journals.

Chapter 6
Matching perspectives and co-constructing knowledge

The last two chapters have shown reflexive discourse as an integral part of dialogic interaction with characteristics that cannot be reduced to what we already knew about metadiscourse in written monologic texts. At this point we shift the perspective towards how discourse reflexivity features in extended discourse, as another step towards understanding how metadiscourse shapes our interactions and why we use it. Thus, we now tackle what was earlier termed *negotiating* in Chapter 4, where its elaboration was postponed to this chapter.

It was suggested at the outset of Chapter 2 that collaboration is exceptionally well developed in humans, we are particularly adept at it, and we collaborate even more than other social species. Undertaking practical tasks together like cooking a meal or setting up self-assembly furniture involves an appreciable amount of collaborative problem solving. Likewise, verbal and intellectual cooperation underpin much of our activity. We probably engage in collaborative problem solving, thinking, and talking for a considerable part of our everyday lives. We jointly construct evaluations of events, objects, persons, states of affairs, new gadgets, mutual acquaintances, or government actions. Our ability to employ reflexive discourse is probably an asset in achieving this collaborative activity, since it helps us fine-tune our communication and helps us communicate flexibly at multiple levels. It also helps keep track of unpredictable turns in changing circumstances.

Intellectual collaboration also builds on other traits commonly identified as specifically human such as abstract thought, imagination, and planning. Whether and in what ways reflexive metadiscourse might facilitate sharing and collaboratively developing complex new ideas is interesting to trace in the context of academic discourses where the focus is precisely on such activities. Much of our academic practices involve the production of new knowledge, and the extent to which this takes place collaboratively may pass unnoticed precisely because it seems such a normal part of academic life. Sometimes it surfaces explicitly (6.1) though by no means always.

(6.1) <S7> actually when i was a- when *when you asked* how how can you measure knowledge **then kind of realised something** of course yeah you you cannot measure it

https://doi.org/10.1515/9783110295498-006

The speaker here notices that an interlocutor's earlier turn has sparked off a new thought that he might not have conceived on his own. Discourse reflexivity renders the recognition explicit.

Given its prevalence, it is interesting to note that the joint construction of knowledge is not a topic addressed in many disciplines but has been primarily – albeit widely – investigated in contexts of pedagogy and child development. In linguistics, co-construction has been on the agenda for a long time as well but usually concerning language and especially turns in conversation, not the knowledge constructed thereby. Conversation analysis, interactional linguistics, and usage-based linguistics have been active in this area, but it is only more recently that linguistic interest has extended towards more general cognitive concepts like attention or inference as forms of collective or dyadic cognising. An interesting development in such thinking, confined to linguistic processes but seen in a wider cognitive perspective, is the dialogic syntax paradigm (e.g., DuBois 2014; Tantucci 2021), which treats constructions as emerging from interlocutors' dynamic engagement with each other's constructions. Interlocutors repeat each other's linguistic elements, especially structures, as is known from the more established research on *priming* (e.g., Ellis 2007; Pickering & Garrod 2017, 2021), but the variability in the process is perhaps better captured in the concept of *resonance* (Du Bois 2014; Tantucci 2021), where structural, semantic, or pragmatic features of linguistic elements can also be altered and re-composed. We see this also in ELF, where it has been discussed under *approximation* (Mauranen 2012) or creativity in for example re-metaphorisation (Pitzl 2015). The processes are not mutually exclusive. It is conceivable that such creative co-construction is not limited to linguistic elements but can be equally relevant to investigating co-constructing understanding and knowledge.

Pedagogic interest in co-constructing knowledge has long roots. The idea that knowledge is actively constructed originates in the classic learning theories of scholars like Jean Piaget and Lev Vygotsky in the early 20th century. Even earlier, John Dewey had proposed similar ideas along the lines of what we now think of as collaborative or cooperative learning. Both Piaget and Vygotsky took knowledge construction to involve interaction, although in different ways. While for Piaget the basis of knowledge development lies in active interaction with objects in the environment, Vygotsky proposed that the relevant interaction for child development takes place between humans. Constructivist theories of learning have taken on board Dewey's and particularly Vygotsky's ideas and built notions on them such as 'community of practice' (Lave and Wenger 1998). These ideas have been widely applied and developed at least for secondary schools (e.g., Ahn & Class 2011; Arvaja 2005) and in some instances higher education (Bruffee 1998; Kastberg 2010; Komori-Glatz & Smit 2022). Moreover, discussions about co-construction of knowledge in the digital age have centred around the learning process in individuals and the ways in which digital technologies contribute to learning and to changing the conditions of learning towards more collaborative environments (e.g., Chu & Kennedy 2011; Salmon 2003; Hull & Saxon 2009; Kuter et al. 2012). This seems to suggest that Piaget's early notions about interaction with objects is gradually coming to its own (on the relevance of the physical environment to interaction, see also Canagarajah 2018, 2021). If we take the entire digital environment together with its physical devices into account, the role of objects assumes a new centrality. Both Piaget and Vygotsky's thinking thus live on in the ways in which collaboration is envisaged in learning.

Educational approaches to knowledge co-construction have focused on analysing the contents of the learning processes (e.g., Ng, Cheung & Hew 2012) but mostly skipped attention to language. There is thus an obvious gap between linguistic and pedagogical approaches to co-construction. A notable exception is work on metalanguage in teaching, which arguably overlaps partially with metadiscourse use in instructional contexts (Myhill & Newman 2016; Myhill, Newman & Watson 2020). Pedagogical approaches (e.g., Komori-Glatz & Smit 2022) tend to be burdened with the idea that student groups may arrive at 'incorrect' solutions or learning outcomes. Thinking along these lines is at odds with linguistic approaches like the dialogic syntax paradigm, which consider speakers' alterations to each other's turns to be creative processes. The concept of knowledge construction that I suggest here is largely in line with linguistic approaches to negotiating meanings and language, even if not concerned with negotiating linguistic expressions. Knowledge construction is intersubjective and collaborative as well as dynamic, therefore unpredictable in its outcomes. In other words, co-constructing knowledge in the sense I approach it here triggers new ideas, not just learning what is already known. Academic discussions stimulate new thought by bringing divergent, alternative, or conflicting viewpoints into contact. As noted in Chapter 4, interactive dialogue progresses from its initial settings towards unforeseen outcomes by participants' mutual engagement and collaboration. Similarly, joint construction of knowledge also orients to something novel through intersubjective engagement.

This open-ended notion of dialogic co-construction is also in tune with the idea of academia as a site of research that generates new scientific knowledge and understanding. This is of course a fairly modern ideal, stemming from the Enlightenment rather than mediaeval universities. Disputations and debates, however, already practised in the Middle Ages, remain at the heart of many academic traditions, particularly doctoral defences and academic conferences. They reflect what Scardamalia and Bereiter (2006) call 'knowledge of' something, implying participatory activity in the process, in contrast to 'knowledge about' without participatory capacity.

A non-pedagogic study of people working in a group suggests that language may come into co-construction in ways that are not obvious. An automatic analysis of idea co-construction in teamwork seems to indicate that a sociolinguistic interpretation of voice-related linguistic phenomena such as prosodic and phonological features are good predictors of whether a contribution in teamwork contains idea co-construction (Gweon 2012). Work of this kind suggests that less obvious facets of language than lexis or grammar may play important roles in the co-construction of knowledge in interaction. It is therefore well motivated to explore what part reflexive metadiscourse may play in this. Conversely, it is interesting to see what discourse reflexivity can tell us about co-constructing knowledge.

This chapter looks at both spoken and written dialogue in connected discussion passages longer than those that have been considered in the last two chapters so that the functioning of reflexive metadiscourse can be observed in the context of negotiating positions and thoughts. The focus has therefore shifted from the last two chapters, which sought to uncover typical uses of discourse reflexivity in the light of individual expressions in context. An exception to the focus on extended passages is made in the first analytical section (6.1.1), which deals with a *clarifying* use of discourse reflexivity, only mentioned briefly in chapters 4 and 5. Though common in any dialogue, it is here taken up as a subtype of *matching perspectives* between speakers. Clarifications are particularly salient in extended extracts with several turns, and the wider category of perspective matching is a prerequisite of knowledge co-construction. For the rest, categories already discussed earlier will be applied whenever relevant.

The longer passages in this chapter occasionally incorporate examples that have already been discussed in illustrating functions of discourse reflexivity. To avoid counting them twice (Chapter 8), there was no counting of expressions for this chapter. Also, because counting episodes where co-construction was found would not be possible without some way of dividing all conversations into 'episodes' that would be comparable in different discussions, the analysis remains qualitative throughout.

The chapter has two main parts, of which the first deals with prerequisites for collaborative knowledge generation like clarifications and negotiating debates, differences, and disagreements. The second part then moves on to tackle the construction of knowledge.

6.1 Prerequisites: matching perspectives

A minimal new outcome of intellectual interaction is the explication of different speaker perspectives, that is, *matching perspectives* between discourse participants. Matching speaker perspectives consists in negotiating interpretations (Mauranen 2012) to secure enough common ground to enable joint elaboration of a topic or point. This could be likened to 'aligning situation models' in Pickering and Garrod's

(2021) cognitive model of dialogue. Conversationalists like to find themselves on the same page, as it were. Of course, a perfect matching of perspectives is an unreachable goal because we cannot know if others think like we do. Our theories of mind are just assumptions and inferences about others. Thinking is an idiosyncratic cognitive process to a degree that is not very well known. But we can and clearly do keep trying to reach out across this separation between individual minds, at least to the extent that we find sufficient and relevant in terms of the situational needs at hand.

In trying to achieve a 'match', that is, an approximate correspondence between interlocutors' relevant frames of reference, speakers engage in negotiation. We can also talk about this in terms of achieving intersubjectivity, like in for instance in conversation analysis and interactional linguistics (e.g., Couper-Kuhlen & Selting 2018). Achieving intersubjectivity, or a match, contains a measure of fuzziness: it means an acceptable degree of mutual understanding so as not to disrupt the coherence of the ongoing discussion. Agreement or consensus, however, are not vital. Therefore, for instance Kastberg's (2010) proposal that knowledge co-construction is the entity on which communicative positions converge is not here regarded as necessary. Full convergence is not required, nor even possible. Discussions proceed successfully if participants make contributions to shared knowledge that others implicitly ratify, that is, accept them as valid contributions. We can regard a negotiation as successfully matching perspectives to the extent that participants tacitly accept each other's inputs, even if the negotiation is lengthy or openly conflictual.

In successful negotiation, participants come to a closure on a given topic. A closure can, but need not, be explicitly signalled and the episode can come to an end there (6.2). Alternatively, it may consist of a transition to a new episode as for instance in (6.3). Here a debate ends with a speaker (S29) offering to comment on something construed as problematic during the preceding discussion in his upcoming presentation. The presentation is about to start at this juncture, and the solution is welcomed by the chair (S23), who hitherto had been trying to invite comments on the issue in vain.

(6.2) . . . because it was focused on the content *you see that's what i was [implying]* </S4>
<S2> [*yeah yeah yeah*] </S2>]

(6.3) <S29> *i'll comment* [*on it i-*] </S29>
<S23> [<NAME S29> er <NAME S29>] er *you'll comment* </S23>
<S29> *i'll comment* on lessig @@ </S29>
<S23> *yes very good please do it* </S23>
<PRESENTATION by S29 >

Working towards matching perspectives includes negotiating clarity and issues that can potentially be problematic or sensitive. One of the roles of discourse reflexivity is to mark something as potentially problematic in the discourse, worth sorting out before continuing. Thus, reflexive metadiscourse can be drawn on to deal with contingencies in on-going discussion. Sometimes anticipated trouble is very minor, and clarifications suffice to sort it out, but open disagreements require more substantial negotiation.

Academic discourses are characterised by a tension between healthy debate and disruptive conflict; academia needs debate and difference to move forward, but at the same time depends on a sufficient degree of polite consensus to maintain the discussion, to keep contributions coming. Excessive consensus can become insipid or restrictive whereas open conflict can push people towards competing but internally consensual camps. Negotiating this fine balance is to a large part carried out in academic publications and has been the subject of much research in science studies as well as the study of written academic discourse (e.g., Myers 1989; Becher & Trowler 2001).

The debates are not only acted out in publications but also in discussions, where the same tension applies, though perhaps to some degree tempered by the linguistic positivity bias, and the drive towards consensus in face-to-face conversations (Eggins & Slade 1997[2006]). Yet there is the simultaneous wish to benefit intellectually from question-raising, discussion, and debate, which can also stimulate further research. Striking an optimal balance for dynamic movement requires negotiation and skill.

This section starts from the relatively straightforward end, that is, clarifications, which are presumably unthreatening to participants. The next section is concerned with the way debates, differences, and disagreements are negotiated.

6.1.1 Clarifying

Clarifications and clarification requests arise between interlocutors when they become aware of uncertainties or possible misalignment in interpretations of what is being said. Problematic coordination in dialogue may of course be redressed by simply adjusting choices in speech (Baggio 2018), but participants sometimes deem the situation to require explicit negotiation. As seen in Chapter 5, dialogue participants anticipate potential misunderstandings and seek to pre-empt them with orienting discourse reflexivity. They may add paraphrases to technical terms (*if that m-* ***mentalité*** *if that s-* ***social fabric surrounding it*** *doesn't work, then . . .*), explanations or expansions (*in childhood representation* ***what we refer to as*** *the postmodern representation of the child*) or express doubt over the perceived clarity of their intended meaning (*I don't know if you get the point*), which opens the floor to hearers in case they are confused. Speakers also occasionally offer clarificatory remarks in retrospect with retrieving references (*I maybe was not very clear saying; what I wanted to mention; I just tell this to show an example*). Hearers, in turn, can directly request clarification by for example offering a candidate understanding (*were you saying . . .*) or declare non-understanding (*I didn't get really the point how . . .*).

To begin with interaction in speech, clarifications are typically jointly achieved by interlocutors, as in (6.4), where participants work out the speaker's (S5's) intended meaning together:

(6.4) <S1> *nowadays, you [mean]* </S1>
<S5> [*i mean*] certainly going back also er through the decades </S5>

Discourse reflexivity is often used in talking about terms and concepts (cf. Chapter 7). Naming in many cases becomes an object of negotiation, as a kind of prospective clarification offer (***I would call it*** *sub-PC something*). Not only terms or labels but also non-technical choices of expression can be problematised and brought to the fore, whether as an individual speaker's identification of a troublesome linguistic choice (6.5) or as joint negotiation of what is meant (6.6).

(6.5) <S32> . . . but consumer needs to have some kind of thir- thir- er *how could i say it* trusted third parties that the consumer trusts *let's say* NGOs or or er economic er go-, i don't know </S32>

(6.6) <S4> [i know it] here but they don't know how to do it that's why they [(are)] </S4>
<S1> [*and that's*] *what you call content* </S1>
<S4> *that's what i call* <S1> ah [okay] </S1> [*content*] yeah okay [okay i (xx) your question] </S4>

In (6.6) S4 has been debating with S1 about problems that teachers face. S4 mentioned teaching content at an earlier point, and S1 expresses uncertainty about whether S4 now continues that theme. She proposes a candidate understanding to clarify the matter. S4 ratifies the interpretation with parallel repetition.

In these instances, discourse reflexivity borders on metalinguistic commentary, especially in contexts where code-switching occurs. In (6.7) the speaker comments on her use of a French word, and can therefore be seen as discourse reflexive, whereas in (6.8) the interpretation hinges upon *I mean* as either discourse reflexive or a hesitation marker. It would seem a more natural interpretation here to take *I mean* as a hesitation marker, since the pronunciation is non-prominent, and it appears between another hesitation marker (*er*) and the puzzling word. The borderline nevertheless remains fuzzy especially where we have highly multifunctional item like *I mean*. Prominence or prosody do not invariably suffice to tell them apart.

(6.7) . . . *a complete* décalage *well* ***I don't know if you can use that word in English*** *but* . . .

(6.8) <S10> . . . subtle ways of of controlling schools er *i mean* ***arviointi*** [*what is it*] <S1> [evaluation] </S1> evaluation more more subtle ways . . . </S10>

Clarifications in written dialogue can be much like those in speech: they include routine rephrasing signals (*in other words, I don't mean*), retrospective clarification requests (*By this are you are meaning . . ., not sure what you're referring to regarding . . .*), and prospective clarification offers (*We call something like this a pilot study; we still want to call them symmetries; let's call it defamation*). Online commenters also ask clarifying questions and offer candidate understandings (6.9).

(6.9) *So if I'm following you correctly, you're saying* that the graviton can be thought of as a quasi-particle of sorts because . . .

Written dialogues also have their special features. One is a tendency towards somewhat more elaboration, even wordiness in ascertaining clarity (6.10), which is in line with the generally observed tendency towards enhanced explicitness in online dialogue (Chapter 5).

(6.10) *What I was trying to ask you, and apparently not being very clear about, is,* would you please continue to speak up for ME/CFS, regardless of whether you see any very compelling studies to blog about, purely on humanitarian grounds?

Blog commentaries also show a distinctly greater tendency to give retrospective clarifications after apparently misunderstood intentions of the author's earlier formulations, like in the previous example. (6.11) shows a retrospective clarification with an accompanying emoticon apparently to convey the intended tone. As noted in Chapter 5, emoticons may help express some of the affective information that in speech is conveyed by pitch, prosody, or intonation (Poeppel 2004), or indicated by for example tone of voice, gestures, or eye contact in the wider embodied context.

Clearly, they remain rather crude approximations of the subtle means available in co-present spoken dialogue.

(6.11) <COMMENT BY C2 ON 05.06.2011>*Ah, I was being snarky towards WPI not using Strider, not you* <EMOTICON: smile>

In all, clarifying appears in both egocentric and altercentric dialogue, as well as prospectively and retrospectively, i.e., in orienting and retrieving uses. Clarifications bestow a prerequisite towards matching speaker perspectives (6.12), without which continuing may not be felicitous.

(6.12) *This makes me wonder if you and they are talking about two different things.*

Clarifications are common in spoken and written dialogue, the main differences lying in the lengthier verbalisation and the large amount of explicit retrospective clarification in online dialogues, which obviously lack many of the subtleties afforded by co-present interaction.

6.1.2 Negotiating viewpoints

The previous section began to lay down basic building blocks of matching perspectives with discourse reflexivity. At this point, we explore how reflexive discourse is integrated into interactants' efforts to find common ground despite their different points of departure, positions, or agendas. Even though participants are not necessarily seeking consensus or convergence, they are keen to sound out each other's frames of reference, locating points of difference and establishing the relevance of those differences to themselves or the topic. In short, they are seeking an acceptable level of correspondence between their perspectives to carry out a meaningful debate around issues they share an interest in.

In contrast to the characteristically neutral or positive tone of clarifications, viewpoint negotiations are typically critical and debative. In considering each other's arguments, evidence, methods, or premises, participants weigh them up and evaluate them, question them, and suggest alternatives.

It takes longer and requires more turns to establish a sufficient degree of common ground than it does to clarify individual points. The extracts in this section are therefore fairly long. There are altogether four excerpts, three spoken and one written: two come from conference discussions, one from a master's seminar, and one a blog thread. All have a minimum of three active speakers or writers, and they were selected to illustrate some of the variability among argumentative discourses in the data. One of the conference extracts is somewhat confrontational, the other displays characteristics of a lively but non-confrontational discussion, and the seminar extract with students and the seminar leader looks like friendly debate. The blog discussion thread comes from a blog on theoretical physics, and despite also being confrontational, has a partly didactic flavour with enthusiastic followers asking questions of the blogger.

Matching perspectives in spoken dialogue

The first extract (6.13a-d) of negotiating viewpoints comes from a conference on the history of science and technology. The extract, like the others in this section, is somewhat abbreviated in that only those parts are reproduced here where discourse reflexivity plays a part. The discussion is long and specialised and would be inconvenient to include in full. For the same reason it is divided into parts that are analysed one at a time to make the long discussion easier to follow. The episode begins after a presentation. The chairperson has invited questions, and speaker (S7) starts the discussion (6.13a).

(6.13a) <S7> *no this this er question is is is more a comment to you to your last point because i disagree strongly with with with the final words you say* erm having grown up and studied in Sweden but lived first er four years in Norway and now five years in . . . i wouldn't i would no- not support the this such such a road for for Swe- Sweden (xx) in and Norway and Germany i can talk but they don't they don't (xx) here . . . their institutes are much more isolated and *to go back to what you said* in your theoretical background the institutes are much more isolated in in er *to take the term that that i've created* er creative environments innovative milieus er there are ins- institutes . . .

The discussion section opens in a confrontational manner: S7 starts by an orienting speech act and topic announcement (*this er question is . . . more a comment . . . to your last point*) and goes right on to assert his disagreement (***I disagree strongly** with the final words you say*). This senior figure brings to bear his experience from several countries along with evoking his academic achievements (*to take the term that . . . I've created*), creating a voice of authority in support of his view. S5, the addressee and the previous presenter, responds (6.13b).

(6.13b) <S5> *well maybe i should a- add* that er there is this clear clearly er bad examples . . . in many places er and *this what you are saying here now* is

> of course the classical argument that has been placed in the universities always against institutes er and er er which i think is o- quite often also re- er er reiterated in universities er even by people who do not share your personal experience of having lived in these countries and so on it's basically something that you learn learn er as a some go- kind of gospel er i sort of rehearsed that gospel too for many years because i didn't know anything about institutes now that i've studied er the this er sort of innovation processes in many countries and tried to find out why things work well and less well in different er social and historical context *i cannot say* i'm that sure anymore . . . and *i think* the Finnish example is a good good one to show that er reality is far more complex and and then *i think* in Sweden there is also some concern . . . so er i'm really er a- *i would also think it's im- important to add that that whe- when we're talking about* virtues and and and vices of of different er kinds of institutions that . . . isolation is nothing that i would er advocate but erm *this is probably not a question that whi- which we solve here but* it's apparently something where where opinions tend to go widely (afar) and i wo- would be curious to learn more about the opinions here in Finland too because er if *if somebody would [like to] <S4> [yes] </S4> mention something about that* </S5>

S5 starts his response with a prefacing particle that anticipates a divergent position (*well*), then suggests he could 'add' something (*well* ***maybe I should a- add*** *that . . .*), presumably to complement his presentation as an answer to S7. In effect he discredits the opponent's criticism by first pointing out that what the interlocutor is saying is not new but widely assumed, even a dogma (***what you are saying here now*** *is of course the classical argument . . . it's basically something that you learn . . . as a some . . . kind of gospel*) and then goes on to contrast it with his own research findings (*I sort of rehearsed that gospel too for many years because I didn't know anything about . . . now that I've studied the . . .*). The juxtaposition of what he portrays as hackneyed myth to results of empirical study is stark, contrasting personal experience and opinion with research. Of course, appealing to authority as S7 does, is generally held to be a fallacy in argumentation studies (e.g. Walton 1997), while appealing to research findings is regarded as sound support for an argument. S5 then engages in a dismissive plane-shift: he declares the question unresolvable in the present discussion (*this is* ***probably not a question which we solve here***). As discussed in Chapter 4, plane-shift is a powerful means of manoeuvring situations, but can also evoke resistance from other participants, and lead to struggle over dominance.

With the plane-shift, S5 then manoeuvres the discussion onto a new phase and continues to manage the situation by turning to all participants for other views (*I would be curious to learn more about the opinions here in Finland too because* ***if somebody would like to mention something about that***). S5 in effect thus bypasses the chairperson, and in principle challenges her conventional role. However, as we saw in Chapter 4, plane-shifts are not uncommon in conference discussions, where participants other than the chair account for about 40% of situation management instances. In this case the role reversal following the plane shift is evident in the way the discussion continues (6.13c).

(6.13c) <S4> *may i say something* i tried to find out what is the main difference between Sweden and . . . but uh what i found @@ and and *maybe you can you can say if i'm wrong or not* but but the er the main . . . such type of institutes that *i was wond-* is it true @@ </S4>
<S5> yeah well the these (statistics) that i showed you basically [what they tell you is that] . . . this has gone down we we have a sort of mhm mhm mhm well *what we call* er <FOREIGN> sektorsforskningens avveckling </FOREIGN> the sort of taking away of sectorial research and the academisation of that research, so nowadays as res- you're precisely right very very small sums of money move from the government to the institutes and er that is a deve- i think we . . . the little money that goes in that *is called* government fund to the institutes . . .
<S4> er but *any other questions* to- er <NAME> </S4>

The first to respond after S5's question is the chairperson (S4), who apparently is somewhat uncertain about her status now, starting with a discourse reflexive move (***may I say something***) which coming from the chair sounds a little peculiar, because it is her prerogative to grant permissions to speak. The chair nevertheless does not go on to answer S5's question directly, but addresses S5 as the previous presenter (. . . what I found @@ and and ***maybe you can*** *you can* ***say*** *if I'm wrong or not* but . . . ***I was wond-*** is it true @@). S5 replies with some clarifications (***what we call*** sektorsforskningens avveckling). S4 then reassumes her chairperson's role and continues with managing the situation (***any other questions***).

The discussion now turns more consensual (6.13d) and what we might call 'fact-sharing': participants contribute their observations from different contexts (e.g., S2 below), co-constructing a broader view of the domain, which in effect works towards answering the question S5 put to them. The chair chips in once more, indicating her dual role with reflexive discourse (*may I say something*) as if asking permission from everyone to assume a participant role, then resuming more of a chairperson role in prioritising her own question (*before anybody else want to ask*). Despite the fact-sharing turn in the conversation, the episode retains an argumentative flavour and we can see a quest for new answers and new understanding reflected in discourse reflexivity, for instance the use of *I think* several times as an opinion marker rather than a hesitation, and S5 elaborating his argument (*I hope you picked up the message that . . . I'm saying; I would certainly not argue*).

(6.13d) <S2> *if i may just comment* er my experiences from Finland er i have at least the the experiences that . . . without practically any resources anymore *so i think* there's a very big risk that if we concentrate er too much resources to certain areas then it is very risky on the long run . . . if and when the CT will not be that successful in the future </S2>
<S5> mhm </S5>
<S4> it was just a report *may i say something* just a report what what is the status er and and prognose of of science and technology in Finland it er the er book published or evaluation published the er two weeks ago . . . people are more aware what is going to happen for this *but i would like to ask @before anybody else want to ask@* when you erm er you emphasised so much this . . . what we can do then in the future </S4>
<S5> *well i i hope you picked up the message that* er culture here is not just what . . . and maybe maybe the circumstance *i'm saying that* maybe there has been too much emphasis @on this particular@ in this belief in in er in in in in R&D i mean R&D is just one little, piece but they have a wide impact </S5>
<S4> mhm okay thank you and <NAME S11> </S4>
<S11> yes i am also fascinated of the map you showed us about . . . if you want to make the similar map from say around 1970 i think you would have found different results </S11>
<NS13> in the (xx papers) or </NS13>
<S11> Stockholm <NS13> yes </NS13> it's it's (xx) important part and we'll have er high figures for Umeå but . . ., so er *i think* er maybe universities is a giant (force in) Swedish economy probably (Finnish as well) but the educational system in total has not been this engine for for economic (xx) </S11>
<S5> mhm yes well er you you you might certainly be (xx) there and *i would certainly not argue that* that every period is the same, different regions have their ups and downs if we could take a er longer term er state er er these those international results by Varga and others *that i'm referring to* seem to suggest that all the long term b- b- bigger regions fare pretty well . . . in the last eight to ten years </S5>

Altogether, discourse reflexivity serves many roles in this whole excerpt. In managing the initial confrontation, we saw reflexivity used for taking a stand (*I disagree strongly*), dismissing arguments (*what you are saying here now is of course the classical argument . . . some kind of gospel*), and manoeuvring the situation towards new parameter settings (*not a question which we solve here . . . I would be curious . . . if somebody would like to mention something about that*). In addition, discourse reflexivity was involved in clarification (*what we call*) in deviating from standard practices (*may I say something*), presenting arguments (*I would also think it's important to add*) and focusing them (*when we're talking about* virtues . . .) as well as in orienting hearers (*if i may just comment; this . . . is more a comment*), retrieving and drawing on their talk (*what you are saying here now*) and showing awareness of the sensitivity of the issue (*I cannot say I'm that sure anymore*). In brief, this extended polylogue passage where something unusual or potentially problematic is dealt with manifests a vast array of discourse reflexive uses which help speakers relate to each other's perspectives in a meaningful way.

The next passage from an information sciences conference (6.14a-e) is also quite long, comprising a whole discussion section between two presentations. The passage starts again with the chair (S18), then the first question (by S31) following S32's presentation. All six speakers are male. As before, the extract has some minor omissions to keep the length down.

In the episode, participants are negotiating an apparently sensitive issue, on which their views are divided.

(6.14a) <S18> *any questions comments please* </S18>
<S31> well how do you do how do you see er kind of the erm lack o- lack of flow of information regarding . . . the producer in the south </S31>
<S32> *yeah that that is a that is a fundamental quistion question* er we don't have that information flow . . . how could i er define the responsible er decisions if if i don't have that information or h- w- *was this answer to your question or* </S32>
<S31> *maybe i was looking for* a like a solution what would you do </S31>
<S32> what what would be the solution <S31> yes </S31> i i believe that in future the the the amount of information will be huge . . . but consumer needs to have some kind of thir- thir- er *how could i say it* trusted third parties that the consumer trusts let's say NGOs or or er economic er go-, i don't know </S32>
<S34> yes </S34>

S31 asks a question, which S32 acknowledges as "fundamental", but his confirmation check (*was this answer to your question*) indicates some uncertainty. S31 rejects the answer with a softening hedge (***maybe*** *I was*) and tries anew. S32 rephrases part of the second formulation (*what would be the solution*), as if again seeking confirmation. S31 ratifies this (*yes*), and S32 goes on to answer. S34's *yes* could be seen as support for S32, but this is his only sign of participation at this point.

A third speaker (S35) now comes in (6.14b), beginning with a retrieving contextualisation (*when you were talking about* these . . .). S32 cuts the question short with his response.

(6.14b) <S35> er <SIGH> i have a feeling that *when you were talking about these* labels labels <S32> yeah </S32> that er this group of people these consumers they don't trust labels they d- labels they don't they can't count on them or something i [<SIGH>] </S35>
<S32> [mo- most] of the people <S35> [yeah] </S35> [in fact] . . . so people don't take them when there is this label </S32>

In (6.14c), S35 and S32 continue the debate.

(6.14c) <S35> *yes but i have to disagree a little bit i think* it depends on the label because on the other hand er a lot of people are very very well aware that there are many sorts of labels <S32> yeah </S32> *you're talking about* sem- something like erm well ethical consumption in erm eggs for instance you have these these er labels that say that it's a they are happy eggs . . . or something like this [but if] </S35>
<S32> [the most] yeah most [people] <S35> [yeah] </S35> don't understand what these labels [means yeah] </S32>
<S35> [sure but then] then of course there are labels that people do trust . . . so if you have a ce- certain labels that er can be guaranteed to already contain all this ethical aspect you know <S32> yeah [yeah but] </S32> [and it's] easier for the [consumers yeah] </S35>
<S32> [yeah i *i agree* and] i *but er that that is not that was not my point my point is that* these people are already already now doing er the evaluation that what product is good or not and most people think that when they buy local food it it means that they are buying organic food [do] <S35> [but] </S35> *you follow me* </S32>

Following S32's response, S35 resumes his own point, now openly debative (*yes but I have to disagree . . . you're talking about* something . . .), but with some mitigation (*a little bit I think*). S32 cuts him off again with his counterargument, upon which S35 elaborates his point, but despite an initial concession (*yeah I agree and . . .*) S32 insists S35's counterargument is not relevant to his own claim (*but er that,* ***that***

was not my point), which he goes on to reiterate (*my point is that* . . .). He ignores S35's attempt to intervene (*but*), instead insisting, with a comprehension check (*you follow me*), that his point be heard. S35 does not give up yet, as we see in (6.14d).

(6.14d) <S35> sure but then [there are also mhm] </S35>
<S32> [er so so what] what for what do they need the label any more because they are already consuming the organic food that that is the key *so i'm i'm saying* here that sh- are do we really want to give the freedom to these people to define the concept of sustainability themselves or are we still keeping that there are really sustainable products or and then there are these fake er sustainable products that people just think are sustainable *so i'm i'm just saying* that *i'm asking* that who who is to define the sustainability here </S32>

In 6.14d, then, S35 begins another effort to argue against S32, who again interrupts, reiterating and rephrasing his main point, his turn peppered with 'insistent' discourse reflexivity (. . . *so I'm saying* here . . . so *I'm just saying* . . . *I'm asking* . . .). Each instance of *I'm* + communicative verb + ING is followed by what S32 presents as a reformulation of his message.

From here, a fourth speaker (S34) picks up (*can I comment [about]this)* adding a point (*I think* that . . . *I don't think* there is . . .), which S32 appears to take as support for his view (6.14e):

(6.14e) <S34> *i think er can i comment [about]* <S32> [yeah] </S32> this *i think* that the the person to define is the person who cosu- consumes and er there *i don't think* there is much you can do about it </S34>
<S32> yeah because they are doing it al- already </S32>

In (6.14f), S34 makes a start which remains incomplete, and the chair (S18) takes the floor. However, he does not assume his chairperson's role, but that of a discussion participant with a critical stance towards S32's position:

(6.14f) <S34> so er that's probably for this </S34>
<S18> of course there is a lot of to do with it *i mean* think about education <S32> mhm </S32> like *i mean when you told* that er information doesn't count <S32> mhm </S32> but but we do have a schooling system in our countries and and er if we @@ are that @pessimistic@ then we can pretty much end the end the schooling like Ivan Illich was pointing out 30 years ago </S18>

<S32> i'm not pessimistic but *i'm i'm asking* that because the old old er information knowledge old knowledge er building er projects . . . they have had good effects *so i'm asking* that could we could we, get something useful off . . . so which one effects which one is the er question </S32>

S18 effectively questions S34's and S32's views (*I mean* think about . . . *like I mean when you told* that information doesn't . . .), upon which S32 continues to press his point, now more defensively (*I'm not pessimistic but* ***I'm asking*** *that . . . so* ***I'm asking*** *that . . .*).

It is interesting to note different reflexivity strategies in these exchanges. S32's reflexive metadiscourse is noticeably at variance with that of the others: his is predominantly egocentric, concentrating on his own point (*my point is, I'm saying, I'm asking*), while other speakers here show a more altercentric orientation (*when you told, you're talking about*) and use orienting prefaces (*can I comment, I don't think*). S32 comes across as somewhat combative, but at the same time intent on getting his point across and reaching out to the others in this way.

(6.14g) <S18> *another question* </S18>
<S11> *well er i'd like to comment on on that comment you just presented* <S32> mhm </S32> because i i first of all myself i i do believe in this kind of pressure coming from the consumers er *let us say* some kind of boycotting campaigns and so on but the big problem with them at the moment is er it is a kind of conceptual problem in the sense that we still have no clear idea what er sustainability means which is a well that's even more technical question and thus a bit easier one than *let us say* what does fair trade mean <S32> mhm-hm </S32> so er *i think* we have a lot of potential in in in directing the consumer pressure er on on the producers but first of all we would have to know what would this concept actually mean *i mean* for instance the the criteria that the fair trade organisations use they are quite they are quite vague and i i wouldn't use them as a basis as such </S11>
<S32> yeah yeah *i agree totally* <S11> mhm </S11> and and because we to *to say this aloud* that the the definition is open i- i- *is to to look the whole question in a new way* because *i am not here to answer the question because i am i'm i'm trying to say that* the consumers themselves should and they are already doing it and and and we we should give them freedom and tools to do it more effectively </S32>

Here (6.14g) the chair reassumes his role as the manager of the situation (*another question*), and a hitherto silent participant (S11) offers to comment (*I'd like to comment on that comment you just presented*), and lays down his take on the issue, organising his turn with reflexive discourse (*let us say, . . . let us say . . .* so *I think . . . I mean*). S32 supports S11's turn by backchannels, and eventually explicitly (*I agree totally . . .*), goes on to reiterate his main idea once again, which now has gained support from S34 and S11. At this point, the time is up for the discussion section, but the discussion does not yet come to an end:

(6.14e) <S34> <WHISPERING> (xx) </WHISPERING> </S34>
<SU> we have to carry on </SU>
<S34> okay [so] <S32> [okay] </S32> it's [(xx)] </S34>
<S18> [yeah we have to] carry on now and er and er thank you <NAME S32>
. . . [side sequence omitted relating to setting up the next presenter's computer] . . .
<S34> well there is this er change *i would just like to add to this point* [that er] <S18> [oh yeah] yeah </S18> it is er *i think* it is er it is probably not so important to er to have this precise understanding of what is sustainability . . . and *i think* this is a again as *as with last er presenta- i think* er the private sector activity is was overlooked *in the presentation* in the sense that er i mean *we can talk about* many things but there is little we can do about it except that . . . this wisdom it er instils itself *and so i think* private companies will be er using this to their advantages and that the labels that meet the expectations will be raising thank you </S34

Although the chair ended the discussion before S34 could put in another turn, the next speaker is connecting his laptop and S34 grasps this unexpected opportunity to continue. He now gets the floor (*well there is this change* ***I would just like to add to this point***) and goes on to add a new note to the debate, one that is critical of S32's line of thinking from an angle not yet touched upon in the discussion (*I think* this is again *as with last presenta- I think* the private sector activity was overlooked *in the presentation . . . I mean we can talk about* many things but . . . *and so I think . . .*). In effect S34's final turn resists closure to the debate by pointing to a relevant unanswered question. The discussion thus ended but did not achieve convergence.

In (6.14), while participants were clearly divided on the issue, they were at the same time apparently keen to reach a modicum of mutual understanding, if only to press their own points. They persist in seeking to make their viewpoints accessible to each other by returning to the same issues and repeatedly reformulating their views as if looking for some common ground upon which to pitch their argument to convince others of its superiority. In other words, they strive to match their perspectives, even if not to find consensus. As in much of the present data, we find a concentration of discourse reflexivity where debates, differences, and disagreements are manifest. Discourse reflexivity also helps the analyst without specialist understanding of the issues to follow dividing lines between the debating parties.

Our third example (16.14a-b) shows an educational setting. Shorter than the previous two, it comes from a graduate seminar in political science. The seminar leader is not only a chairperson for managing the situation, but he also has a pedagogic role relative to the student participants. He therefore has responsibilities towards them in addition to authority in respect of situational and content matters, which sets a teacher chair apart from a conference chair. The social situation is more asymmetric than a conference. In this excerpt, all four speakers have different linguistic and national backgrounds; one is female and three are males.

The extract begins towards the end of a discussion following one student's presentation and seems to drift spontaneously somewhat off the original topic. The presenter is not participating in the discussion at this point. The current topic started when S6 compared capitalism to protestant religion, someone objected, and the seminar leader (S1) responds that capitalism originated before Protestantism. This is where our extract begins.

(6.14a) <S1> [oh its] its origin is in northern Italy, <SS> @@ </SS> from the time when there wasn't any Protestantism </S1>
<S6> well alright *you may say* it's a religion but its nowadays appearance is very much protestant *i would say* erm even more Zwinglian issue of life or Calvinist because erm er religion is not an abstract thing which is here and the state is there and our culture's just another third point somewhere else . . . but how do we come to define these cultural circles, it's also a question of religion </S6>
<S4> *you mean that* the cultural circle is a metaphor of religion or </S4>
<S6> well no you you're just looking at it like culture and [religion] </S6>
<S4> [you don't know] how i look things @@ </S4>
<S6> but religion is inherited in culture, there is no culture without religion, (not possible) in our <S7> if i </S7> in our (point) </S6>

After S1 has pointed out a problem in S6's observation on capitalism and Protestantism, S6 defends his own view (***you may say*** *it's a religion but its nowadays appearance is very much protestant* ***I would say***). His *you may say* is not a concession, because it is S6 who himself compares it to capitalism, and the concession (*well alright*) seems to be limited to the correction S1 made. Instead, *you may say* is more of a borderline case of a generic reference outside the current discussion. The stance marker (*I would say*) incorporates a slight mitigation but asserts the speaker maintains his view, challenging the earlier objection. S4 joins the discussion with a clarification request (*you mean that*). S6 starts to elaborate his view, S4 chips in with a little banter and laughter, S6 continues to expand on his point, and S7 makes an unsuccessful attempt to join in.

(6.14b) <S7> *may i point that point that* i made i made a little sociology study on religion just a week ago and <SS> @@ </SS> basically the fun thing is [many sociologists many sociologists] </S7>
<S1> [has it been published in any] any good international journal </S1>
<SS> @@ </SS>
<S7> yeah many sociologists argue actually that religion erm is rather a reflection of the culture and that way (xx) again religion is a piece of culture and and erm influence the culture again and then becomes a perfect reflection of the culture it's like a continuous circle so they are like integrated everywhere *which is kind of support what he said* (xx) </S7>
<S1> yeah but *when we talk about* religion the the problem is . . .

In (6.14b) S7 now succeeds in taking the floor, starting his turn with orienting discourse reflexivity (*may I point that*), then refers to his own authority on the matter. S1 initiates a humorous side sequence, but without getting distracted, S7 resumes his point, and ends by indicating its relevance to the discussion at hand and his support to S6 (*which is kind of support what he said*). The extract ends with S1 putting the discussion into a wider perspective (*yeah but* ***when we talk about*** *religion the problem is* . . .), which in a pedagogical context seems like normal practice. *When we talk about* is, again, somewhat marginally discourse reflexive, given its interpretability as either referring to the current discussion or generically to an abstract 'we'. In effect, it can give rise to both meanings simultaneously. Altogether, discourse reflexivity does not play a particularly prominent role in this pedagogical context, but it reveals the dominant role of the chairperson and the inherent role asymmetry. The seminar leader does not engage in situational management in the extract, but does so at the outset of the event, in transitions, and at the end. He rather assumes a participant role here, and apparently throws aside temporarily the chairperson's mantle like the conference chairs did in previous examples (6.12 and 6.13). Yet he presents his views as if with self-evident authority, not for example framing his statements with reflexive metadiscourse like speakers did in the conference examples as they engaged in debate on an equal social footing, and like students do in this discussion. He also alternates in multiple roles as he deems appropriate: a discussion participant, a knowledge authority, and the chairperson.

Clearly, an educational context affords very different resources to the participants compared to a conference, and this is interestingly also reflected in the amount and the nature of discourse reflexivity.

Matching perspectives in written dialogue

Our final example of a debate comes from a blog thread. The blog is kept by a theoretical physicist, has been running for several years, and apparently has a very large following. The blogger is a keen advocate of string theory. A good number of the exchanges take place between the blogger and followers who ask questions or clarifications but also challenge the blogger's presentations. Again, the extract (18.a-c) is shortened, putting the spotlight on the uses of discourse reflexivity for negotiating debate. The extract shows why blog threads are unwieldy to produce in full: since the dialogues are asynchronous, and participants respond to each other after greater or smaller time lapses, other commenters' comments on various topics intervene in these temporal spaces in any order. The outcome thus consists of interspersed dialogues or parallel threads that overlap in a strictly temporal sense but appear in one linear sequence necessitated by the format of the digital space. One of the textual consequences is that addressee identification occurs frequently: contributors habitually address each other by name (usually a pseudonym). Bolander (2012) talks about this addressee identification as 'signalling responsiveness', but the practice seems necessary just for keeping track among several simultaneously ongoing discussion threads. Quotations from earlier posts are also often reproduced at the outset of a comment (e.g., 6.15b). Although I have shortened the actual entries below, the sequence is in its original order to retain authenticity. Our extract starts from C11 asking a question (6.15a) of the blogger (B1) and ends with C11 thanking him (6.15c). As before, B is the blogger, Cs are commenters.

(6.15a) <COMMENT BY C11>
Dear Lubos,
I like your discussions of frontier physics.
This thread seems to be open for general questions, so let me ask: Does the success of the string description of the world mean that space time is quantised, not a continuum but a succession of strings?
Time too?
(taking cover) :)

<COMMENT BY B1>
Thanks, <NAME C11>, but *the several statements you pretend to be equivalent in your question* are not equivalent.

A "succession" of strings is . . . The shorter distances one considers, the more accurately all these symmetries have to hold, and the more "continuous" spacetime has to be.

<COMMENT BY B1>
Haven't I explained about 50 times why all theories assuming a discrete spacetime are doomed from the start? . . .
I don't enjoy discussions about crackpot theories all the time. I hate when discussions about exciting topics quickly degenerate into exchanges about meaningless crackpot fantasies.

Above, at the outset of the discussion we see C11 offering an initial positive evaluation of B1's blog discussions (*I like your discussions*), then moving on to an orienting phase, where (s)he first provides a motive for the contribution (*This thread seems to be open for general questions*) then a prompt (*so let me ask*). B1 responds in the first instance by a retrieving evaluation of C11's question, which disputes C11's premises (*the several statements . . . in your question*). He then goes on to give his interpretation of the issue, and in a second comment continues what he started in the first, but with far less description, venting his frustration with the questions he receives, first referring to his previous blog discussions (*Haven't I explained about 50 times why*), then pouring out his disapproval more generally (*I don't enjoy discussions about crackpot theories*), which is in the margin of reflexive metadiscourse, being ambiguous with respect to referring to the discussion at hand, although it clearly refers to his blog site. The sequence continues in (6.15b), where three commenters (C4, C12, and C17) present conciliatory contributions. C17 includes an initial direct quote in his turn.

(6.15b) <COMMENT BY C4>
Dear Lumo,
thanks for the upload of this talk, it really gives a nice summery and is very easy to follow . . .
I somehow understand that it drives You up the wall that some people don't understand that discrete spacetimes don't work . . .
But don't worry to much about it, that's not the fault of *Your clear explanations*; . . .
Surely a lot of people appreciate Your enlightening articles on TRF:)
Cheers

<COMMENT BY C12>
Just wanted to say thanks for taking the time to answer my questions.:)

<COMMENT BY C17>
*"I find it *extremely* disappointing that you apparently can't taste it, I can probably do nothing whatsoever about it."*
Dear Lubos, don't worry!
I might have exaggerated my metafor a bit; And I might also have also misled you to a feeling of disappointment with an inappropriate – not literally meant to represent doubt – emoticon. . . .
P.S. *I earnestly promise to* (shall try as far as I can trust a Sly Creep) to not use an emoticon for any other expressive purpose than what it is conventionally meant for!!

In (6.15b), we find very positive comments to B1's earlier postings, whether thanking him for responding to commenters' requests (*thanks for the upload of this talk, . . . taking the time to answer my questions*), which in effect is situational management, and expressing sympathy for B1's uttering his frustration. In addition, the reflexive discourse includes an addressee-reference (*Your clear explanations*) and an orienting speech act (*I earnestly promise to*).

In the next phase, we also find another participant (C72) than the blogger elaborate and expand on the issues, including a link to a presentation that C11 refers to. To B1, C11 responds in less conciliatory terms than before:

(6.15c) <COMMENT BY C11>
Dear Lubos,
You are overreacting to a simple question.
1) I have not been following your blog for long, and the subject has not come up since I started.
2) *I am not proposing* a theory or view or anything, I am trying to understand how things work, . . . *Again, I am not proposing anything,* I am trying to understand.

<COMMENT BY C72>
In some models, the gravity force is emergent at low energies, . . .

<COMMENT BY C11>
I listened to the presentation, and it is lucid and understandable. (skipped the italian though)

<COMMENT BY C11>
Is my confusion coming from mixing up the observed four dimensional space, . . . ?

<COMMENT BY B1>
Dear <NAME C11>, (super)string theory has 9+1 (space+time) dimensions while M-theory has 10+1 dimensions . . . .
Einstein's equations are always satisfied – in 10 or 11 dimensions much like in 4 dimensions. *Does it answer all your questions or did I miss something?*

<COMMENT BY B1>
Pleasure, <NAME C12>.

<COMMENT BY B1>
Dear <NAME C11>, 1), 2) OK, please don't worry, it's obviously not (only) your fault. 3) gravitons at a given frequency have quantised energy in units of E=hf. But the spacetime in which they propagate . . . .
Have I answered your questions? Cheers, LM

<COMMENT BY C11>
Thanks for your patience.

C11 resumes the debate with a plane-shift challenging the appropriacy of B1's speech act (*You are overreacting to a simple question*), then goes on with an orienting preface specifying the intended speech act (*I am not proposing a theory*), repeating it at the end of the comment (*Again, I am not proposing anything*). The insistent repetition seems to signal the writer's concern about getting misunderstood, which in view of B1's earlier reaction to a question (6.15a) is a real possibility. Discourse reflexivity is here again employed in negotiating a potentially conflictual juncture. Explicating the intended speech act may not only obviate misperceptions but signify the speaker's willingness to negotiate the issues further and be included as an active participant.

C72 now contributes a lengthy explanation of some of the relevant concepts, followed by self-reporting from C11 (*I listened to the presentation*) with appraisal (*it is lucid and understandable*). The presentation link was provided by B1 and already referred to by C4 (6.15b), thus it is shared information among these discussion participants. C11 goes on to ask a new question about the presentation, to which B1 responds, with a clarity check at the end (*Does it answer all your questions or did I miss something?*). B1 then acknowledges C12's earlier thanks before moving back to respond to C11's turn with numbered points, again ending up with a clarity check (*Have I answered your questions?*). The discussion then moves on to a different direction.

The blog thread extract illuminates the progression of blog discussions, and the consequences of asynchronous contributions: different dialogues get interleaved in the track. When the whole thread is read in the order of appearance, the viewpoint differences between C11 and B1 seem interspersed with what look like digressions, such as other comment chains, contributions, thanking, or other diverging paths. At first glance, the sequence looks chaotic but after disentangling individual threads (as in this data) they proceed much like dialogues in face-to face interaction.

Apparently to help keep track of what the responses relate to, discussants use a good deal of identity markings such as addressing and quotes from earlier turns. Web discussions are always potentially polyadic much like conference discussions, only not limited to co-present participants. Anyone may make an appearance into a dialogue to which they have been silent overhearers up to that point. One difference between spoken and written dialogue seems to be that moving back and forth seems to be more common in blog threads, drawing on the affordances of the written record. For instance, in (6.15c) B1 responds to earlier comments in a slightly curious-looking order, which suggests he may have been going through and responding to them in a batch.

In all, the extracts in this section, both spoken and written, illustrate how diverse kinds of discourse reflexivity get intertwined in elucidating discourse, especially when something potentially problematic is being dealt with. Participants are concerned with sounding out each other's positions and increasing precision about them in several ways: clarifications (*by this I don't mean*), elaborating points already made (*it's important to add*), checking comprehension, whether one's own (*if I'm following you correctly you're saying*) or that of others (*you follow me*), and indicating, even insisting, that one's own argument is consistent and its different formulations paraphrases of each other (*what I'm saying is; as I have emphasised*). As interactants work at matching their perspectives towards some common ground, they can go beyond ascertaining the state of their hitherto shared knowledge: at times the interaction generates something new, some knowledge or understanding that was not there before. This is the topic of the next section.

6.2 Generating knowledge

Discussion, debate, and critical assessment of research claims are among the key instruments of what is generally understood to constitute progression and regeneration of knowledge in academia. Much of this is carried out through research publications, but it is less clear and rarely explored what role face-to-face discussion might play in co-constructing new knowledge. Does discussion in academia have intrinsic value in contributing to new knowledge? Can it reach beyond the asymmetric pedagogical co-construction of established knowledge that educationists talk about? Insofar as discussion among researchers, graduate students, and other parties interested in research generates new knowledge, we should find evidence of it in the present data.

Just to be clear, 'knowledge' is used here in a broad sense that goes beyond the acquisition of facts or established concepts. Rather, it is a convenient shorthand for a number of intellectual processes such as understanding, theoretical and abstract grasp of concepts, and perceiving new connections between entities. In intellectual discussion it is the conceptual aspect of knowledge that is most at stake in any case, because participants are engaged in talking about research rather than in doing it.

Co-construction of knowledge would seem to take place when participants contribute information or views that they deem to be relevant to the topic but not known to their interlocutors. This is of course omnipresent in dialogue. What is less commonplace is speakers manifestly sparking off ideas of each other. It is this process that the spotlight is on in this section: to what extent can we find evidence of joint construction of knowledge between the discussing parties on the spot?

As above, we look at spoken interaction first, and written dialogue follows. Most examples are somewhat shorter than in the previous section because the explicit recognition of new thoughts in an instant takes place in short flashes. This section also draws more on thesis examination data than the previous one did. The blog discussions (Section 6.2.2) come from the same sample of the WrELFA corpus as before.

6.2.1 Collaborating towards knowledge in spoken dialogue

On occasion, we find manifest traces of speakers triggering new thoughts, ideas, and observations in each other during dialogic interaction. These examples (6.16–18) are like the one at the beginning of this chapter (6.1).

(6.16) . . . this gentleman from Australia *you were talking about* freedom and so on does that mean you know *i have never thought of about this connection* yeah then when i now remember you know the battles where like there are none working groups . . .

(6.17) <S2> . . . that actually the theme of empowerment arises then through the analysis much stronger than i [initially claim @that is er@ i *i now*] <S3> [yes okay okay, yes] </S3> *that you say you point this out i realise it myself* of course erm i have here in this study . . .

(6.18) <S1> [@@] yeah <READING THE NAME OF THE ARTICLE> what is-a is and is it er er an analysis of taxonomic links </READING> and it is indeed I triple-E in [1983] <S2> [mhm-hm] okay fine </S2> but *this erm the detail that you mentioned that is actually quite crucial that i failed to notice* </S1

In these instances, which come from one conference and two thesis defences, the speaker self-reports on their thought process leading to a new realisation or connection based on an interlocutor's turn. In the first two, the speaker then goes on to elaborate on the new perspective. In other words, the new idea assumes a springboard function like altercentric references often do, as discussed in Chapter 4. Something a previous speaker said incites a new thought, which the next speaker fills out from their perspective. The latter idea thus grows out of the first and in effect incorporates both contributions. It is reasonable to assume that such processes go on much more widely in discussions and conversations than gets overtly verbalised.

Sometimes the idea that occurs combines different points from the previous discourse. Something said at present retrieves an earlier thought in the speaker's mind, giving them the opportunity to connect that to what an interlocutor has said. This apparently makes use of their long-term working memory, related to the on-going macro event. An example (6.19) comes from a doctoral defence where the examiner (S3) responds to what the defendant (S1) has suggested and proceeds from there.

(6.19) <S1> . . . but actually it would be easier to predict er what kind of interferences is er in the translation <S3> mhm </S3> yes </S1>
<S3> *er that actually brings me to a question that i didn't put on the slide which occurred to me right now* and er <COUGH> which also is er. when when you look at learner corpora <S1> mhm </S1> then one one of the things that you can do, which you couldn't do earlier is look at things like tendencies <S1> mhm </S1> which which i *i thank you for mentioning here* you you can look at learner language and see how is it different

Since many academic events consist of composite or chain-like event types, knowledge co-construction straddles separate parts of a macro-event, as evinced in the next example (6.20). The participants are attending a conference session where one of the speakers (S18) makes a connection to an earlier keynote presentation:

(6.20) <S36> . . . *i don't have anything to say* but i'm just very excited that i i would have almost missed this presentation going through could be so obscure and and (xx) and actually it is first-class (critique) </S36>
<S18> yeah *i agree* and er and there's yeah er i think there's a very nice link between <NAME S8>'s presentation to to that *what er <NAME NS16> said in his keynote* in the very beginning of this conference . . .

Here a composite event leads to a joint construction of connections and thereby to new understanding: S8's presentation inspired an enthusiastic response in one participant, another participant picks this up and links it further to an earlier presentation.

Similar bridging of two events is manifest in the next instance (6.21) from a graduate seminar. The connection between the events is less explicit, but this seminar in the philosophy of science follows immediately a conference held in the same place and attended by those present. This session has started with a presentation. The speaker (S4) is a senior visitor to the group, and he is offered the floor for commentary. This is his opening turn.

(6.21) <S4> [you know i i i been listening] very carefully to *what you have said* yeah i mean erm that my my you know the the *as you talked* i mean *i was just thinking of that that discussion* about knowledge information and wisdom erm that knowledge is still not quite there you know what i mean i mean there is a (line at) the door i mean you act as as you're going to open the door but you only like going to open the door if the you wanted to make the (inference) that he wants to (enter here) you know @@ </S4>

What you have said and *as you talked* refer to the presentation that just ended, but the reflexive discourse (*that discussion about knowledge information and wisdom*) refers to a discussion at the conference that had just ended and is presumed to be familiar and accessible to those present.

The next three examples come from thesis defences and are somewhat longer. Doctoral thesis defences are a special setting and uphold a gatekeeping function, in some sense academic quality assurance in action. The public defence is a tradition especially in continental and northern Europe, and similar practices of oral examinations are common in other parts of the world even if the events are not always public (like the viva in the U.K). The situation is socially asymmetric, as one party (the examiner) represents established academia, and the other an aspiring new member. The examiner tests whether the candidate qualifies for membership.

However, even though examiners have a superior institutional standing, the university institution's foundational values rest on the pursuit of new knowledge.

Examiners are experts in the field, but the candidate is an expert on their specific topic. Opponents and defendants thus each bring their different knowledge resources to the discussion, and additionally, they share an interest in the research field and its development. The discussions are therefore not entirely limited to the thesis itself. Examiners often evoke general principles of science and scholarship and sound out the candidate's wider thinking behind methodological choices and interpretations of theories or practices in the field. In addition, and more importantly to our present concerns, they can pursue issues of shared interest beyond the task at hand.

Cases of dialogic co-construction tend to be fairly long in defence discourses, but I tried to select three examples from the shorter end. They come from different fields. The first extract (6.22) comes from information technology, and one of the two examiners (or opponents), S2, is here taking his turn with the defendant (S1). Their topic at this point is a 'fairness' model.

(6.22) <S2> . . . in some of your examples you use fairness to model the fact that some channel does not use it do not lose definitely it as a message. but are channels fair or probabilistic </S2>
<S1> erm, *i would say that* fairness is a weaker requirement than than being probabilistic so er <S2> in what sense </S2> er fairness doesn't really imply anything about the distribution of the er of the of the well whatever we are observing so i think fairness is something weaker makes a weaker assumption so we are using fair fair models and and in a way this also then covers probabilistic systems </S1>
<S2> *so you're saying* that probabilistic system is fair at least under some er [a reasonable probabilistic system is going to be fair] </S2>
<S1> [yes yes yes] yes </S1>
<S2> *actually i agree* i think indeed <COUGH> i mean fairness is a is a sort of a of a limit of of probabilistic systems to *to say so* the minimum requirement on of the er er probabilistic system but another problem with fairness is that you know fairness does not correspond to any implementation you cannot implement fairness as is, so what does it mean when you've verified a fair system </S2>
<S1> well er *as you said* it is a kind of limit of of, of s- well *we could say* there's a limit of of systems that are implementable so in a by using a fairness assumption we sort of cover all those systems that can represent real implementations to verify them so again this is kind of a useful abstraction more than an implementation </S1>
<S2> *quite (agreed). if i maybe can finish this line of questioning before giving the floor* to the other opponent . . .

The exchange differs from the more spontaneous, less regimented discussions in seminars or conferences, where in principle the floor can be taken by any participant. The regulated turn-taking and pre-planning that has gone into the defence is reflected in the opponent's final turn (*if I maybe can finish this line of questioning before giving the floor to the other opponent*). After S1's first answer, the opponent rephrases the defendant's response in a springboard fashion and goes on to elaborate his own understanding of the notion, pointing out another problem in the concept. In his turn, S1 adopts the opponent's formulation (*as you said*) as a springboard and offers a way out of the conceptual dilemma, which S2 then accepts (*quite agreed*). The opponent and the defendant thus seem to collaborate on achieving a joint understanding of the relations between fair and probabilistic models and the role of implementation. While this intellectual wrestling may seem somewhat low key compared to major discoveries or eureka moments, it strives towards shared conceptual development beyond the testing of a candidate's qualification. This is supported by the fact that they are discussing a compilation PhD whose the individual articles have already passed peer review and thereby academic gatekeeping.

The episode shows a few uses of discourse reflexivity. Retrieving and altercentricity are at play as the speaker formulates a candidate understanding (*so you're saying*), picks up the interlocutor's contribution as a springboard (*as you said*), and indicates agreement with the interlocutor (*actually I agree; quite agreed*). The extract also shows forward orientation in egocentric organising (*I would say that; we could say; if I maybe can finish this line of questioning*).

The next case (6.23) shows the examiner and the candidate developing new research ideas together that arise from the topic they have just reached shared understanding about. It comes from a materials engineering defence, with two opponents (S2 and S3), and the thesis is again a compilation PhD. The dialogue takes place between S1 (the defendant) and S3.

(6.23) <S1> [okay] that *that is true what you what you said* and er also this E-V-A-based adhesive is is not solely er consisting of E-V-A but it also has has lower er molecular weight resins and also waxes in in in in the composition er in in my system er it's totally different system in in in that way because it's it's one one basic polymer which doe- does [all all all this kind] </S1>
<S3> [so it's clear that you have you have the polymer in there] <S1> yeah </S1> it's also clear that you have the *let's say* the the antioxidant will be your treatment for stabilising the [polylactide] </S3>

<S1> [yeah] yeah and all- also if you can er describe it so that maybe maybe maybe the caprolactone is is the the <S3> the wax </S3> or or the resin phase of the </S1>
<S3> and that's and that's the and *that's the point that's what that was the question that i was* <S1> yeah </S1> *expecting you to say* so you have a kind of *let's say* a human body without water <S1> yeah </S1> if you don't consider the wax </S3>
<S1> and an interesting topic *which is not covered here* is is mi- might be in the in the future considered a blending of of <S3> yeah </S3> of of this system </S1>
<S3> don't you think you you could use some plasticides or or something like that </S3>
<S1> yeah with with the plasticisers it might be might be er, the problem might be that er that you make the adhesive too too soft and and maybe towards er pressure sensitive [adhesive] </S1>
<S3> [mhm] of course you could play with the amount of polycaprolactone and the plasticisers </S3>
<S1> yeah yeah and and also also because available of of the as *as er professor <NAME S2> said in the introduction phase* the available of of the polylactide for for this kind of bulk purposes is is very limited at the moment so so it might be useful to think think of er blending some biodegradable <S3> mhm </S3> er components to to the system </S1>

This extract is preceded by a long turn by S3 talking about some of his own work in the field, pointing out a potential analogy, and in effect asking the defendant to place his own work within this framework. This episode opens by the candidate conceding what the examiner had explained (*that is true . . . what you said*). The defendant thus accepts the analogy, and the opponent then reformulates it again. This is in essence matching perspectives. The reformulation seems to generate a new thought in the candidate: . . . *if you can er describe it so that maybe . . . the caprolactone is* . . . The opponent completes the defendant's word search (*the wax*) before the defendant comes up with (*or the resin phase*), and then goes on to interrupt the defendant saying this is what he had been looking for: *that's the point . . . that was the question that I was expecting you to say* and explicates the analogy again (*so you have a kind of . . .*). The defendant then spontaneously brings up another idea (*and an interesting topic . . . might be*), with no prompting from the opponent. They go on expanding this idea together (S3: *don't you think you you could . . .* S1: *yeah with with the plasticisers it might be might be er, the problem . . .* S3: *of course you could . . .*), and finally the defendant draws on what the other opponent had said earlier in the event (*as er professor <NAME S2> said in the introduction phase*).

We see here not only matching perspectives but also joint construction of new ideas in connection with joint construction of language. Reflexive metadiscourse comes up in a sequence of altercentric acknowledgements of agreement (*that is true . . . what you said*), in referring to missing elements that might be relevant (*which is not covered here*) and in retrieving previous stages of the discourse that are relevant for present concerns (*as er professor <NAME S2> said in the introduction phase*). In the final turns we can again see how these exchanges can stimulate new ideas in participants beyond what has immediately preceded. This suggests that ideas from recent discourse have been integrated in the present interactants' knowledge structures, and since the previous discourse is shared in the long-term working memory of both participants, it can be evoked without very elaborate explanations.

It is very likely that explicit talk about discussion-inspired ideas captures only a small proportion of what is going on. Things we hear and see can generate new thoughts and ideas later or gradually, as we saw in some examples above, e.g. 6.20 and 6.21. Participants may also benefit from exchanges of ideas and viewpoints without actively participating in the discussion themselves. None of this will be recorded in discussion data, and we can only expect to capture a small part of such thought processes by exploring explicit indications. Nevertheless, it is also clear that processes reflected in our examples are ubiquitous: when we enter dialogic interaction on academic issues, the discussions themselves increment our knowledge resources and thereby also stimulate thought.

6.2.2 Collaborating towards knowledge in written dialogue

Turning now to written dialogue and blog discussion threads, we can expect an environment with some shared characteristics with the co-present discussions above, along with those of its own (cf. Chapter 5). Because our sample specifically draws on those blogs that receive comments, the data should also enable us to witness co-construction of knowledge, insofar as it occurs in blog commentary. Research blogs are a variable and still unstable kind of discourse, even if confined to those kept by active researchers or research groups. Some blog traditions clearly go further in collaborative construction than the comparatively ordinary blogs in our data. An example is the *polymath blog* site (polymathprojects.org) analysed by McGrath (2015), and some philosophy sites of a similar kind, where people present their preliminary thoughts and rough drafts of papers for discussion, and gradually refine them into publishable texts with the help of peer discussion around a blog site.

To start from a typical blog phenomenon that tends to co-occur with discourse reflexivity, let us briefly look at the standard practice among bloggers to supply links to other websites, often containing reference material, online articles, and the like. In studies of blogs, this is usually connected to blogs as promoters of the public understanding of science, which is supported by the finding that most blogs do not receive any comments (Mahrt & Puschmann 2014). Luzón (2013b), however, gave links a different interpretation. She investigated blogger strategies for recontextualising scientific knowledge. Among those that she analysed as "tailoring information to the audience's needs" (Luzón 2013b), which seems a variant of recipient design, web links were overwhelmingly the most frequent kind, accounting for over 80% of the instances. In Luzón's view, they enable clarifications of potentially unfamiliar concepts to meet the audience's needs without disrupting the text. However, readerships of research blogs are heterogeneous, and the links may not lead to texts that are more readable, but to, say, original scientific papers, which to the non-specialist are likely to be less rather than more accessible. Links nevertheless bring different voices and perspectives to the discussion and reflect a particular kind of intertextuality. And as Luzón (2013b) observes, they provide credibility to the blogger and strengthen their position by material that supports their points.

Unlike these studies on blogs, our focus is on the comment threads, which bestows more nuance on the picture. Some links support the interpretation of blogs as knowledge dissemination, like the next example (6.24), where a blogger gives a link with additional information. The first link, however, may not improve the accessibility of the content for a general audience, but is more likely to interest academic peers. It may thus not so much clarify matters as to enhance the blogger's credibility. Links of this kind nevertheless potentially expand the domain of shared knowledge. It is perhaps worth reminding that even when the links in the present data are provided by bloggers, these are part of discussion threads, not the blog itself.

(6.24) <COMMENT BY B1>
/. . ./
To see what I mean here, check e.g. Dualities vs Singularities
http://arxiv.org/abs/hep-th/9811194
http://motls.blogspot.com/2009/02/dualities-vs-singularities.html
which contains a proof that any extreme enough compactification of M-theory on tori – and analogously with other classes of compactifications – can be mapped by dualities to a compactification whose radii are universally bigger than the fundamental (Planck or string) units.
/. . ./

However, links are by no means supplied by only bloggers. Quite the contrary: more links in our data come from commenters (n=20) than bloggers (n=13 in the comment threads). Very occasionally the links lead to the participants' own blogs, but most of the time they either offer further information (6.25) or give tips to other participants. The links from commenters, like those from bloggers, appear predominantly oriented to a peer community of experts rather than to the wider public. They would thus seem to expand shared knowledge rather than make new knowledge more accessible.

(6.25) <COMMENT BY C4 ON 13.04.2011>
also note that a highly recommended paper that addresses these topics is available online at
http://www.wfu.edu/~silmanmr/labpage/publications/FREE_07.pdf

It seems, then, that providing links is an ingredient in updating shared knowledge, as illustrated in interconnected exchanges involving links (6.26 a-b). The first turn is a blogger responding to one commenter's (C3) link, citing a third commenter from another discussion, then adding a new link which also originates in another of C3's postings elsewhere. Following that, another commenter (C9) chips in with an even more recent link (6.26b). Constant updating is thus going on, and constitutes an integral part of the discussion. The dates reveal that turns can be spread out in time and the turn-taking speed is entirely different from that of live conversations, but the participants' dialogic engagement is nevertheless intense. Discourse reflexivity keeps track of the development often with retrieving comments (*you referred to a new post*).

(6.26a) <COMMENT BY B1 ON 07.06.2011>
Glad @<NAME C3> you didn't really moved on (*like you said* y'day)
Thanks for the reference, I looked it up:
http://pipeline.corante.com/archives/2011/01/11/xmrv_its_ugly_but_thats_science.php
I'm not against wild hypotheses, if presented in opinion papers. On the contrary. But original scientific papers, should refrain from wild theories, if not founded upon sound data. The Science papers was flawed *for reasons mentioned in the previous post.*
Or as <u>one of the commenters to the Pipeline post said</u>:

> Any serious PCR expert could look at the initial Science paper and in 3 minutes know that it was PCR contamination combined with an insufficiently specific PCR assay. I laughed when I saw it.

NOTE: *I now notice you referred to a new post* at PIPELINE CORANTE: http://pipeline.corante.com/archives/2011/06/06/xmrv_and_chronic_fatigue_down_for_more_than_the_third_time.php

(6.26b) <COMMENT BY C9 ON 08.06.2011>
You left out Corante's latest post on the XMRV mess: http://pipeline.corante.com/archives/2011/06/07/murine_viruses_and_chronic_fatigue_does_the_story_continue.php.
He links to http://www.retrovirology.com/content/8/S1/A234 (Detection of MLV-like gag sequences in blood samples from a New York state CFS cohort) and he states that his pronouncement of the subject as dead may have been premature.

Simply exchanging links seems to engage the blog community widely, so that we cannot write off blogging as unidirectional dissemination of knowledge. As other voices are brought into the discussion through links it is like what happens in conference discussions, where it is normal practice to refer to theorists, researchers, and their findings, or everyday conversations, which often talk about what absent parties have said or thought. Thus, besides the roles that Luzón identified in links, it is evident that there is also a dialogical and knowledge-generating dimension.

Mahrt & Puschmann (2014) note that most comments are concerned with the original blog, which is why there is little communal development of knowledge. We can see this also in the present data in questions directed at bloggers, but this is not the whole story. Commenters also respond to questions and take the discussion forward between themselves (6.27). The first commenter's (C5) question prompts further questions from the blogger (B1) and the second commenter (C2), and so the discussion continues. This blog is from the less technical end of the sample. Discourse reflexivity focuses on participants' positive comments on each other's contributions (*good point*).

(6.27) <COMMENT BY C5 ON 29.03.2011>
This is a very interesting subject. I first thought of it when visiting a palaeontological museum in Colombia, surrounded by all this amazing, huge, and unknown fauna (unknown to me, of course). All those species needed millions of years to form, and yet they seem to disappear in a flash, mostly in the last deglaciation. That sounds a bit fortuituous <NAME C5>.

<COMMENT BY B1 ON 29.03.2011>
I think <NAME C5> put forward a good point. Why haven't the magafauna adapted to the climate change? It was a few degrees increase in the average

temperature; the magafauna had plenty of space and time to migrate to different latitudes or elevations. Probably climate put magafauna under stress but people did the final job. *I think.*

<COMMENT BY C2 ON 30.03.2011>
well, yes, good point . . . why did those creatures just didn't make it . . . ? but since when did they make it? what do we know about their evolution?? is it that they /. . ./

Commenters also answer each other's questions and may assume the expert role on topics. A discussion which stays within the expert range of several parties can include their comments and the blogger need not occupy the driver's seat. The following thread in theoretical physics may not invite responses from complete laymen, but some practitioners and amateurs seem very keen to join in to talk about a paper that the blogger had put up a link to. The blogger does not appear in this exchange. Reflexive discourse is mostly orienting, but sometimes also retrieving (*So you must mean*).

(6.28) <COMMENT BY C14>
<NAME C12>: The paper gives just the appearance of tests that could verify it. It uses some words, like CPT violations, all of which /. . ./ *I'm sure this sounds like a conspiracy theory to you,* but imagine the players are all delusional so they realy do believe they are playing hockey, and your getting a closer understanding of the situation.

<COMMENT BY C114>
I think the underlying issue is whether you are willing to equate all observers as being equivalent. Their statement can be correct if /. . ./

<COMMENT BY C11>
<NAME C114> So each observer might construct a spacetime that contains objects that appear independent but are at best prismatic projections of oneself. /. . ./.
But it does work, our world works even though /. . ./ With these hypotheses we have constructed the world we live in and the physics we know. *So you must mean* deviations from these hypotheses, as the paper under consideration does.

<COMMENT BY C36>
I worked in a discipline where the phase space is the most important working tool – non linear dynamics or chaos theory. So I overflew this preprint and it didn't make much sense for me.

Let's consider the Lorenz system defined by its 3 coordinates X(t),Y(t),Z(t) which have been adequately normalised. /. . ./
But I admit that I have not read the paper very deeply – when I was 1st page, it made me think of the Lorenz phase space /. . ./

Sometimes a blog wanders off the blogger's central field of expertise. In the following three-party exchange (6.29), the participants' tone is speculative, but they are clearly seeking to make sense of the issues in earnest, each contributing from their own resources what they can to increment their shared pool of knowledge. New questions also arise while they engage in this discussion.

(6.29) <COMMENT BY C2 ON 06.01.2011>
Doesn't this focus on vocabulary result in a model of language as little more than a collection of words? What about syntax and grammar? Changes in pronunciation when borrowing?/. . ./ I can't accept that vocabulary is the most important feature of a language.

<COMMENT BY B1 ON 06.01.2011>
Thanks for your comment <NAME C2>! I absolutely agree with you that a language is more than a collection of words. That would be a gross oversimplification, /. . ./
Of course any linguist would like to take syntax and grammar into account in such comparisons, /. . ./. Defining orthology for species and languages is already difficult enough as it is.
The suggestion that you make for studying the differential use sounds of loanwords sounds really interesting and plausible (maybe some research has already been done on this?). Such things become easier to study with large-scale investigations that become possible with the release of large corpora, such as described here (which are still analyses based on 'just' a word-to-word basis, without incorporating grammar or syntax!).

<COMMENT BY C3 ON 07.01.2011>
Actually, my understanding is that linguists often do use grammatical changes to resolve deeper branches in such phylogenies. /. . ./
And yes, <NAME C2>, the "vocabulary" in this sense typically consists of phonetic transcriptions, /. . ./ I have a link to some of the corpora (datasets) that are most commonly used for this sort of thing somewhere, but my mail is down – the Dagan paper probably has a link too.
(NB I am not a linguist; I do algorithms/models for molecular evolution, though, and some of those models have found their way over to linguistic collaborators).

> *Thanks for this post*, Lucas: I routinely use slides of language trees in my undergrad class, and now I can use this one (and Dagan et al's work) to show how a simple tree is never the full story.

Just as in conference discussions, questions from the audience prompt bloggers to move onto new things (6.30). B2 is one of two individuals who keep this blog. Reflexive discourse assumes both orienting (*I have a couple of remarks*) and retrieving functions (*I have had a look at the model; following your suggestion*), keeping interacting parties aware of each other's intentions.

(6.30) <COMMENT BY C4 ON 12.08.2011>
I have had a look at the model, and I have a couple of remarks.
The first one is, you're using the same vision for people and cops. Since the media are different, should try to /. . ./.
Surprisingly, tho, having longer vision for cops doesn't change your main result – at least it looks so after some quick experimentation. This is probably due to vision being tied up in a couple of critical feedback loops.
The second one, that as much as I can see, the periods of relative quiet correspond also to /. . ./
. . .
etc. (how should this change the arrest probability is a delicate point)

<COMMENT BY B2 ON 12.08.2011>
Dear <NAME C4>,
Many thanks for your comments -much appreciated!
A quick reply to your comments:
1) We interpreted the same vision for people and cops as due to technological constraints that are pretty much the same for everyone, so /. . ./ However we recognise that some forms of selective censorship may still be possible, and *we thank you* for trying to see what happens in this case - further investigation would be desirable!
2) It is true that many people are in jail during periods of peace in our model. *Following your suggestion*, we have looked at the model again and noticed that the number of people in jail (average over time) is higher for lower levels of vision. . . We are now working at the interpretation of this result; *perhaps we may do another post on it in the next few days.*
For now, a snapshot of what the situation looks like is at: http://paolatubaro.files.wordpress.com/2011/08/jailed.jpg
Thanks again!
<NAME B2>

This extract shows collaborative creation of new knowledge starting off from a blog dialogue but going beyond it, even leading to new findings. Active comment thread interaction shows elements of sharing, updating and co-constructing knowledge, and involve several participants in significant and collaborative roles. They do not only consist of questions or brief comments to bloggers. Contributions to discussion vary widely in their level of engagement and expertise, but blog communities are by their nature open, self-organised, and heterogeneous, thus also unpredictable.

6.3 Conclusion

This chapter has explored the co-construction of knowledge and understanding in academic discussions, with a focus on discourse reflexivity in the process. It delved into the prerequisites of joint construction of knowledge, like clarification processes and matching speaker perspectives, in addition to interactive co-construction of new ideas, thoughts, and knowledge. Knowledge has been interpreted in a broad sense, encompassing understanding, thoughts, ideas, and connections. Co-constructing knowledge means giving rise to new ideas, not merely learning, or coming to an agreement about what is already known. The present conceptualisation thus departs from the typical educational understanding of knowledge co-construction, which is expected to lead to 'correct' outcomes (Komori-Glatz & Smit 2021) or to 'convergent' views (Kastberg 2010). Knowledge construction has been envisaged here as intersubjective and collaborative, therefore dynamic, with unpredictable outcomes. In this sense, it is very much like dialogic interaction in general; both can be seen as complex dynamic systems where dialogic interaction between humans can lead to unforeseen outcomes.

The analyses drew on the categories already established in chapters 4 and 5, like orienting vs. retrieving, egocentric vs. altercentric, together with concepts like plane-shifts. The focus in this chapter, however, was on the major discourse managing category, *negotiating*, that was not elaborated in chapters 4 and 5. Analysing the co-construction of knowledge through interaction has been qualitative, as the subject does not lend itself readily to quantification (though see Gweon 2012).

Since the Enlightenment, academia has constructed itself as a site for generating new knowledge. It has accordingly sought to encourage not only new empirical research but also discussions that bring divergent, alternative, and conflicting viewpoints into contact for the purpose of stimulating new thought. This is not a mere idealistic wish as we were able to see in the practices of the event types discussed in this chapter: conference discussions, graduate seminars, thesis defences, and to some extent even blog threads, which arguably lie at the outskirts of academic debate. That collaborative knowledge construction is less prominent in blog threads and takes different forms from what we see in genres more central to academia is perhaps indicative of the position of blogs with respect to the centre of academia. In the light of our examples, then, these event types seem to be realising some traditional academic ideals of collaboratively developing thoughts in dialogue. Even where not much agreement or convergence on new ideas was manifest, participants showed apparent motivation and effort towards making their viewpoints accessible and acceptable to each other and to taking things forward.

Discourse reflexivity was noticeably prominent in phases where debates, differences, and disagreements were evinced. Reflexive discourse apparently helps navigate through situations where problematic or potentially sensitive issues are at stake. When participants were striving towards closure on an issue that they were far divided, or where they negotiated potential or actual conflict, they made ample use of discourse reflexivity. While some situations showed quite confrontational reflexive discourse in taking a stand (*I disagree strongly*) or dismissing another's argument (*what you are saying here now is . . . some kind of gospel*), in other cases we saw speakers indicating their willingness to negotiate the evidence and their own positions in the course of the discussion (*I cannot say I'm that sure anymore*).

Preparing ground for possible co-construction of new knowledge takes place in clarifications and more generally in the process of *matching perspectives*. Matching perspectives, a broader conceptualisation than 'convergence', results from negotiating positions between participants. A match can be reached without a fully convergent closure or consensus, and that may suffice for advancing knowledge during a conversation. The important thing is that participants at least tacitly accept each other's contributions as valid to the issue at hand. We saw in some instances above that a phase of matching perspectives on an issue was followed by active co-construction of ideas about it.

This goes for multi-party events and blog threads alike. The asynchrony of blogs and the ensuing delays mean that comments may come up days after their referent (***The suggestion that you make** for studying . . . sounds really interesting and plausible)* when the commenter may have had time to think about the point, or it may have crossed their mind later. This enabled the commenters to draw on the affordances of the written record.

The immediacy of spoken interaction, on the other hand, revealed how things people say trigger associations in participants. In the middle of a discussion people suddenly integrate elements to the topic at hand from earlier earlier parts of a macro-event, such as the same conference. They seem to assume that this is shared knowledge among conference participants. It also indicates that these ideas from recent discourses have been integrated in at least the current speaker's knowledge structures. To what degree they are shared is an open question, but it is reasonable to assume that some shared elements are available in different participants' representations.

Perhaps most interestingly, several cases above showed people thinking on their feet, responding instantaneously to each other's turns by expanding the ideas further (*that* ***actually brings me to a question . . . which occurred to me right now*** *. . . when you look at learner corpora . . . one of the things that you can do . . . is look at things like tendencies*). The different speeds at which speaking and writing proceed is significant and its effect on dialogue should give rise to more research. Whether slow or fast, the processes found in both illuminate what we called the 'springboard' function of discourse reflexivity, that is, acknowledging interlocutors' contributions to the ideas emerging in the speaker.

It was possible to see how in these longer discussion extracts, different kinds of discourse reflexivity were interleaved, much as we saw in the beginning of the long extract at the opening of Chapter 4 (4.1). Participants sought to increase precision about each other's positions with clarifications (*by this I don't mean*), elaborated points already made (*it's important to add*), insisted that the speaker's argument is consistent (*what I'm saying is; as I have emphasised*), and checked comprehension, both the speaker's own (*if I'm following you correctly you're saying)* and that of their interlocutors (*you follow me*).

Genres, or, event types, reveal some differences that can be related back to social parameters. In addition to those already discussed in chapters 4 and 5, asymmetries of power and status played out somewhat differently in spoken discourses from the perspective of knowledge co-construction. While the status difference is obvious between examiners and candidates in doctoral defences, this was in many cases overrun in favour of joint construction of knowledge. In graduate seminars such was not necessarily the case, and especially one seminar leader among the examples asserted himself as a knowledge authority even when challenged by students. Clearly, these observations are tentative, as the data was not sampled to represent power relations but joint construction of knowledge.

It is likely that many of the ideas that people spark off in each other may never be in evidence on record, because they occur to interactants only later, or they inspire ideas in participants who remain silent overhearers, or they simply are not commented on. In spite of this, or perhaps precisely because overt indications of such thought processes are rare, the explicit mentions that we find in reflexive metadiscourse are valuable indicators that this takes place. This is a major methodological affordance from studying discourse reflexivity in dialogic interaction.

Chapter 7
Discourse reflexivity in monologue

While metadiscourse in academic monologue is already very well charted, even if with a heavy bias towards writing, the question may arise whether there is much new that can be said about it. What is the motivation for more investigation into monologic metadiscourse?

The general reason for studying discourse reflexivity in monologic speech lies in its position relative to the medium (speaking vs writing) on the one hand, and to mode (monologue vs dialogue) on the other. This allows for two minimal comparisons with only one major parameter changed in each. Alterations in situational parameters can be expected to lead to alterations in language use.

In this chapter, we will compare monologic speech only to dialogic speech. Comparisons between metadiscourse in spoken and written monologues have already been made (e.g. Luukka 1994, Ädel 2010, J. Lee & Subtirelu 2015; Liu 2021), and all those I am aware of have adopted what Ädel (2010) calls a 'lumping' approach, that is, a unified model to explore metadiscourse in both. As Ädel argues, despite some variability originating in the conditions of speaking and writing, the discrepancies were not sufficient to warrant separate taxonomies, and other research along similar lines has found variation in frequencies and expressions within categories, but only made minor additions or alterations in the categories themselves. For example, J. Lee & Subtirelu (2015) studied university lectures and Liu (2021) 3-minute theses, and both found far more interactional than interactive metadiscourse features in speech than in written academic texts, but that was a matter of relative frequencies, not new categorisation.

The previous studies mentioned above are interesting in that they have all used different models of metadiscourse: Luukka's was essentially based on Crismore & Steffensen (1990) and Vande Kopple (1985), Ädel's on reflexive metadiscourse (Ädel 2006), and J. Lee & Subtirelu's and Liu's on Hyland (2005) but they drew the same conclusion about the relatively smooth applicability of writing-based analytical categories on speaking. Against this backdrop, we can assume a basic similarity in written and spoken metadiscourse in the monologic mode. However, since our focus in this book is on dialogic speaking, monologic speaking is of interest primarily in relation to that. We thus continue analysing the material, as hitherto, by viewing metadiscourse in this dataset in the light of the categories established so far for dialogue, to see how far the focus on speech will take us in capturing metadiscourse. This means holding on to a 'splitting' approach, tackling speaking on its own terms, without following taxonomies from written-text research.

https://doi.org/10.1515/9783110295498-007

Monologues are sustained contributions from a single participant, whether written or spoken. With one speaker having an extended hold of the floor, spoken and written monologues are likely to be similar if only because monologic presentations are prepared ahead. At the preparation stage hearers are essentially imagined, in other words author-constructed, just like readers, and the talk, including discourse reflexivity, is designed to indicate the speaker's preferred interpretation of what they are trying to get across to hearers.

The audience in the actual event alters the anticipatory settings, including the speaker's perception of the situation. The co-presence of the audience accentuates the speaker's propensity to exercise audience design (Grice 1975; Baggio 2018), that is, adaptive signalling behaviour of speakers, or in Sacks and Schegloff's classic terms, *recipient design*:

> By recipient design we refer to a multitude of respects in which the talk by a party in a conversation is constructed or designed in ways which display an orientation and sensitivity to the particular other(s) who are the co-participants. (Sacks & Schegloff 1974).

Sacks and Schegloff were talking about dialogue, but recipient design also applies to asymmetric situations where all the work falls upon one speaker. I discussed recipient or audience design in terms of the speaker's *theory of mind* in Chapter 2, pointing out that the speaker's theory of mind, unlike the writer's, can adapt to the unfolding speech situation as they observe audience responses. Discourse reflexivity can give one indication of the speaker's orientation to their hearers, for instance their sensitivity to how intelligible hearers might find the talk and to what extent listeners' interpretation matches what the speaker is trying to get across. While audience size varies from seminars or small conference sections to plenary conference sessions, listeners can be described along roughly Goffmanian lines (Goffman 1981:131–3) as *collectively addressed participants*.

A co-present audience interacts with the presenter nonverbally by nods, laughter, shakes of the head, shifting their postures, or just by looking interested or bored. Speakers are aware of such audience responses and have various means at their disposal for adapting their talk accordingly, including nonverbal and paralinguistic means like gaze, voice quality, prosody, speech rhythm, or pausing, just like speakers in dialogic interaction. Spoken monologues thus draw on the means of both written monologue and spoken dialogue for recipient design.

How discourse reflexivity works in spoken monologue is illustrated in an initial example (7.1). An extended excerpt would seem best to convey the general flavour of discourse reflexivity in context, especially since most other examples in this chapter are short. Because presentations are far too long to reproduce in full, I show one complete conference talk with omissions in the body of the talk so that what we see is the development of the presentation through its reflexive metadiscourse. Obviously, the presenter's argument will not be transparent from this skeletal view, but the multiple ways in which he uses discourse reflexivity can be appreciated.

(7.1) /. . ./ civic training and so on *was mentioned in an earlier paper today* er let us recall that er *i think it's very important* let us recall /. . ./ just fill up a thin layer, at the bottom of our time box, er, *i say this because* it has to do with the the formation of societies /. . ./ and the society at large which *i will do in this talk,* these relationships /. . ./ what is being called the social capital, *another term for this* that er i have come to use more and more in my own work is er the social fabric the social fabric er *this denotes* the pattern of countless contacts meetings and social events and relationships /. . ./ social fabric of Swedish conditions or *i should rather say* because they don't use the concept *i should rather say* regional development /. . ./ dynamics and economic growth *as has already been stated today er which i will repeat now* with certain exceptions the findings /. . ./ has indeed had a large impact on the region and *as you have just heard* Umeå is one of those cases /. . ./ and *just to underline er this er last point* i would just like to show you /. . ./ the Umeå study also sheds light and *now i'm back on the Olsson Viberg study* on what might otherwise appear to be a local paradox /. . ./ now first of all *maybe we should say* that the measure of success /. . ./ perhaps the most remarkable development of all *again talking about Umeå* has been the cultural sector /. . ./ tend to rank high in quality of life surveys *it could be argued that* er in the information society /. . ./ few major centres exist and *i come back to that in a while* so er and *and then again what i said* a similar trend /. . ./ *it is easy to conclude that* if a university or college aims to promote regional growth and *i would like to stress* that this is the particularly the aim /. . ./ still *what i say here is* sort of a sampling of evidence /. . ./ innovations that are circulated throughout society, *we can talk of* these production environments not *as* one single limited institution /. . ./ *i would like to er finalise my er, my talk by showing you* a few examples of the the er kinds of er s- symbolic er representations that i think we can see now to quite some extent obvious process that *i'm being referring to here* erm er certainly we can er i- in in in er *in Swedish er i i've er started using the the concept* er *kunskaps anläggning i haven't really thought about any good word for in in English* er to er to er to to sort of underline that it's not just an institution /. . ./ early *what do you say* zeros er er er er design /. . ./ now *two final little er added er things* that *i think* has a lot to do with *i mean* if if we then are turning a little bit more /. . ./ well *i would like just to show you* er, *an observation er that er i made recently.* on public spending /. . ./ if you want to achieve regional development *i think this is my best basic message here in this talk* if you wanna go for that which *i think is really important* the end of transition from an industrial to a more knowledge-based society

The example incorporates certain fundamental uses that discourse reflexivity can be expected to have in any context, such as contextualising by signposting (*I will do in this talk; now I'm back on the . . . study; I come back to that in a while*), indicating importance (*I think it's very important; just to underline this last point; I would like to stress*) and clarifying (*another term for this; this denotes; we can talk of these . . . as*).

Some discourse reflexivity in the excerpt orients the hearer towards what is to follow (*it could be argued that; I come back to that in a while; I would like just to show you*), other instances retrieve something from an earlier point, investing it with present relevance (*as you have just heard*). Just as in dialogue, it is the retrieving type that holds particular interest, because it is not prominent in written monologue (in contrast to written dialogue; see Ch.5). We can see retrieving altercentric references to the macro-event (*mentioned in an earlier paper today*; *has already been stated today*), along with egocentric references to the ongoing presentation (*and then again what I said*).

The multilingual ELF context surfaces in references to the speaker's usage (*in Swedish I've started using the concept 'kunskapsanläggning' I haven't really thought about any good word for it in English*) and in his explicit word search (*early* ***what do you say*** *zeros design*), as well as in linguistic approximations (*I would like to* ***finalise my talk*** *by showing*).

In view of (7.1), discourse reflexivity seems to maintain its basic functions in spoken monologue. Previous chapters have suggested, though, that differences from dialogue are likely to ensue from both mode and medium. The point of departure in this chapter is rooted in the analysis of spoken dialogue (Ch 4), at the same time respecting the data in a bottom-up analysis that is open to new distinctions and categories, much along the lines of analysing written dialogue earlier (Ch 5). I seek to harmonise categorisation in monologues with dialogic uses as much as possible and see how far that takes us before the data requires new categories to be set up and the descriptions to bifurcate.

The monologues sampled for this chapter comprise conference presentations and graduate seminar presentations (for details, see Chapter 3). They cover a wide spectrum of speakers in terms of academic seniority in two event types, a research-related and an education-related.

The primary distinction between managing the discourse and managing the situation is maintained here in line with the earlier chapters. However, Luukka (1994) and Ädel (2010) categorise similar expressions as *contextualising* metadiscourse. I have used the same term (Chapter 4) in a different sense, which may seem confusing.

The difference seems to lie in Firth's (1968) concepts of the context of text (co-text), and the context of situation. Clearly, Luukka and Ädel talk about the context of situation, whereas I talk about both. For me, contextualising is a general, overall metadiscoursal function, which makes explicit how an utterance relates on the one hand to the discourse ('managing discourse') and on the other to the speech situation ('managing situation'). Situation management in these academic monologues is not very common. Luukka and Ädel may have found more instances, but this is hard to tell because their focus is on the categories, not numbers, and no comparable figures are available. Managing the situation is clearly not the presenter's domain, but conventionally delegated to persons like appointed chairpersons, seminar leaders, etc. Presenters focus on managing their own talk, but some *situational interaction* takes place as well, whether this is verbalised or remains nonverbal, and this, along with the previous studies, motivates maintaining the category.

7.1 Managing discourse

Managing discourse in monologues puts cognitive demands on both presenters and recipients. Asymmetric situations as they are, they put different pressures on participant positions. Speakers must hold listeners' interest for a long time and make themselves understood in the way they intend, while hearers will have to focus their attention on an extended stretch of communication that they have little influence on. Speakers have the advantage of advance preparation, but listeners may have only a vague notion of what they will be hearing, apart from perhaps a topic area to be dealt with, and possibly an abstract to indicate the main thrust of what the speaker means to say. Sustained attention on an exposition or a line of argument in real time requires the brain's predictive processing mechanisms to stay alert for a long time while the discourse unfolds, which is taxing and hard to maintain without lapses. Successful communication requires speaker attention to recipient design, such as using reflexive discourse.

Discourse management in monologic speech would seem to fall into two main types that overlap with but are not entirely identical to dialogic speech. One is a *contextualising* kind, which basically consists in indicating how the unfolding discourse fits into its co-text as it moves forward in real time, and we can discern *orienting* and *retrieving* types like in this activity just like in dialogue. The other, a *commenting* kind, comprises elements that are similar to dialogue, like clarifying, as well as elements not very prominent in dialogic reflexive discourse, like expressing focus and evaluation. As usual, the functions are separable, but can also overlap, like where reflexive discourse simultaneously contextualises and comments on the discourse (*now we come to the really difficult questions*).

7.1.1 Contextualising

Contextualising discourse reflexivity indicates how the utterance fits into the moment-to-moment progression of the discourse as it unfolds. It can contribute importantly to making discourse intelligible. This is particularly valuable in speech, because unlike a reader, the hearer cannot go back if they missed something or if their thoughts wandered. Moreover, as distinct from the fast turn-taking of dialogue, monologues require special effort from hearers to stay attuned to one speaker. It is in the speaker's interest to try to provide the hearer with navigational clues about where the discourse is moving.

The main categories of contextualising discourse reflexivity seem to reflect those already identified for dialogic discourse, namely orienting and retrieving.

Orienting

Orienting discourse reflexivity can perhaps be considered the prototypical case of metadiscourse, which most researchers recognise in function even if not by the same term. The expressions in this section do not therefore deviate much from what has been observed in earlier metadiscourse studies, particularly those on spoken monologues. From the speaker's perspective orienting discourse reflexivity contextualises their utterances by prospecting ahead to what is to come. In written monologue, this is generally seen as facilitating the reader's task in making sense of the text (see, however, the discussion in Chapter 2, section 2.4). For hearers, it sustains their anticipation of what the speaker might be saying next and can lead to readjusting their expectations. Hearers constantly engage in predictive processing about the way the discourse is likely to proceed, and explicit clues from the speaker support the confirmation or rejection of predictive hypotheses. We have good reasons, therefore, to regard the hearer as engaged in active processing of the input and talk about the *active hearer* just as we did in Chapter 2.

The basic functions of orienting discourse reflexivity would seem to be quite robust across the monologue-dialogue and written-spoken divide. What is noteworthy is its dominance in monologic speech, accounting as it does for 71.3% of all discourse contextualising reflexivity, thus contrasting sharply with the corresponding figure (39.1%) for dialogue. At this point, we will not delve into differences between egocentric and altercentric references, but instead the different timescales of orienting references. The main orienting uses of egocentric and altercentric discourse reflexivity with their numerical proportions will be discussed in Chapter 8 and compared to dialogic speech.

Rowley-Jolivet & and Carter-Thomas (2005) found in their study of conference presentation metadiscourse that presenters often use forward oriented signposting (*I'll then go on to . . .*) in their talks. Prospecting ahead to upcoming discourse can span longer or shorter periods within the speech event, a similar observation to some earlier research on discourse markers in lectures (e.g. Flowerdew & Tauroza 1995), who talked about macro and micro discourse markers. In line with these observations, we distinguished between immediate and non-immediate prospection in Chapter 2. In a similar fashion, interactional linguistics differentiates between macro and micro levels or domains that projections can take in conversation (Auer 2005; Schegloff 2013; Couper-Kuhlen & Seltig 2018). Since the experience of speech is crucially a temporal matter, neither 'level' nor 'domain' are felicitous descriptive terms in this case. Rather, we are dealing with different time scales, which I suggest be subsumed under the term *span*. Speech processing would seem to involve multiple spans for speakers and hearers alike. I distinguish here three scales of time, not to complicate matters too much: global, local, and immediate. This slightly finer categorisation captures and helps appreciate the multiplex character of prospective reflexivity perhaps better than a dichotomy.

There are other dimensions besides the timescale along which we might want to investigate uses of orienting discourse reflexivity in monologues, as for example Auer (2005) does for conversation, differentiating between projections relevant to action, sequence, content, syntax, or phonology. Not all of these would be equally relevant in the present context of extended monologue, but the general point of the existence of different domains, levels, and scales is important. Eventually what the hearer is likely to do is process clues holistically, exploiting their joint import for predictive processing. The fact that different clues do not always coincide (cf. 'staggering' in Mukherjee 2001; Monschau, Keryer & Mukherjee 2004) may help make language processing more robust as it generates more redundancy than individual elements or their combinations which invariably coincide.

Much of discourse reflexivity contextualises discourse content, and this is particularly true of *global orienting*, long-span acts of anticipating a whole presentation, which usually occur at the initial stages of a talk. They are readily recognizable by labelling nouns like *paper, talk, presentation*, or *lecture* (7.2 a-e)

(7.2) (a) so *the aim of* ***this paper*** and the future report
(b) so ***my paper*** *is built around* two hypotheses
(c) and *in* ***my presentation*** i will try to find
(d) ***my talk*** *will about* erm (xx) agroforestry systems
(e) ***my lecture will not deal about*** Catalonia as a whole

The nouns in 7.2 can be regarded as *context-creating* in that they do not require much co-text to help interpret them (Chapter 2). Similarly, verbs of communication like TALK, SPEAK, or PRESENT, are also found at the outset of presentations (7.3). Examples (7.2 and 7.3) are straightforward instances of what we generally regard as metadiscourse, even though some may slightly depart from the most conventional form (e.g. 7.3d: ***say** some remarks on*).

(7.3) (a) ***what i'm gonna talk about today*** *is* er is something
(b) *today* ***i will speak to you about*** the tale of two spikes
(c) women's education in Iran in which ***i'm going to discuss***
(d) and then ***i'm also gonna sa- say some remarks on*** b- Bolivia erm in terms of lessons learned

In this category I have also included some verbs that do not inherently, i.e., in their decontextualised citation forms, evoke the sense of communication. Instead, they receive their meaning from the context, and are thus *context-dependent* (Chapter 2). Verbs of this kind include ANALYSE, INTRODUCE, SEE or OFFER (7.4).

(7.4) (a) and ***would like to introduce to you*** my two hypotheses ***rather than just t- talking about***
(b) seem to be growing ***this is what i would like to analyse*** and and and ***er er report about***
(c) so basically ***what i'm going to offer is*** if you want
(d) okay ***we are going to see*** er the objective

In (7.4) context-dependence is clear. INTRODUCE would seem to have communication among its salient semantic properties, even though dictionaries tend not to grant it a communicative sense. In (7.4a), INTRODUCE appears in a phrase (*I would like to introduce to you*) that would seem to evoke a context of introducing people to each other, or perhaps a speaker to an audience, but the situation as well as the immediately following co-text (*hypotheses*) invoke the communicative sense as primary. In (7.4b), *analyse* would seem to be somewhat ambiguous between the speaker's analytic talking or an underlying analysis already undertaken, but the former interpretation is supported by the co-text. OFFER (7.4c) and SEE (7.4d) would not in isolation be likely to evoke associations with speaking, but in these contexts, this is a reasonable interpretation. We can look at both in a little more co-text, keeping in mind that it is the preceding context that provides the crucial clues for the listener's predictive processing. For (7.4b), the preceding part runs (with minor omissions) like this (7.5):

(7.5) . . . that was er my er sort of natural initial naïve er assumption but then when i started to think and and and and work er with empirical material . . . i thought that probably er this this assumption doesn't hold entirely and . . . it's er probably not good to assume in advance that . . . and that er it's more complicated than that er so basically ***what i'm going to offer*** is if you want a light version of this modernisation theory approach . . .

The extract comes from an introductory section of a conference presentation where the speaker is recounting the train of thought that led him to his current viewpoint. *Offer* comes at a point when we would expect a verb of communication and is likely to be easily perceived as discourse reflexive. In turn, *see* in (7.6, a contextualised version of 7.4d) is preceded by a reference to speaking (*I want to talk about*), which probably attunes listeners to expect more about the talk (*okay we are going to . . .*). Again, a verb of communication, like DISCUSS, or HEAR, would be within the range of expectations that SEE here fulfils.

(7.6) . . . *i want to talk about* the free trade area of the Americas negotiations and its main challenges and this has to do a lot with development because . . . okay *we are going to* ***see*** er er the objective of *my paper* the American background and antecedents in America

Global orienting typically indicates the beginnings of talks, (*let me start by saying that; let's first look at the ways (xx) talk about*; *in this presentation I will start*), beginnings of closing episodes (*now I would like to con- er conclude by saying*; *here are some of the conclusions; in the end I want to say that*) and declaring endings, as examples in (7.7).

(7.7) (a) *i think that* erm *i can stop here*
(b) *i'll end there*
(c) well *i think this might suffice*
(d) *that was it,* thank you
(e) i think that's *that's all*

Apart from signalling the global structure, speakers also indicate interim orientation with more local signposting, or *local orienting*, which we now turn to.

Effective contextualisation in a monologue calls for intermittent reminders and signals which keep listeners (and possibly also speakers themselves) on course within the bigger picture. They may announce what speakers are going to do next, what they are putting off for a while but intending to return to, or what they are skipping altogether.

While a presentation is in progress, basic navigation signals are not very different from initial orientations, apart from not occurring at the beginning. In these, speakers talk about the next part or section in the discourse (7.8).

(7.8) (a) *i want to illustrate for you* that there were intraparliamentary efforts
(b) *i'm going to mention* partly how
(c) *i'm just here running through* er a number of features that
(d) *first i'd like to tell bit about*

It is also common to indicate explicitly that there is a transition from one topic to another (7.9).

(7.9) (a) okay *that's a very short discussion about* the about the history of polar cartography *and then we come to this* real polar science
(b) *so these are some of the preliminary observations before i share with you my slides* on that
(c) and *i'll just er give the problems here the conclusion so far is* that pamphlets might not

In transition sequences, retrospective marking that a section is now concluded tends to precede anticipation of the next step, but the reverse order also occurs as the last instance (7.9c) shows.

Transitions are fairly often signalled by rhetorical questions (7.10), possibly for extra attention to these junctures. With some speakers, though, rhetorical questions seem more like a habit or a routine way to deal with signposting.

(7.10) (a) now *we can ask er this question* er what is the issue
(b*) it is indeed interesting to ask* why
(c) okay *er how do i er ar- arguments argue this*

Sometimes topics seem to occur to speakers at earlier points than they have been placed in the plan. This is probably where orientations like those in (7.11) occur. In these, speakers mention topics before they can fully address them. In this way they can let listeners know that they are relevant now, even though postponed for the moment, and will come up again.

(7.11) (a) *i will talk about it* about abo – *i will talk about er those parties these parties later*
(b) few major centres exist *and i come back to that* <COUGH> *in a while*
(c) *i'll say a little bit a- about* the er project *later* as well

Talks do not always run smoothly from one planned phase to the next. Sometimes things take more time than expected, and presenters may find themselves in a situation where they cannot cover all the material they anticipated. This is where the overt expressions of reflexive metadiscourse bifurcate in speech and writing. Comments on these unexpected omissions are common, for instance explanations of why relevant-seeming topics are not covered or slides are whizzed by. Many speakers refer to time pressure on these occasions (7.12).

(7.12) (a) okay *i'm just gonna jump right into* some of the more interesting findings
(b) *i will i'll be quick so i'll skip* some of the slides
(c) *i'm pressed for time so i'll just flash this stuff past* <SIGH> anyway

Speakers sometimes indicate that they are aware of some topics they are not talking about but that might also be relevant (7.13). These get shelved and put off to a hazier future or some other occasion (*not . . . this time*).

(7.13) (a) i had this great opportunity to actually er make notes for it *than try to er erm try to er say something about it to you now,*
(b) *i will not go into debate* how
(c) nose either *but i'm not going to talk talk about that this time*

Comments on topic-shelving help speakers share their awareness of the potential relevance of these topics with their listeners. This may be done to obviate questions suggesting they have overlooked something important, although will not of course prevent listeners from asking about them after the presentation.

We have moved down the scale from a global to a local span, but it makes sense to take one more step in this direction. The shortest timescale speakers manage is *immediate*. After these short-span comments hearers are invited to expect the speaker to move on to the topic without delay (7.14).

(7.14) (a) and er *now i'd like to talk about* the enlargement of EU
(b) and *now we've started to getting into, more closer to what i what i er wa- was a title of the talk today* er called the narratives of the European city
(c) *so let's go to the project now* i'm er okay and i wanted to say s- another thing er after i described you the two countries briefly

These instances include a time reference, mostly *now* (see also Webber 2005), like in the examples. They probably shape listeners' predictions about what is about to come up in the next instance.

In delivering monologues, speakers thus employ multi-span signalling for orienting their hearers to what to expect in the ongoing talk. This elaborate contextualising may stem from the pre-planned nature of academic monologues, because the phenomenon can be likened to what we see in research articles and academic textbooks. However, it may be even more important to hearers whose attention needs to be engaged for a long time but whose short-term memory cannot stretch out to cover long periods. The process is likely to rely also on long-term working memory, briefly discussed earlier (Chapters 2 and 4). These local anticipatory cues can act as refreshers in relation to the global cues and direct the hearer's attention to the evolving whole at the current point of the discourse. While readers can interrupt their reading at any point to think of the implications of what they have read so far, or to jot down a note or a comment, or just because they are distracted or bored, listeners have few options if they are to make sense of a whole monologue. Discourse signposting can well be an asset in composing a representation of the discourse at multiple levels.

Equally, the speaker may benefit from making orienting reflexive comments to keep track of their own progress, a kind of verbal orienteering through a terrain where the goal is known and path planned, but where unexpected bumps and delays also occur and require new tactics, as we saw in the examples of shelving and skipping. It would thus seem that, on occasion, even the speaker can get lost.

Different time spans of metadiscoursal signalling can have different implications on the real-time processing of the discourse for hearers and speakers. The import of global orienting is likely to be integrated into very general listener representations of what the discourse is about, and while it can generate expectations at some point, these are unlikely to have lasting effects on how the hearer's representation evolves as the discourse progresses. Local orienting seems to act as the basic signposting in the discourse: this is where we are now, after covering such ground, and we are moving towards this direction – or shelving or skipping something that might have been expected to come next. We can assume it reassures hearers that they are on the right track and if they were lost, they can reorient themselves. Immediate orienting is the most likely timescale to guide the interpretation of the next stretch of discourse and to modulate expectations accordingly.

This section has shown how orienting discourse reflexivity in extended spoken monologues uses variable spans, that is, works with multiple ranges. This contrasts with dialogues and their characteristic rapid exchanges. The span with its variations resembles written monologue but cannot function identically if only because the fleeting nature of the spoken word and the limitations of working memory prevent the recipient from taking in the discourse at their chosen pace. Listeners, unlike readers, must adapt to the presenter's delivery speed. Orienting signals from the presenter are used to prospect ahead and they feed into the continual interaction of prediction and adjustment that make up the evolving representation of the content for the listener.

Retrieving

As we might expect based on earlier metadiscourse research of writing, reflexive discourse in monologues is predominantly forward-looking. A presenter is free from having to compete for turns and has an undisturbed opportunity for delivering their own message. Their challenge is to maintain the audience's interest. Forward orientation would seem to make sense in view of the brain's tendency to engage in predictive processing, because it sustains listeners' hypothesis generation. Even so, we also find some retrieving discourse reflexivity in extended monologues. Moreover, they have a special characteristic: a clear majority of retrieving discourse reflexivity consists of self-references. Let us begin with this intriguing phenomenon first, and then go on to discuss references to others than self.

As discussed in Chapter 4, in making an *egocentric reference*, a speaker resumes something from their own earlier speech in the ongoing speech event. Reflexive egocentric references are thus made in the context of the current event. This overlaps with Hyland's (2005) *self-mentions*, but not completely, because he relies on certain expressions like 1st person pronouns in his counts, and a look at his examples reveals that they include a wider array of references by authors to their own work, whereas in our case a vital requirement is that the references must be to the ongoing discourse. However, self-mentions have been found to be more frequent in spoken monologues than in written academic texts (Lee & Subtrielu 2015; Hyland & Zou 2020; Qiu & Jiang, 2021; Liu 2021).

Why do people refer in retrospect to what they have already said during their own talk? Why do they say things like *as I said* or *as mentioned previously*? It would seem to be more natural in a dialogue, where it can indicate things like self-consistency as R. Craig and Sanusi (2000) suggested or direct an interlocutor's attention to a point the speaker made previously and its relevance to the discussion at that moment. But why do speakers do this in a monologue, when the floor is theirs, and they can build their rhetoric and presentation to their own liking?

To come to grips with their role in live presentations, it is best to start by examining some examples. The first (7.15a) from a conference seems quite straightforward: the speaker is interrupted by a practical issue, reshuffling his slides (he is using both a Powerpoint and an overhead projector), right after he has anticipated the continuation of his talk (*I'll just . . . and then conclude*), so that resumption of the topic he was discussing before the pause simply seems an obvious thing to do to indicate the talk continues.

The second example (7.15b) is from the same presentation. The speaker implies that this is familiar content. However, the familiarity is debatable. The reference is vague, and cannot be precisely located even from the transcript, although a passing mention has been made to the health insurance. The talk up to this point has dealt with a complex and detailed history of Kenyan health policy with its many turns. An analyst can consult the transcript for searching and re-reading, but a hearer can hardly have internalised the entire content up to that point, and whatever memory trace may remain of this health insurance fund, it is likely to have been integrated into a general representation of the meaning so far.

(7.15) (a) . . . so i'll just put a o- er one more or two more er overheads here *and then conclude* <PREPARING OVERHEAD PROJECTOR, P:37> okay *so* ***i mentioned*** the er the, Kenya health policy framework the health policy framework that was crafted in 1994
(b) . . . through this national social health insurance fund and ***as i mentioned*** it will transform the existing system

The reference to past discourse in (7.15b) may nevertheless work as a reassuring note to an attentive listener that they are on the right track if this is part of their representation of the talk. However, what seems more relevant to the speaker's point is that the retrospective reference is followed by a reformulation of a past statement (*it will transform the existing system*). An apparently retrospective reference also works prospectively (cf. Chapter 4), alerting the hearer to a point that is relevant at present, something that the speaker is going to expand on whether the first mention has been missed or not. It thus sets up an expectation of a restatement (or reformulation) in the listener. This is exactly what happens in the current example; it is immediately followed by a thorough elaboration of how the social health insurance fund is expected to transform Kenya's health system (which in fact had not been explained previously in the talk).

The most common egocentric reference is *as I said*, with some variants, including some other verbs (7.16).

(7.16) (a) there is not only ***as i said*** one legal definition of discrimination
(b) so they were er er ***like i said*** interviewed
(c) erm ***as i told you*** the electoral law was accepted in 1848
(d) ***as i*** *er* ***suggested in the beginning*** perhaps they're not communicating

The typical egocentric reference, then, anticipates a rephrasing or expansion of something that has been said earlier. The previous formulation as far as it can be traced back in transcripts may not be very clear, be long, distributed over several sections, or simply not there. From a cognitive viewpoint, the difficulty of finding the same formulation earlier in the transcript suggests that even the speaker's own representation of the discourse so far is not accurate, let alone verbatim. The meaning of a retrieving egocentric reference seems to be not so much a rephrasing than a reassurance that 'if this is what you have taken from my talk so far, you are on the right track', or simply 'this is relevant and noteworthy'.

A different reminding function is associated with *I mentioned*, which seems to refer to something that has been discussed, has current relevance, but will not be resumed. A typical example is (7.17a), where retrieving reminders are made with *I mentioned*, and the new, forward orienting one is added to the list (*the third one is*).

(7.17) (a) so *i mentioned* business economy i men- economical divide *i mentioned* technology divide and the third one is gender divide
(b) i think *i* er *mentioned* all of these issues already
(c) three er traditional sort of tools one is reviewing literature and documents for perception and analysis basically the RFA *which i just mentioned* and to examine policy implications we've called it policy characteristics analysis

Egocentric references also appear in the beginnings of conclusion sections where presenters return to the big picture of the presentation, the global level, as if in preparation for a summary or a take-home message (7.18):

(7.18) (a) *this was just a brief presentation i gave you* but about the role of landscape integration
(b) er *i have now i've talk about talked about two* body parts and given an account of er the meanings produced through them with with a framework of gender one of them

Occasionally references are also made to the discourse macro-event that the current session is part of, but this was rarer than in dialogues:

(7.19) (a) *yesterday i tried to argue* that that that er cultural approach to the history of technology will bring us new insight
(b) *like we tried to to say last time*

Overall, retrospective egocentric references mark present relevance of non-new material. They clearly indicate recipient design on the speaker's part. With these references, the speaker constructs something as being retrievable from what has already been said and as relevant to what is coming up next. However, the content presumed to be familiar may not be retrievable, either because the previous mention is beyond the working memory span, because the antecedent may not have been salient in the listener's mental representation of the discourse so far, or because there has been no clear antecedent in the first place.

The listener may thus not be able to retrieve the material, but they may nevertheless accept its suggested relevance and orient to the anticipated next step. In successful cases, their expectations of the upcoming content will be met. *As I said* and its variants are vital in live presentations, where hearers cannot keep everything in their mental representations of the talk and cannot go back to check. They probably also contribute to harmonising listeners' situation models with each other and especially that of the speaker. These expressions are important in constructing a coherent argument, and play a rhetorical role by giving special prominence to those elements of a presentation that are constructed as being reintroduced.

Monologue presenters do not exclusively refer to themselves, even though the patterns and their distributions are not like those in dialogic events, where most retrieving references are *altercentric*, that is, they are made to co-present interlocutors. References to the reader have been observed and discussed in the metadiscourse literature often enough (for instance Mauranen 1993a; Hyland 2005; Ädel 2006), but these address the imagined reader of the text, not any individual real reader. References to the audience have been found in studies of spoken monologues, but it seems that they are typically orienting rather than retrieving because especially studies that adopt the 'broad' approach to metadiscourse tend to list them under 'engagement markers', and from the examples it looks like the references are to the collective addressee, that is, the whole audience.

It is hard to assess how common this is, because separating altercentric references from lexis-based quantitative data is not usually possible. An exception is Qiu & Jiang's (2021) study which reports that self-mentions and listener mentions were the most prevalent interactional features in their data. However, there is no data telling us whether any of them were of a retrieving kind.

Apart from references to absent third parties, which are common in all academic discourse but not discourse reflexive, we might expect to find retrieving altercentric references to the macro-event that envelops a presentation. In view of our data, this is a reasonable expectation, even if the references may not be very frequent. Compared to the number of egocentric references, altercentric references in conference presentations account for less than half of those, and graduate seminar presentations about a tenth.

Even so, a few altercentric references are made in monologic speech. Among these, by far the majority refer to identified other participants or discourses, usually in the macro-event that the on-going session is part of. Some speakers refer to presentations for identification (7.20 a-b), others use proper names (c-d), and yet others (e-f) refer to other speakers from the same or related projects (*my colleague*(*s*).

(7.20) (a) and this also confirmed by er *the previous talk*
(b) division between *as we heard in the last session* the the true wilderness
(c) *as we have just seen in a way in <NAME's> lecture in the morning*
(d) it's er *like <NAME NS7> said last time* not
(e) i mean m- *my colleagues already mentioned* the high bulk
(f) which *my colleague explained* the overall polity

Sometimes references leave the referent more implicit, of which the following (7.21) are examples, but such occurrences were even rarer than identifying references.

(7.21) (a) similar civic education civic training and so on *was mentioned in an earlier paper today*
(b) since er *everyone today erm mentioned* erm er some er examples and case studies
(c) *as we heard yesterday*

Retrieving altercentric references reflect and contribute to coherence across interrelated speech events within a macro-event. Within the framework of macro-events of shared experience, altercentric references highlight the mutual relevance of their on-going talk and this shared experience. Of course, the experience need not be shared in the literal sense of all hearers having attended the previous events let alone remembering the parts relevant to the speaker, that is, their representations may be very diffrerent. The sharedness is essentially constructed by the speaker, but the effect of the wider, more 'global' context to the ongoing talk is manifest in altercentric references more than in the egocentric references that construct a more self-contained talk. Altercentric references can also be seen as further evidence of the co-construction of knowledge, like the dialogic events in Chapter 6: building on what other speakers have said in the same discourse event.

In all, retrieving references are a facet of audience design and a means of generating coherence, keeping the listener focused on the progression of the presentation by anticipating summaries and offering repetitions.

7.1.2 Commenting

As already noted, distinguishing *commenting* discourse reflexivity from contextualising is well motivated for monologues. Commenting is not only prominent in monologues, but it would seem to take on some of the tasks that in dialogic interaction are negotiated in collaboration: expressing stance, weighing arguments, findings, methods, and assigning importance to topics – in short, making evaluations. None are in themselves discourse reflexive, but discourse reflexivity seems often involved in achieving communicative acts of these kinds. Thus, expressions of evaluation, stance, or hedging can overlap or co-occur with discourse reflexivity. The present analysis includes discourse reflexive commentary in cases where the usual criteria of reflexive metadiscourse are also fulfilled.

Because the functions of evaluative commentary in monologic discourse fall on only one speaker, they tend to become viewed in a personalised light, and perhaps thereby have attracted researchers' attention. It does not mean that monologues are intrinsically more evaluative. Much dialogic negotiation takes place around evaluative co-construction, as has been discussed in earlier chapters (4 to 6).

In addition to evaluation, commenting comprises clarification. Clarifications reflect the speaker's situational assessment of achieving intersubjectivity, their theory of mind. They implement recipient design, and their significance lies not only in seeking intelligibility but also in laying foundations for intersubjectivity, much like matching perspectives in dialogues (Chapter 6). Clarifications seem to perform very similar things in the monologic mode as they do in dialogue.

Contextualising the discourse and commenting on it do not always appear in strictly separate expressions, but for instance evaluative commentary can simultaneously also contextualise the discourse and anticipate what the speaker is about to say. In (7.22a) for example, the speaker prospects ahead with a commentary on the epistemic status (*maybe*) of the utterance to come. Commenting does not have to be linked to prospecting ahead, though, but it can follow what has already been said, as if an afterthought (7.22b).

(7.22) (a) now first of all *maybe we should say* that the measure of success here is certainly not
(b) and has been fairly successful *i would say*

Commenting is, then, a broad category which comprises clarifications, evaluation, and focus. It is far less common than contextualising, roughly half as frequent in the present data. This might seem surprising in view of the fundamental character and ubiquity of evaluation in language use (Gozdz-Roszkowski & Hunston 2016; Thompson & Hunston 2000), but it is worth keeping in mind that our view is here limited to explicit, or 'inscribed', evaluation in the context of discourse reflexivity in spoken monologue.

Commenting is neither unusual nor unimportant in connection with discourse reflexivity even though less frequent than contextualising. To keep the analysis simple and avoid multiplying categories by cross-categorisation, the orienting vs retrieving distinction is not imposed on commentary analyses, even though it could easily be done. The distinction between prospective and retrospective orientation has already been made, and it would seem superfluous to illustrate it further here. Therefore, we shall focus the discussion here on the two main types, *clarifying* and *evaluation and focus*, starting with clarifying.

Clarifications tend to surface when speakers or hearers show concern about shared understanding. While dialogue participants collaborate towards clarification and seek to achieve intersubjectivity by joint effort, a speaker delivering a monologue falls back on their own sense of what in their talk might require special clarity or precision. It seems reasonable to assume that concerns about one's intelligibility or achieving intersubjectivity become particularly salient when there is something vital at stake. In this way monologic clarifications can convey importance and indicate that certain concepts or terms are singled out as worth the listener's attention.

Clarifications can roughly speaking target either meaning or expression, as noted in Chapter 6. The present data shows basically an even distribution between these two kinds, with a slight overall preference for expression over meaning (53.0% vs 47.0%). However, a closer look reveals a clear difference between event types: conference talks show a preference for clarifying expression (63.0%) over meaning (37.0%), while graduate seminar presentations do the reverse, and clarify meanings more often than expressions (70% vs 30%). In addition, graduate seminar presentations resort to clarifications of any kind less often. These observations suggest that academic experience and growing expertise alter speakers' relation to clarification.

Clarifications of meaning often seek to specify the content matter in a referent (7.23), thereby making a given expression or term also more precise.

(7.23) (a) *what i mean with this scientific interest in polar regions is* that the first polar year was organised
(b) if nothing else is mentioned *by normal i mean* bodies with two arms and and two legs
(c) *what i'm talking about* in business set-up *means* the process

Reporting original research often suggests new concepts and new conceptual distinctions, which requires new terms. As researchers make claims about their contribution to knowledge, they tend to be explicit and precise about terms and the concepts or conceptual distinctions these denote, especially when they claim ownership to a term or label (7.24). Naming concepts not only gives them expression but is a central analytical tool for scholars in the humanities and social sciences. It is not surprising that graduate students do this less often. Coming up with terminology not established in the literature is not normally expected of master's students.

(7.24) (a) one which *i would name* more geopolitical approach
(b) *i call this the first phrase* phase of of the travelling, er, but this system
(c) *another term for this* that er i have come to use more and more in my own work is er the social fabric

Sometimes terms may not be resolved by the speaker. In (7.25), we find a speaker voicing her dissatisfaction with a term she declares has outlived its purpose. It is not entirely clear whether she is less happy with the term or the concept, and in the end, she goes on to employ the term after a longish complaint about it and appealing to the audience (*let's try to invent something new*) for a better term. This is also one of the rare occasions where a speaker addresses the audience directly in the second person (*this is self-criticism not criticism towards you*). The episode employs several discourse reflexive expressions to clarify her uneasy position regarding the term *digital divide.*

(7.25) *i mean let me before i say* the three divides *i wanna say something i'm kind of fed up with the word* digital divide because i use it every day you probably use it more than once a day if there's a new concept to bridge the digital divide please let me know i'm happy to you can have the copyright *i'm happy to use the word* but it should be something more constructive we i think we have been for the last ten years bridging the digital divide and i know it's a reality but *let's try to invent something new we have heard the word already this is self-criticism not criticism towards you* okay so three divides . . .

This extract is a good illustration of how the co-present audience affects the conditions of discourse reflexivity: there is direct interaction between a speaker and even a silent audience, unlike between an author and their readers.

In the previous example the speaker's problem with a term was intertwined with her dissatisfaction with a conceptual matter. By contrast, the next example (7.26) presents a concept, constructed as a well-defined one, in search of a term. The speaker explains his novel concept and gives his term (which, incidentally, he calls 'concept' rather than 'term') for it in Swedish, and simply admits he has not thought of a suitable English term for it.

(7.26) i think we can see now to quite some extent obvious process that *i'm being referring to* here erm er certainly we can er i- in in in er in Swedish er *i i've er started using the the concept er kunskaps anläggning i haven't really thought about any good word for in in English* er to er to er to to sort of *underline that* it's not just an institution it's not just a building er but it's rather complex set of theories

Later in the talk this speaker uses the same Swedish term again, but with a paraphrase of the notion (*knowledge complexes*) without attempting or problematising an equivalent in English (*there is a growing awareness certainly among those that are building these 'kunskaps anläggning' these knowledge complexes er that they are important*). The last two examples show how intertwined concepts and terms can get in academic discourse and how they are not always kept separate. Both get discussed and questioned widely as part of disciplinary development especially in the humanities and social sciences.

Sometimes presenters seem to engage in think-aloud word searches (7.27). Explicit word searches constitute a kind of commentary on the discourse and thus can be regarded as reflexive discourse, even though it arguably borders on metalanguage. Such comments not only indicate a speaker's awareness that a word or term might exist that they do not know or are not able to recall, but they also prospect a forthcoming clarification. Needless to say, this is not possible in written monologue.

(7.27) (a) the Russian culture shouldn't er again like erm *what would be the word*, to to not let them to build their this new cultural identity
(b) the next point is is the enlargement of EU the er *how i say* the target of the enlargement is to establish the great Europe or some western Europe
(c) so er France feel that it's er France was was er *how to say* er separated from this kind of plan

When speakers seem to be trying to capture something for which a suitable or precise expression evades them, they can use items like *so to speak* to indicate the tentative status of the term or expression. In ELF contexts, common approximate equivalents are so *to say* (see, Carey 2013) or *let's say* (Mauranen 2006a) as in (7.28), which also indicate roughly that they use a term or word in an ad hoc manner or in an unorthodox or perhaps a figurative manner.

(7.28) (a) one should er not *so to say* be too hush <COUGH> a- about this
(b) play on terms of their own with the images of our postmodern culture and and *so to say* create er spaces for them for themselves
(c) discussed in the parliament however at the same time because the *let's say* the revolution and the main motor of revolution had been
(d) clients' patterns are a little bit different. erm. *let's say* @completely different in in some places@

Both *so to say* and *let's say* have translation equivalents in many European languages, which is likely to reinforce their use and diffusion, given that they are easily comprehensible to other speakers of at least European languages. The presenters, then, indicate that the expression they are looking for may elude them, but simultaneously raise awareness that the current formulation is deployed in an unusual or provisional manner. This does not necessarily indicate trouble because the language they use is not their L1, but equally probably because the speaker is struggling with the conceptualisation of the topic matter: in either case they indicate a search for a suitable expression for a preliminary account of a state of affairs that would convey the idea to their interlocutors. It imparts a sense of thinking on their feet, and obviously would not be repeated in a published version of the presentation. Such provisional formulations impart a certain sense of freshness and novelty in a talk.

Since it is important to contribute new things from research to the pool of knowledge and understanding, signalling novelty is rhetorically effective. At the same time, it is pertinent to mark terms or expressions tentative when this is the case and maintain epistemic openness or the possibility of self-correction. Elaboration of expressions and phrasing thus serves both a clarifying and an epistemic function.

At some stage tentative conceptualisations need to be resolved and settled with a term or label. The introduction of a new term may be felt to require reflections that clarify its background.

(7.29) we start getting this kind of irrational way of of seeing technology *so i've been building this a new horrible word* which is S-A-C-C-O-T @@ <COUGH> it's very unofficial and and it's not widely known this is probably the first time it's been ever shown in a wider public except my own study er which is a social and cultural construction of technology . . .

Here the new speaker-generated term is explained and introduced with distancing tactics of humour and self-irony, which would probably help cover the speaker's back if he later came up with a better term. In the conceptual development of the talk up to that point the speaker has criticised earlier conceptualisations and terms for their inadequacy for capturing the phenomenon he is discussing. Clearly, we would not expect to see such unsettled formulations of concepts or terms in published, written texts.

In all, clarifying discourse reflexivity helps explicate notions, individual items, and expressions, and at the same time serves rhetorical purposes such as giving prominence to certain terms and concepts, and staking a speaker's claim to a term or a conceptual distinction, while often at the same time maintaining some epistemic freedom in respect of the notion. It would seem that in their talks, academics like to introduce new conceptual distinctions but without necessarily fully committing themselves to them. This would be interesting to compare to written research reports, where backing down on a position afterwards may be a harder task. Graduate students engage in these practices noticeably less than conference presenters, which should perhaps not come as a surprise because they do not usually to come up with their own terms or concepts. The standard expectation of graduate students is that they master central established concepts and terminology of the field.

In addition to clarifying, the other major kind of commentary consists in *evaluation and focus*. In fact, commentary that has a bearing on evaluation and focus is about twice as common as commentary that is clarifying in our data. Evaluation in language is omnipresent, and reflexive metadiscourse can capture only a fraction of it. What the present data seems to bring to light especially is how entwined evaluation is with emphasis and focus. The expressions are largely concerned with how important a given point is either in the ongoing presentation or more generally in the advancement of knowledge. In other words, they pertain to the value of the point, and concern different levels of knowledge claims. Such comments direct the listener's attention to the point or claim, which adds to its weight, as we can see for example in (7.30).

(7.30) (a) also that er *it's worth to mention* for example
(b) *the point here is not to say that* that there were not very concrete mate- material health and other problems like health problems the *the point is here to say that* that is not the whole story

Explicit expressions of emphasis play a similar role. These can co-occur with modal verbs or expressions of volition. Modals in this use lend a sense of urgency to the matter at hand (7.31).

(7.31) (a) *so i must stress that* citizenship approach er opens
(b) as a lawyer *i must er emphasise*
(c) er once again *i need to stress* that the issue of equality

By contrast, volitional verbs mitigate the emphasis, and tend to co-occur with other mitigating and hedging expressions (*sort of, just*) and conditionals. Thus, if discourse reflexivity imposes the speaker's order on the discourse, mitigating expressions work to counterbalance the imposition.

(7.32) (a) er *i'd still want to sort of emphasise* that
(b) and *i would like to stress* that this is the particularly the aim and policy
(c) and *just to underline er this er last point i would just like to* show you

Mitigating and hedging have of course been much investigated and found to typify academic discourse. Hedges and other mitigators have been observed to co-occur with discourse reflexivity as a 'discourse collocation' (e.g., Mauranen 2001, 2004, 2010). Many researchers following Hyland's (2005), 'broad' approach include them in metadiscourse. Clearly, a discourse reflexive view of metadiscourse excludes hedging and stance (e.g., Ädel 2006; Mauranen 2001, 2010; Smart 2016), since they are not in themselves discourse about discourse. Conflating attitude, evaluation, and stance with discourse reflexivity simply muddies the waters. It is difficult to see how hedges and mitigation could stand in a 'meta' relationship to the discourse. They are an integral part of the discourse without talking about it, and collocations between discourse phenomena like metadiscourse and hedging or stance are important topics of investigation. They should not be subsumed under the umbrella of metadiscourse but viewed in their own right.

Mitigation in connection with discourse reflexivity is by no means unusual. A speaker may wish to leave themselves epistemic space outside the confines of certainty and present something as their personal assessment, a possible interpretation, a likely outcome, or a feasible generalisation (7.33).

(7.33) (a) of course erm *i would say* in the last years
(c) we have, more or less *i wouldn't say ideal typically* but er some of the narratives that we have sort of distilled out of the period
(d) i mean thi- this is er an area where *we could say* well this is a common interest

Speakers can also foreground their personal role (7.34) in selecting the points of emphasis (***I think*** . . . ***my*** *best basic message; main question* **to me**; *still important* ***I think***). In this way they personalise their evaluation, which in an epistemic sense makes it less determinate and more open because they refrain from making general claims. On this basis it can be seen as having a mitigating epistemic effect. In rhetorical terms, however, it gives the focal points more rhetorical prominence if only by spending more time on it.

(7.34) (a) if you want to achieve regional development *i think this is my best basic message here in this talk* if you wanna go for that which i think is really important
(b) and then i would like to talk about this in respects or in relation to democracy because *a main question to me* is to
(c) *please also notice* which is *perhaps less less the er striking but still important i* ***think*** the connection with the word modernity

Most instances of evaluative discourse reflexivity in this data seem to come from a standard stock of conventionalised expressions. Approximations are virtually non-existent, even though common enough in ELF talk as a rule. It would therefore seem that frequent conventionalised stance-marking expressions (*I would say, we can say,* etc.) are adopted into second-language use as whole multi-word expressions.

This is nevertheless not the whole story, and more varied, more lexical means of expressing evaluation and focus are also found. Some of these are negative (7.35) and given the general linguistic positivity bias in speech (see, Ch 4), it is possible that negative expressions require novel lexical expressions, because conventionalised, highly frequent expressions tend to be positive. Routine expressions may not be equally available for conveying negativity. Apart from perhaps the last case (d) below, which might be simply polished in copyediting, the other examples here would most likely be weeded out, resolved, or altered in a major way in written text.

(7.35) (a) sorry mhm *this is probably not a good thing to say here* but
(b) *unfortunately i cannot tell you that* this was a success
(c) comes from realism which *i well i personally wouldn't think* first about realism
(d) and this *i claim is a particular problematic* even though it is

Overall, commenting discourse reflexivity produces rhetorical effects in drawing attention to what is central to a presentation or an argument. It also helps preserve epistemic leeway in appropriate places. Many of the instances seen in this section show the effect of a co-present audience on the speaker even though there is no dialogue between them (*this is probably not a good thing to say here*). Even though speaker-audience interaction is verbalised only on the speaker's side, speakers are clearly aware of the listeners. Evaluative discourse reflexive comments in this data relate to issues of importance and emphasis as well as epistemic status (such as certainty or generalisability). They tend to co-occur with hedges or indications of personalisation in claims or judgments. Clarifications, likewise, generate emphasis if only by drawing attention to a matter that is being explicated, because the attention a speaker is giving to the elaboration of a particular issue directs listeners' attention to the same thing. Clarifying can also play a role in conveying epistemic openness by signalling that the speaker is thinking on their feet and that the formulations are tentative rather than final.

7.2 Managing situation

Situation management is a normal part of the academic discourse events recorded for our present data. Management operations seek to ensure the smooth running of the interaction in its situational frame, if only for mundane practical reasons such as scheduling so that sessions will not overrun their time slots. More academic interests also require a structure which allows space to questions, comments, and above all critical dialogue based on presentations.

It is not for presenters to take on situation management because their primary task is to manage their talk, and appointed chairpersons take care of the talk-external situation. Therefore, cases where presenters manage the situation are rare, only a fraction of discourse management (N= 22 vs. 593 respectively) and far less frequent compared to dialogues (N= 119 vs. 402). It is nevertheless useful to take a brief look at instances where this happens, not only for reasons of analytical symmetry but because they display the co-presence of the speaker and the audience from a less familiar angle.

Although some speaker comments that can be regarded as situational rather than discourse organising are quite trivial technical remarks (7.36), and not particularly noticeable or memorable, this is not all.

(7.36) (a) well good afternoon everyone and er, *i hope i will be able to to speak loudly enough so that you can hear me*
(b) *i can read you this quote*

In conventional interaction structures around monologues, chairpersons often interact silently with presenters, for example signalling that the time is up. A speaker may nevertheless respond verbally (7.37), although much of this interaction remains nonverbal altogether. We could call this *situational interaction*, which can be verbalised or remain silent. It is interesting in evincing the difference that co-presence makes to even monologic interaction.

(7.37) *yeah i'm finishing* @@ er </S2>

Occasionally speakers take on management tasks that normally fall upon the chairperson, such as inviting questions and comments (7.38). By such moves, speakers orient more to the framing of their discourse in its outer context than to placing it in its internal, co-textual context, just like corresponding moves from a chairperson.

(7.38) (a) i don't know what you think about it *maybe we could start the discussion here if you have any questions*
(b) i think i've had my share already so thank you very much *if there are questions* </S7>
(c) and *if anyone has any suggestions* for that i'm mo- *you're most welcome to tell me i'd be really happy to hear* something about that

It can happen that certain questions are not so welcome, and the speaker may try to shield themselves against those, as in this case from a graduate seminar:

(7.39) *don't ask* what the stig-1 domain does

Speakers also engage with the audience as if off the record, outside the main discourse of the presentation, for example with jokes or humorous comments. Some of this humour is couched in reflexive metadiscourse.

(7.40) (a) so i'm gonna hand over to <NAME S14> now *who's got a much better voice and and he's going to talk about* the (xx) </S10>
(b) so i *i just brought it to be able to s- say that* i have been reading some <NAME>

Discourse reflexive managing comments tend to be short and situations sorted out quickly. Occasionally, though, attempts at resolving them seem to make things worse if participants get too active and start a dialogic negotiation episode, which can take more time than planned:

(7.41) . . . and erm, *should i read it* or can you follow it <SU> mhm-hm </SU> which one </S13>
<SU> i think we can follow it </SU>
<SU> we can <S13> *i read* </S13> follow it </SU>
<S13> *read no* <SS> [@@] </SS> [@@] </S13>
<S12> well [someone wants] <SU> *[yes read]* </SU> *you to read it* and some don't but *please do [read* yeah mhm] </S12>

The confusion in the previous example seems to elicit a good deal of laughter from the listeners, as does the next instance (7.42), where the speaker is deliberately making fun of issues discussed in the event. Again, the episode turns into a dialogue.

(7.42) . . . @@ microsoft word mhm *i have to say it very <SS> @@ </SS> quietly* because this is a place for open source debate so but we i confess we used <WHISPERING> Microsoft </WHISPERING> </S3>
<S7> [what was it] </S7>
<S3> [they didn't] sponsor us </S3>
<SS> @@ </SS>
<S3> @@ they didn't they didn't pay us a penny okay if that helps anybody </S3>
<S8> @no no you paid@ </S8>
<SS> @@ </SS>
<S3> no we didn't pay we didn't pay them </S3>

The last two examples show how in live situations the audience can sometimes also voice short comments in the context of monologic presentation. Even when they do not use their voices, however, their presence affects speakers, who laugh, tell jokes, and worry about the visibility or audibility of their presentations – in brief, show unmistakable awareness of their listeners in ways that are not open to a writer. This off-the-record discourse takes many forms that are not discourse reflexive, and situational management itself resides at the outer edges of discourse reflexivity. This section nevertheless illuminates some of the subtle but distinct effects of co-presence on monologic discourse.

7.3 Conclusion

Monologic speech viewed through the lens of discourse reflexivity shows typical characteristics of written monologues, such as pronounced egocentricity and a predominantly forward orientation, while the co-presence of an audience imbues the monologue with interactional aspects that are reminiscent of dialogues, such as jokes and joint laughter, speakers signalling that they are thinking on their feet, or references to the shared experience of the ongoing event and drawing on its contributions. Discourse reflexive language thus reflects changes in both the medium and the mode as we might expect.

Discourse reflexivity is a way of imposing order on discourse, not only by means of organising it, but also by imposing the speaker's perspective on the whole discourse (see also McKeown & Ladegaard 2020). In some sense the speaker perspective is inherent in all the choices a speaker makes, from an innumerable range of possible facts, theories, and issues that could have been mentioned but are not, not to speak of angles on their own findings. Importantly, this perspective is conveyed also through reflexive metadiscourse. We can see it clearly in speakers' comments on their own talk, which give emphasis and prominence on certain things, and evaluate matters through reflexive remarks. All this is apt to limit the hearer's interpretative freedom. There is apparently need for a balance between a strong speaker order and the listener's independent interpretation, which may explain why epistemic hedges tend to co-occur with metadiscourse (see also Mauranen 2001). Combinations of hedges with expressions of emphatic and evaluative views also reduces the risk of treading too hard on colleagues' toes while enabling the speaker to present strong, even radical points.

This chapter's analyses started from categories that reflected the medium (speech) rather than the mode (monologue), which in effect meant those that had emerged in spoken dialogues. The approach reflects the overall focus of the book and enables comparisons across modes within the medium of speech. From this point of departure, the actual analyses were sensitive to the data and led to alterations in the categorisation (Figure 7.1). The main divisions made in the dialogic mode held up, apart from the category of negotiating, which remained exclusive to dialogic discourse. The distributions of elements in the similar categories also varied in important ways, as will be seen more closely in the next chapter (Ch. 8).

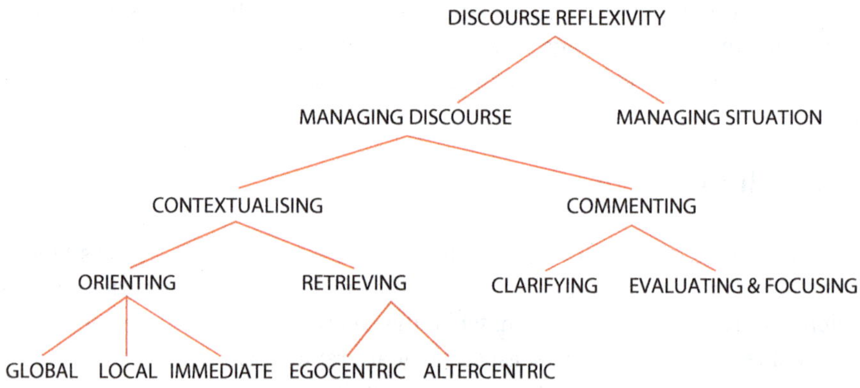

Figure 7.1: Discourse reflexivity in spoken monologue.

The figure shows that while fundamental distinctions are identical in the analyses of monologues and dialogues (Figures 4.1 and 5.1), such as those between managing discourse and managing situation, and orienting and retrieving discourse, there are also some obvious differences.

One is found at the first level of division into managing the discourse vs managing the situation. Situational management plays a clearly smaller role in monologue, and therefore gives no basis for subcategorization. Nevertheless, what situational management there is, yields its own kind of evidence to the effects of audience presence: even in practical transitions and minor problem situations speakers make remarks of an off-the-record kind, often jocular, generating joint laughter, and listeners may even participate with short verbal responses (*yes, read, better*).

The second, and more striking difference from dialogues is that the two main types of managing the discourse fall into *contextualising* and *commenting*. The contextualising kind divides further into the types familiar from dialogues, orienting and retrieving, whereas the commenting type comprises clarifications and evaluations. The latter are tasks that in dialogic interaction get collaboratively negotiated, such as evaluating and weighing arguments, findings, and methods, expressing stance, and assigning importance. That is to say, clarification and evaluation are *distributed* in dialogic interaction. In monologue, commenting is internalised in a single speaker's extended turn. Its two main kinds, on the one hand clarifying and on the other evaluating and focus, also appear in dialogues, the former also an important category of dialogic discourse (Chapter 6); clarifications are undoubtedly found in all argumentative academic discourse in some form. Commenting discourse reflexivity is about half as common as contextualising in monologic delivery but an important means of achieving intersubjectivity. It draws attention to what is significant or unique in the presentation and tends to combine with for example epistemic hedges to indicate the epistemic status of claims or suggestions.

A third noteworthy category difference from dialogues is that within orienting discourse reflexivity there is no altercentric orienting category. There simply were no orienting references to the others present. This may be a specific feature of the present data, but it is unlikely in view of Luukka's (1995) and Ädel's (2010) studies, because the examples they report would fall into 'managing the situation' in the current categorisation (where altercentric references actually do occur). Instead, speakers sought to orient hearers to their own speech at frequent intervals with egocentric reflexivity of varying spans, comprising the *global* orientation to the whole talk at the early stages and when moving towards a close, the *immediate* orientation of constant modulation of the talk, and between the global and the immediate, *local* orienting. It would seem that local orienting is the 'basic level' (cf. Rosch 1978) of an orienting span, relating the present stage to the bigger picture, putting things on hold, or omitting parts from the whole that had originally been planned.

Omissions are in many ways interesting. They can be signalled by verbalisation while flicking through slides that will not be discussed, which gives a particularly here-and-now feel to speech. Omissions and deviations from the plan reveal the effect of the transition from planning to performance, from a longer to a shorter timescale, from an imagined to a real audience.

More generally, the speaker adapts to the listeners and the passage of time, modulating their speech accordingly. Recipient design is adjusted on the fly in the light of subtle nonverbal responses from the audience. Spoken monologue is clearly interactional, and in a sense if not collaboratively produced, at least cooperatively modulated. The speaker's orienting signals reflect their assessment of the situation in the moment of speaking, whether according to plan or ad hoc, and listeners actively integrate these clues into their predictions and adjustments of their own evolving representations of the talk.

Even though there is some retrieving discourse reflexivity in extended monologues, the balance between egocentric and altercentric types contrasts with dialogues. Most retrieving reflexivity is egocentric, that is, consists of self-references (*as I said*). Egocentric references can be rhetorically effective in lending coherence to an argument and highlighting points that are as if reintroduced, even if their actual retrievability is unlikely. More importantly, they alert hearers to a forthcoming formulation of content that is constructed as significant to the argument at that moment. Listeners are likely to attend to that and adjust their expectations and representations accordingly.

Altercentric retrieving references are comparatively infrequent but not uninteresting. Above all, they respond to the situation: to the social context of co-presence and to the intellectual context where other participants are also engaged in constructing ideas even if they do not have the floor. In practical terms, altercentric references do not refer to identified addressees but to third-person participants in the ongoing macro-event and tend to arise from earlier presentations and discussions. Altercentric references seem to contribute to social cohesion in terms of shared experience in relating the present argument to what has been said in the event and acknowledging mutual relevance. They also of course help construct a speaker's intellectual convincingness. Altercentric references thus relate to co-construction of knowledge, which was identified in conference dialogues (Chapter 6), i.e., participants taking up each other's ideas and developing them. This is one of the less obvious and less discussed ways in which dialogicality is woven into spoken monologue. Compared to egocentric references, then, altercentric references would seem to orient outwards to a more 'global' situation while self-references look inwards to the speaker's own presentation, in that sense to the more 'local'. The global macro-event thus expands and is used for expanding the territories of individual presentations and their associated discussion sections in conferences (and graduate seminars), with the consequence that the discourses intermingle. Even if we only consider talk relevant to the academic topics at hand, references to self and others abound over coffee-breaks, various parallel events, and casual encounters. All this talk advances the co-construction of knowledge and generates more material and more references for later presentations.

In all, discourse reflexivity maintains its basic functions in spoken monologue but also demonstrates specific characteristics, which draw on the affordances of both written monologue and spoken dialogue. Above all, in all categories and types identified in this chapter, we have witnessed the effects of audience co-presence on monologic delivery. This is in line with Ädel's (2010) and Liu's (2021) findings, where spoken monologues show a somewhat wider range of functions than written and where speakers seem to be sensitive to audience presence.

Chapter 8
Discourse reflexivity across speech events

How much discourse reflexivity do we use in academic speech? How commonly do speakers resort to reflexive discourse, and is its incidence constant? If not, how does it vary across the kinds of academic discourse we have covered in this book? Previous chapters have explored its uses in one event type at a time in search of an in-depth understanding of its workings in different circumstances. At this point it is time to take a step back and review the main uses of reflexive discourse in numerical terms to see how its overall presence manifests itself across event types.

8.1 Incidence and distribution of discourse reflexivity in the data

The extent to which discourse reflexivity is used in speech or writing, that is, its incidence, provides us with one indication of its place in our ordinary language use. To estimate this needs to be based on databases and comparisons between them, and clearly, our estimates are more accurate if the databases are relevant and representative. The corpora used and sampled for this book were described in Chapter 3, and in this chapter we scrutinize the figures emanating from the analyses in the intervening chapters. Individual metadiscoursal expressions have been analysed and counted based on their function, irrespective of their span, that is, how many words, phrases or sentences constitute one expression. Discourse reflexivity is often expressed in multi-word units but can also be longer or shorter, and they can be discontinuous. It turned out that in this data individual expressions vary between about two words to two dozen or so. Since the measure we have for the overall amount of discourse in database is the total number of individual words in it, we in practice compare expressions of a variable span to the number of single words, but this is standard practice in corpus research. The variable expression span is typical of discourse phenomena generally, as is their discontinuity.

Clearly, the sheer amount of reflexivity in discourse is not in itself meaningful if there is nothing to compare it with, in other words, if we cannot review the incidence against some expected figure, it will not tell us very much. How much discourse reflexivity should there be, or what could be regarded as 'normal' or 'expected' in ordinary running text is not known, let alone obvious. There are innumerable corpus-based studies available on metadiscourse, but since they are

https://doi.org/10.1515/9783110295498-008

based on different models and many focus on just one or two subcategories, it is difficult to make reliable comparisons across studies. In addition, many previous studies look for and count metadiscourse 'markers', typically individual items, which is not the case in this book. I am not aware of meta-analyses in the field either. What we can do with the present data, however, is make internal comparisons. Within the range of event types we have scrutinised here it makes sense to compare them with each other, and capture the scope, and hopefully some of the parameters, of variability. A suitable general reference point for speech data would be the overall average rate of expressions per 1,000 words.

8.1.1 Rate of discourse reflexivity in spoken discourse

Starting from two pivotal event types throughout this study, conferences and graduate seminars, which comprise both dialogic and monologic discourse, the big picture reveals an even overall distribution.

Dialogues	4/1,000w
Monologues	5/1,000w
Overall rate	5/1,000w

Dialogues and monologues thus show very similar general incidences, and the slight advantage for monologues is partly caused by rounding figures to whole numbers. This suggests that the basic level of reflexive discourse stays essentially constant in academic talk, and gives us 5/1,000w as a reference level for assessing whether other figures are high or low. If we compare these figures to earlier metadiscourse research on spoken language (see, e.g., Liu 2021), the incidence here seems clearly lower. However, the comparison is not entirely meaningful, because (1) previous research has investigated only monologues and/or (2) the model has been a broader one, that is, adopted from Hyland (2005), which comprises many item categories not included here. Closer comparisons could have been made with reflexive models like Ädel (2010) if she had presented numerical material, or Cameron (2016) if he had given the figures for discourse reflexivity alone, but in his case quantitative results were related to linear unit types.

It is well known that numerical indicators at very general levels tend to hide variability at lower, more specific levels, which means that we need to dive below the flat surface to get to the undercurrents of variability. Let us first compare monologues of two kinds, presentations in conferences and graduate seminars. We find a small numerical advantage with junior presenters, but again, the difference is not large:

Conference monologues	5/1,000w
Seminar monologues	6/1,000w

However, turning to dialogues reveals more variability. While their overall rate of 4/1,000 words is not far from monologues nor from the grand average, comparing conference and seminar dialogues reveals figures that depart from the even distribution and bifurcate to both directions from the reference level.

Conference dialogues	2/1,000w
Seminar dialogues	7/1,000w

We find three and half times as much metadiscourse in graduate seminars as conferences. Before attempting an explanation, let us consider another way of comparing conferences and graduate seminars: how does the speech mode, that is, monologue vs dialogue, affect the reflexivity rates within each event type?

Overall rate in conferences	4/1,000w
Dialogues	2/1,000w
Monologues	5/1,000w

Overall rate in seminars	7/1,000w
Dialogues	7/1,000w
Monologues	6/1,000w

In the light of these figures, conference dialogues stand out from the rest. By contrast, monologues in conferences and graduate seminars are fairly similar, and both are closer to the average of 5/1,000w.

Why, then, might conference dialogues be so different? Possible explanations could lie in external constraints, discourse characteristics, and/or social parameters. The obvious *external* constraint is the duration of the discussion, which in typical conference discussions (if not all, see, Chapter 4), last only about five minutes. This is not likely to encourage long turns with characteristic internal organising. By contrast, graduate seminar discussions are distinctly longer, lasting between thirty minutes and an hour. It does not necessarily follow that turns are longer if a discussion is longer, and we have no evidence of greater average turn length in seminar discussions. Nevertheless, duration is a possible influencing factor in discussions, but it cannot be settled by this comparison alone, and we need to consider other possible determinants.

Among *discourse-related* factors, the relative external regulation vs self-organisation of the discourse could be important. Unlike most conference discussions with conventional regulation systems like scheduling and chairpersons, seminar discussions are comparatively self-regulated (Chapter 3). This renders them less predetermined and more conversation-like, where participants overlap and compete for turns, and drift to new topics. The self-organising character may also lie behind the proportions of situation management: it is marginal in conference discussions, only 4% of reflexive metadiscourse, whereas in seminar discussions it is 23%, nearly six times higher. The structuring of a dialogue would thus seem to affect the use of discourse reflexivity, and presumably the need for it. If dialogue structure is predetermined, there is not much scope for negotiation, but in less predictable situations, more is left to participants. Self-regulation and unpredictability were associated with longer discussions (Chapter 4), which means that under those circumstances we should expect to find more discourse reflexivity, which is in line with the figures.

A *social* factor that may come in is social symmetry. In conferences, participants are essentially on an equal footing, and alternate in the roles of presenters, listeners, and commenters during the macro event. In addition to short duration and predictable structuring, this symmetry may also reduce spending the available time on framing questions or answers. In graduate seminars, the social roles are more complex: what we might call low *horizontal distance* (i.e. high degree of acquaintedness) characterises seminars, and among students, the status relations are also equal and symmetrical, indicating low *vertical social distance*, but there is an inbuilt asymmetry that typifies educational institutions even in highly egalitarian contexts. The responsible seminar leader is an academic, a specialist in the field, who instructs the students, supports their socialisation, and above all assesses their performance. Assessment maintains an asymmetry (vertical social distance) between students and academic staff perhaps even more than the difference in expertise. The shared goal of promoting learning and the joint construction of knowledge and understanding that take place in graduate seminars mitigate the asymmetry but do not erase it. Social asymmetry may invite participants to explicate their positions and the relevance of their turns more, and thus contribute to a higher incidence of discourse reflexivity.

It may be a good idea at this point to compare seminars and conferences to the third type of spoken dialogue in the data, namely doctoral defences. Their average rate of discourse reflexivity is notably higher than in either of the other event types, five times higher than in conferences and nearly a third higher than in seminars:

Thesis defences 10/1,000w

Doctoral defences in the Finnish system are public events that last between an hour and a half to two hours. The parties are normally not previously well acquainted with each other, if at all. Defences are socially asymmetric high-stake events, where one of the active participants assesses the other's work and performance. They are thus characterised by simultaneous high horizontal and vertical social distance. The general discussion frame derives from institutionally determined roles with the initiative allocated to examiner(s) for critical questions and comments about the thesis. However, the examinee's answers modulate the examiner's further questions, so that the event does not exclusively follow the examiner's pre-planned agenda. Within the general framework, then, examiners and candidates can to a certain extent organise the talk between themselves. The candidate can also initiate comments, explanations, additions, and the like. Clarification requests are frequently made by both parties. When there are two examiners, they negotiate their turn-taking and update their moment-to-moment division of labour as the disputation proceeds. All this takes place in front of a heterogeneous audience, comprising not only academics and fellow PhD students, but also lay people like the candidate's friends and family. The audience is meant to be able to follow the discussion. There are thus several sources of uncertainty about the expectations and previous knowledge of the active participants as well as the audience, which would seem conducive to explicitness of many kinds, including reflexive discourse.

We can now extend our comparison to the three kinds of dialogue and use the same parameters as above: discourse characteristics, social parameters, and external constraints. The discourse-related characteristic discussed above is the degree of (self-)regulation. Regulation does not vary in line with the incidence of discourse reflexivity: graduate seminars are highest in self-regulation, but in the middle ground in respect of incidence. Of social parameters, the degree of formality or acquaintedness does not show a linear relationship with reflexivity incidence either, because graduate seminar discussions are the least formal of the three and the participants best acquainted, yet the prevalence of reflexivity is neither the highest nor the lowest. Instead, what seems to be involved is status symmetry and how high the stakes are. Asymmetric status relations, or high vertical social distance and high stakes associate with more discourse reflexivity: settings where one participant is responsible for evaluating the other's performance seem to generate more reflexive discourse. Such situations are beset with social uncertainty, which is in line with observations in earlier chapters.

Finally, the external parameter, the sheer duration of the discussion, which has also come up in previous chapters, also promotes higher metadiscourse incidence: longer discussions seem to use proportionally more discourse reflexivity. In brief, then, longer discussions with more social distance and high stakes are more likely to give rise to reflexive discourse.

8.1.2 Rate of discourse reflexivity in written dialogue

Against the observations in the previous section, it is interesting to add a medium effect to the comparison to the mix. Does the picture change if we shift our attention to written dialogues? How far can we expect the medium to affect the overall amount of discourse reflexivity, and if so, to which direction? Previous research from blog discourses suggests a general propensity to greater explicitness, but none of the studies has used comparable, that is, research-oriented, data. Our dialogues from research blog discussion threads can again be depicted along external, discoursal, and social parameters. Blog threads depart from speech not only in that they are tapped in by keyboard rather than vocalised, but also in that they are asynchronous, socially distant horizontally but not vertically, and chiefly anonymous. Any of these factors can have a bearing on discourse reflexivity. External constraints allow more time to plan and execute responses, presumed audience heterogeneity may induce greater attempts at clarity, and in social terms anonymity may mean more affordances (self-disclosure) as well as constraints (not knowing who your interlocutors are).

Response planning time alters external conditions. More time could imply an increase in reflexive discourse, based on our dialogue-monologue comparisons. Even though monologues in our data are spoken, they are pre-planned, and this rendered a clearly higher overall metadiscourse prevalence compared to spoken dialogues. The difference was particularly strong (nearly 50%) in discourse management. In addition to planning time afforded by writing, asynchrony means that responses to an earlier post can be made minutes after the original posting, or take days or weeks, while intervening postings may have come in. Commenters may wish to ensure that their post is read in the right discourse connection, which could occasion a rise in the incidence of discourse reflexivity – thus also perceived explicitness. Anonymity implies that horizontal social proximity, that is, acquaintedness, is lower than in any of the spoken event types, but its contribution to the incidence remains hard to predict from spoken dialogue, where no clear connection was found.

As it turns out, the overall rate of discourse reflexivity is higher in blog discussion threads than in any of the spoken, co-present discourses:

Blog discussions 12/1,000w

It would seem, then, that asynchrony may be another external contributing factor. It is also possible that in line with spoken dialogues, the sheer length of the discussion contributes to the rate of occurrence, because these blog threads are among the longest in the corpus. Although long discussions are not characteristic of blog threads as a rule, quite the contrary, in the present data they are.

Blogs could in principle help shed light on one social factor that remained indeterminate in the speech events, namely horizontal social proximity between participants. Blog thread discussants are rarely acquainted off-line. In the big picture, then, those event types with the highest horizontal distance (defences and blogs) also show the highest rates of reflexive discourse, whereas those with more proximity (conferences and seminars) have less discourse reflexivity. However, metadiscourse incidence is clearly higher in seminars than conferences, implying that horizontal social proximity alone does not explain the degree of discourse reflexivity. The biggest vertical distance, that is, social asymmetry, is found in defences and seminars, which implies that no single social parameter among those considered explains the incidence of discourse reflexivity in both speech events and blog discussions on its own.

In all, dialogic discourses in our data suggest that longer duration of discussion predicts higher incidence of discourse reflexivity, and that greater social distance, whether horizontal or vertical, between participants may also have some effect. A specific feature of spoken dialogues is that social asymmetry and high stakes predict a high incidence, while for written dialogue, asynchrony and planning time may be contributing factors.

8.2 Comparing dialogic and monologic speech events

As we saw in section 8.1.1, dialogic and monologic discourses have different patterns of discourse reflexivity: while monologues indicate a comparatively constant proportion of metadiscourse across speech event types, dialogues show considerable variation. Beyond the general levels of prevalence, we have also seen in the previous chapters how preferences vary for types of reflexive discourse in dialogues and monologues, but not yet how the varying usages and preferences show in numbers. In this overview, we can now compare the two modes in the light of the main categories from earlier chapters. It is useful to bear in mind that the present comparisons draw on conference and seminar data, which cover both dialogues and monologues, but excludes thesis defences, from which only dialogues were analysed. This delimitation is made in the interests of comparability between dialogues and monologues. The qualitative analyses in Chapter 6 were excluded because the instances were not counted.

All conference discourses from the ELFA corpus were included in the data, while the seminar events were based on a sample (Chapter 3). Therefore, in terms of total word numbers, conference and graduate seminar data are fairly evenly balanced, dialogues only slightly outnumbering monologues (Table 8.1, bottom column). Within the event types the distributions are less alike. Conference discourses have a higher total number of words, and a clear bias towards monologues, while the reverse is the case with seminars. There were more presentations than discussions in conferences, but since the presentations were mostly short (up to 20 minutes) and a few discussion sections followed a sequence of several presentations, the total number of words in monologues was only about a quarter higher than in discussions. The graduate seminar sample had an even number of dialogic and monologic events (with one exception), but the dialogues were much longer, and altogether had twice the number of words seen in monologues.

Table 8.1: Dialogic and monologic events.

	Dialogues	Monologues	Total
Conferences	74,057	94,360	168,417
Seminars	51,873	24,901	76,774
Total	125,930	119,261	245,191

Numbers of words in conference and graduate seminar events. Conference presentations N=34, conference discussion sections N=14; seminar presentations N=10, seminar discussions N=9.

An initial division of discourse reflexivity into managing the discourse vs. managing the situation was made for all event types throughout the analyses in the previous chapters. Discourse management was by far the larger type, covering nearly four fifths (77.0%) of reflexive dialogic discourse and almost all of it (96.4%) in monologues (Table 8.2). The figures need to be taken with some caution, because in monologic situations the division of labour between chairpersons and presenters is clear, and the chairpersons' introductions of speakers were not always included in the transcripts or the recordings. In dialogues, chairpersons took a more active role, often participating in the discussion in addition to managing it. Moreover, since the dialogic events are in effect polyadic, i.e., have several participants, managing the situation demands a fair amount of work from the chair, in addition to which participants also take to self-organising the situation in longer discussions. Monologues by contrast are less negotiable: with speaking slots pre-allocated to one speaker at a time, management turns get performed routinely and essentially only by chairpersons without much need for discourse reflexivity (Chapter 7). There would not seem to be much reason to try to break down the uses of situation management in the two modes for comparison beyond these general observations.

Within discourse management, the situation was quite the reverse, revealing several important differences. The analyses and categorisation were initially built

Table 8.2: Spoken discourse: Managing the discourse and the situation.

	Dialogues		Monologues		Total	
	N	%	N	%	N	%
Discourse management	399	77.0	595	96.4	994	87.6
Situation management	119	23.0	22	3.6	141	12.4
Total	518	100	617	100	1,135	100

Distributions of discourse management and situation management in academic conferences and graduate seminars.

from the bottom up based on what emerged from spoken dialogic discourse (Chapter 4), and monologue analyses followed these to the extent that the data permitted, which meant that some of the even relatively major categories were revised (Chapter 7).

To briefly recapitulate the major distinctions within discourse management, they were drawn somewhat differently in dialogues and monologues: in dialogues the umbrella categories were contextualising and negotiating, of which the latter was analysed only in qualitative terms, thus had to be excluded from this comparison. In the contextualising category, orienting and retrieving kinds were distinguished, which applied to written dialogues as well. In monologues, by contrast, contextualising and commenting were the two top-level categories. In both, contextualising divided into orienting and retrieving types, but some variation was found in their manifestations which motivated new subtypes in monologues. The monologue-specific category of commenting comprised clarifications, evaluation, and expressions of focus, all of which were discernible in dialogues, but more conspicuous in monologues. Largely the same basic uses were thus found in dialogues and monologues, but their salience varied importantly. In addition, what was typically achieved in interaction in distributed fashion in dialogues was performed in single extended turns by one speaker in monologues. It should therefore not be surprising that the same elements varied so noticeably in prominence in these two different modes. The modes represent different conditions of speaking.

Table 8.3 shows these types in numbers. Clearly, discourse management of a contextualising kind, consisting of orienting and retrieving types, constitutes the core function of discourse reflexivity: it covers all dialogic instances and over two thirds in monologues. Incidentally, contextualising discourse reflexivity is also a close match in monologues and dialogues in raw numbers (401 and 399, respectively).

On a closer look, however, Table 8.3 reveals a striking contrast between dialogues and monologues: dialogues show a heavy bias towards retrieving (approximately 60%), whereas monologues are even more biased towards orienting (over

Table 8.3: Spoken discourse: Discourse Management.

Dialogues			Monologues		
	N	%		N	%
Contextualising			Contextualising	401	67.4
Orienting	156	39.1	Orienting	286	71.3
Retrieving	243	60.1	Retrieving	115	28.7
			Commenting	194	32.6
Total	399	100	Total	595	100

Discourse management in dialogue and monologue: Contextualising divides into orienting and retrieving discourse reflexivity in both dialogic and monologic modes, but monologues have an additional category of commenting.

70%). The forward-looking, orienting type that characterises spoken monologues is familiar from research into written monologues and has strongly coloured our notions of what metadiscourse does in discourse.

At first glance, it might seem as if dialogic speech, with its predominantly retrieving orientation, is retrospective, that is, backward-looking, instead of prospective. However, retrospective reflexivity does not work in speech the same way it would in written text, because working memory capacity cannot hold even brief verbatim stretches of previous discourse beyond 10–15 seconds. Therefore, retrospective reflexivity cannot evoke a verbatim memory of speech, let alone allow hearers to return to a past point of discourse. Instead, it offers a representation of some verbalised sequence in the past, and this representation then triggers expectations in listeners of what might come next, thereby preparing ground for what the current speaker is about to say. Retrieving discourse reflexivity thus raises expectations in listeners of the next stage of the discourse just like orienting reflexivity does but uses affordances of real-time speech that seem to be specifically apt for the dialogic mode: representing past verbalisation to prospect ahead.

We can break down the retrieving category further in terms of who the referent is, into egocentric and altercentric discourse reflexivity (Table 8.4). Here we again find a distribution which suggests a major difference, this time even more pronounced than that between orienting and retrieving discourse: in dialogues three quarters (74.5%) of retrieving instances are altercentric, whereas in monologues the figures are the reverse (73.9% egocentric).

The figures suggest a strong orientation to others in discussions and to self in presentations. It is only to be expected that we find few altercentric references in monologue, where the floor is handed to a single speaker. There are no in terlocutors whose turns to refer to. In view of this, it may not come as a great surprise that among the retrieving references found in monologues, the vast majority are

Table 8.4: Spoken discourse: Retrieving discourse reflexivity.

	Egocentric		Altercentric		Total	
	N	%	N	%	N	%
Dialogue	62	25.5	181	74.5	243	100
Monologue	85	73.9	30	26.1	115	100
Total	147	41.1	211	58.9	358	100

Retrieving discourse reflexivity in discussions and presentations in academic conferences and graduate seminars.

egocentric, that is, references to what speakers themselves said a few moments ago. While monologic speech altogether makes distinctly fewer retrieving references than dialogic speech, the references are also of a different kind, underscoring the impression that it is markedly characteristic of dialogues to orient to collaborative construction of discourse between participants.

Who do speakers refer to when they are not talking about themselves? The principal altercentric referent types can be broken down into second and third-person referents, that is, addressees and third parties. In dialogues, speakers make altercentric references most often (over 70% of cases) to specific interlocutors who are addressed by a second person pronoun, a proper name, or some other identification, whereas in monologues no instances of second-person addressees are found that would occur in a discourse reflexive co-text (Table 8.5). Since this finding diverges from that in some other studies, it may be attributable to different event types and speech situations, or even analytical models. We find studies based on the broad metadiscourse model report second-person pronoun mentions in for example 3-minute thesis presentations (Liu 2021). In our data, then, third-party category accounts for less than 30% of dialogic references, but all monologic references.

Within the third-party category, a further division can be made according to identification ("attributed" vs. "unattributed" identification). Here dialogues and monologues differ again: in dialogues, third parties get mentioned but remain unidentified more often than not (Table 8.5). Presenters of monologues make no second-person references, but they do refer to what other speakers in the same speech event have said. Such others tend to be identified by name or by using identifiers like *the previous speaker*.

Briefly, then, altercentric references abound in dialogues as speakers address each other, engaging in co-constructing meaning and knowledge. However, they refer to third parties distinctly less often, and when they do, they do not attribute the references to identified persons. By contrast, monologue presenters refer to

Table 8.5: Spoken discourse: Retrieving altercentric references.

		Dialogues		Monologues		Total	
		N	%	N	%	N	%
Addressee		129	71.3	–	–	129	60.2
Third party		52	28.7	30	100	86	39.8
	Attributed	22	12.2	22	73.3	44	20.4
	Unattributed	30	16.6	8	26.7	38	19.4
Total		181	100	30	100	215	100

Retrieving altercentric discourse reflexivity in discussions and presentations in academic conferences and graduate seminars.

themselves overwhelmingly more than to anyone else present, but when they refer to others, they mostly identify them.

Despite the sharp differences transpiring from this section, there are also clear affinities between dialogues and monologues. Egocentric references are a case in point. Orienting egocentric references prospect ahead irrespective of speech mode. They frame a speaker's turn in dialogues and anticipate the next phase in monologues. Retrieving egocentric references, in turn, bestow present relevance to an earlier phase in the discourse and prospect a reformulation of that state. Rhetorically the latter share at least one role in dialogues and monologues: imparting a sense of the speaker's self-consistency.

8.3 Discourse reflexivity in spoken and written dialogue

Apart from speech mode, the effect of medium has been considered at various points in this book, including the present chapter in connection with the overall incidence of discourse reflexivity (Section 8.1.2). There is even less research on written dialogue than spoken in metadiscourse research, with the exceptions of Cameron (2016) and Biri (2021). To gain a more detailed view of what effect the medium may have in the light of numerical data, let us move on to comparing medium effects while keeping mode constant. At the outset, the distributions of managing the discourse are compared to managing the situation, as was done with spoken dialogues and monologues.

As Table 8.6 shows, the distributions are virtually identical. It was already noted in the previous section that longer spoken dialogues tend to exercise considerable freedom to self-organise, and this is equally true of blog threads. They tend to be spontaneous, being completely open sites with no institutional or organisational frame to bind them to protocols or externally originated conventions. Neither is

Table 8.6: Spoken and Written Dialogue: Managing the discourse and the situation.

	Speech		**Writing**		**Total**	
	N	**%**	**N**	**%**	**N**	**%**
Discourse management	399	77.0	312	77.4	711	77.2
Situation management	119	23.0	91	22.6	210	22.8
Total	518	100	403	100	921	100

Distributions of discourse management and situation management in two kinds of dialogues: spoken discussions and blog threads.

there any predetermined principle of organising the discourse. Conventions emerge from usage in any given blog site, and even in any particular discussion, but apparently in a self-organising manner. Moderators can remove postings that are off-topic, offensive, or otherwise unsuitable, but they do not assume chairperson roles like allocating or ordering turns.

Continuing through the same steps as in comparisons between dialogues and monologues, the focus from now on will be on discourse management and settle next on the proportions of orienting and retrieving reflexivity (Table 8.7).

Table 8.7: Spoken and Written Dialogue: Orienting and Retrieving discourse reflexivity.

Discourse Management	**Spoken**		**Written**		**Total**	
	N	**%**	**N**	**%**	**N**	**%**
Orienting	156	39.1	128	41.0	284	39.9
Retrieving	243	60.1	184	59.0	427	60.0
Total	399	100	312	100	711	100

Orienting and retrieving discourse reflexivity in spoken and written dialogic discourses.

Digital dialogues again essentially replicate the distribution of spoken dialogues: roughly 60% is retrieving, 40% orienting. A comparable dominance of retrospection in reflexive discourse in online message boards was found by Cameron (2016).

The next comparison in the previous section concerned egocentricity vs. altercentricity in retrieving references. Again, the cross-medium distributions are almost identical (Table 8.8). These figures would seem to suggest that dialogue is dialogue, and medium does not have much effect.

Again, zooming in on the larger category, we break down retrieving altercentric reflexivity into second- and third person addressing. Here the two media

Table 8.8: Spoken and Written Dialogue: Retrieving discourse reflexivity.

	Egocentric		Altercentric		Total	
	N	%	N	%	N	%
Spoken	62	25.5	181	74.5	243	100
Written	50	27.2	134	72.8	184	100
Total	112		315		427	

Egocentric and altercentric discourse reflexivity in dialogues: spoken and written.

bifurcate (Table 8.9). Spoken interaction orients to individuals present, with a clear preference for identifiable addressees as we saw in the previous section (approximately 70% vs. 30%). By contrast, online interactions orient to the 'third', that is, individuals identified by third person references, also with a clear majority (roughly 60% vs. 40%).

Table 8.9: Spoken and Written Dialogue: Retrieving altercentric references.

		Spoken		Written		Total	
		N	%	N	%	N	%
Addressee		129	71.3	57	42.5	186	59.0
Third party		52	28.7	77	57.5	129	40.1
	Attributed	22	12.2	6	7.8	28	8.9
	Unattributed	30	16.6	71	92.2	101	32.1
Total		181	100	134	100	315	100

Retrieving altercentric discourse reflexivity in dialogues: addressee vs. third party references in spoken and written dialogic discourses.

In favouring third-person references, written dialogues would seem to follow more in the tracks of monologues (Table 8.5). However, unlike spoken monologues, blog dialogues do not usually attribute references to an identified person (Table 8.9). Rather, references are typically made to postings (*Even in the first sentence, it mentions . . .*). In the synchronous time frame of co-present interactions, addressees are easy to identify, if only by gestures or gaze, whereas in asynchronous circumstances it is a posting that needs to be identified to render the comment relevant.

Virtually all unattributed blog post references (68 out of the total 71) are evaluative (*interesting stuff, this.*). The evaluations tend to be polarised, many negative, even dismissive (*It is just a complete nonsense*), while in spoken dialogues negative comments tend to be subdued and indirect (Chapter 4). Open hostility and hate speech in digital communication, especially social media are generally recognised phenomena, which seem to be echoed in a milder form in blog commentary, in a similar way to online message boards (see Cameron 2016). This would suggest an effect of not the medium (i.e. writing) any longer, but the communication channel, that is, digital means of communication, specifically the Internet. The most hostile comments are quite possibly absent from the present data because blog threads are moderated.

We did not compare distributions of situation management across modes in Section 8.2, because their incidence in monologues was negligible (Table 8.2). In all dialogues, though, there is a fair number of discourse reflexive expressions that manage the situation, and since they account for over a fifth of discourse reflexivity in all dialogues (Table 8.6), they are worth a brief look.

The overall incidence in the spoken and written medium looks constant, but if we separate conference and seminar dialogues from each other, and add blogs to the comparison, variability becomes evident (Table 8.10).

Table 8.10: Dialogic discourse: Managing the situation in speech and writing.

	Conferences		Seminars		Blogs		Total	
	N	%	N	%	N	%	N	%
Chair	17	56.7	78	87.6	–	–	95	45.2
Plane-shift	13	43.3	11	12.4	37	40.7	61	29.0
Other	–	–	–	–	54	59.3	54	25.7
Total	30	100	89	100	91	100	210	99.9

Distributions of discourse management and situation management in academic discussions and research blog comment threads

The categories in spoken and written dialogues do not fully match, because blog threads are not chaired. Instead, for blogs it seemed worth separating those expressions that managed the situation by seeking to change the direction or the topic of the discussion from those that were more technical, or miscellaneous other kinds, such as thanking others for their advice or help, which were not assigned to separate categories in spoken discourses. The central axis of comparison thus revolves around plane-shifts, which switch the focus from the issues being discussed to what the discussion is or should be about. They occur in conferences (*I think here we are discussing a missing link*), seminars (*why get bogged down with a word, move on to the competence*), and blogs (*We could talk about the WPI and its' 'failings' in my eyes, but this was and should be about Lombardi*). For spoken dialogues it needs to be noted that although chairpersons frequently make moves similar in effect to plane-shifts, this is part of their assignment, and therefore the plane-shift category was reserved to those made 'from the floor', that is, by participants other than the chair. What we see in the table is that the proportion of plane-shifts is at the same level (about 40%) in conference and blog discussions, but accounts for little more than a tenth of seminar discussions.

The dip in the plane-shifts in seminar discussions points to the social parameter of symmetry. Vertical social distance in an educational context is low in specific respects, as already discussed in Section 8.1.1. However, for discourse management, high social asymmetry was associated with a high rate of discourse reflexivity, whereas for situation management it is linked to a low rate. This suggests that in contexts of high vertical distance, dialogue participants actively relate their turns to each other's speech but are not very likely to participate in structuring the outer constraints of the situation, such as openings or closings, allocating turns, or suggesting the discussion should take a certain direction. These acts are performed by only those in a particular position to do so. As transpires from Table 8.10, it is indeed the chairperson who dominates the situation management in seminar discussions (nearly 90% of the instances), whereas under the greater social symmetry that prevails in conference discussions, the chair's share is distinctly smaller (less than 60%).

In all, spoken and written dialogues are very similar to each other, and compared to those between spoken dialogues and monologues their differences are minor. Medium differences reveal themselves clearly only in altercentric references to either co-present interlocutors or to third parties, which in the written medium are in effect made mostly to postings, not persons. There is nevertheless an apparent channel difference that relates to discourse conventions: blog discussions generally show more, much stronger, and more polarised evaluation than co-present discussions. It is also interesting to note that comparing types of situation management brought up a feature of social asymmetry in spoken dialogues which passed unnoticed before this comparison, which strengthened the observation that social asymmetry remains strong in educational settings. This is manifests itself in the difference in plane-shifts between seminar discussions on the one hand and blog and conference discussions on the other. It also suggests that reflexivity which manages situation may be worth more attention, and should be carefully included in recordings, too.

8.4 Conclusion

This chapter has gauged numerical evidence of the prevalence of reflexive discourse in different academic event types to obtain an idea of its place in our ordinary language use. The interest value of numerical considerations lies on the one hand in getting a broad idea of how often we generally use reflexive discourse, and on the other how much its use varies across event types. Considering figures permits insights into factors that might account for similarities and differences among event types. It was discovered that the average rate of expressions per 1,000 words in spoken discourses is 5, which was used as a general reference point against which to view its variability. However, averages can hide more than they reveal. The variability underlying this average is high, from 2/1,000w in conference dialogues to 10/1,000w in doctoral defences but 12/1,000w in blog discussion threads, which means that the incidence of discourse reflexivity is by no means constant in spoken academic discourses, nor is there one rate that would apply even to all dialogues irrespective of medium. It would be interesting to compare this with the research there is in spoken metadiscourses even if that would have to be limited to monologues, but most other counts use models widely different from the present one, usually Hyland's (2005) or a modification of it. This tends to yield far higher overall rates because it includes categories like hedges and boosters, mostly of kinds he calls 'interactional' that do not fulfil our criteria. An exception is Ädel (2010), whose model, though slightly different, is also reflexive, but she presents no figures. Smart (2016) also uses a discourse reflexive model for digital dialogues. He draws on a good deal of quantitative data, but with different statistics and in relation to linear units rather than for comparing discourse reflexive elements with each other, which renders even his figures incompatible.

To get a handle on what factors might contribute to the variation in our data we tentatively looked at external constraints, discourse characteristics, and social parameters. The duration of a discussion is a temporal constraint of an *external* kind, which affects dialogues so that longer discussions tend to have not only more reflexive discourse as a whole, but also a higher proportion of it than shorter ones. The brevity of most conference discussions would thus seem to lie behind their exceptionally low rate (2/1,000w) of discourse reflexivity.

Temporal constraints include not only duration but others, like asynchrony, which of course typifies written discourse. The asynchrony of blog discussion threads can probably account for a good share of their very frequent use of reflexive discourse (12/1,000w was the highest rate among all event types). The consequent temporal interleaving of different blog threads would seem to motivate frequent identifying references to the postings that have triggered the comments, which may not immediately follow their targets in the chain. In blog threads, participants mostly make retrieving references to third parties, particularly to inanimate parties, that is, texts, whereas spoken dialogues mostly refer to co-present interlocutors. This would seem to reflect time synchrony along with the social setting.

Referent identification need not be discourse reflexive, but it often is, in addition to which reflexivity is also one way of enhancing clarity. Clarity, or enhanced explicitness, has been found to be characteristic of blogsite discourse (Bolander 2012; Chapter 5). This might point to a channel effect, i.e., one that derives from general characteristics of Internet discourses. Channel is probably at stake also in the polarised discourse of blog discussions. Nearly all unattributed references to a previous post are evaluative and often polarised.

Among *discourse-related* factors, the most striking differences relate to mode, that is, dialogic vs. monologic speech. A fundamental distinction was made at the outset between managing the discourse and managing the situation. Managing the discourse is easily the larger category in all event types, and in monologues it accounts for virtually all (over 96%) discourse reflexivity. This means that discourses of managing the situation take place almost exclusively in dialogic discourses. While it is not difficult to see why this should be the case, the presenter of a monologue having a speech slot allocated to them with no legitimate competition, it is an important difference in appreciating the whole range of functions that reflexive discourse can perform. Moreover, it shows that managing the situation is part of dialogic interaction: we relate to the actual terms of the interaction when talking about the discourse, not only to the discourse itself.

A significant mode difference is found in the principal categories of discourse management. Dialogues are strongly biased towards retrieving discourse reflexivity, that is, bringing topics from the preceding discourse to the present moment, while monologues have an even stronger propensity to favour orienting discourse reflexivity i.e., to talk about what is coming. When monologues do make retrieving references, they are nearly always egocentric. By contrast, there is an even more pronounced tendency for dialogues to make altercentric references, usually to co-present interlocutors. Retrieving references manifest similar functions in both, but what is worth retrieving from the preceding discourse is different: for a sole presenter, it can only be their own talk.

Despite considerable differences, numbers also reveal commonalities between dialogues and monologues, which likewise are important, because they point to what might be regarded as core properties of discourse reflexivity. The principal similarity is manifest at the highest level of discourse management: the orienting and retrieving kinds, subsumed under the umbrella of 'contextualising', constitute the main categories in both modes. In other words, we find the same basic functions of orienting and retrieving, which epitomise the concept of talking about the ongoing discourse, irrespective of the mode. At more specific levels, we find commonalities and disparities in various uses, for example in egocentric references, but with more variability than at the top level.

Within dialogues we find fewer and less radical differences than across modes. The effect of the medium, speech vs writing, is slight compared to the mode effect, and the distributions among the major categories are virtually identical on discourse management. It is only within the category of retrieving that the medium leads to a fork. As already noted above, spoken dialogues mostly refer to co-present interlocutors, whereas written dialogues tend to refer to inanimate third parties, that is, texts. Here external constraints of the medium, especially time-related, would seem to play a role. Most likely the digital channel also affects the tendency to use more polarised evaluative language.

Where we see clear medium-independent differences among dialogues is in the degree of relative external regulation vs. self-regulation of the discourse. Longer discussions tend to be more self-regulated. All digital dialogues in this data are long. Whether shorter digital dialogues are more like short spoken discussions was not investigated but would be a possibility in future research. It would nevertheless seem that external constraints altogether trigger different discourse practices. Although this is not surprising in general terms, but rather usually assumed in functional and sociolinguistic models of language, it would seem to offer plenty of scope for further investigation with regard to reflexive discourse in spoken dialogues.

Primarily *social* parameters seem to be involved in managing the situation, which is virtually exclusive to dialogues. The medium does not play a role at the general level, because conference and blog discussions show approximately the same degree of reflexive situation management, whereas seminars have considerably less than either. What is distinctive about seminar discussions is that they are also socially less symmetric than the other two. As was observed earlier, it is endemic in an educational setting that one of the parties evaluates the other, which inevitably generates disparity in social positions. The third type of spoken dialogue, the doctoral defence, is also highly asymmetric, and like seminars has a high overall rate of discourse reflexivity. Unfortunately, numerical comparisons of different reflexivity types were not made for thesis defences to avoid double counting (cf. Chapter 3). It would make an interesting comparison for further research, because in graduate seminars the chairperson is also the evaluator, in doctoral defences the chair and the evaluator are separate, and blog discussions have neither a chair nor an evaluator, so that spontaneous self-regulation as well as evaluation are distributed among participants.

Like situation management, discourse management in dialogic events also revealed some differences relating to social parameters: more senior academics (that is, those participating in conferences) make three times more altercentric references than participants in graduate seminars. Orienting altercentric references are mostly made in connection with questions, and it would seem that the more professionally academic the context, the more speakers frame their questions in explicit reference to their addressee's talk, specifying what in it they wanted to question, compliment, or comment on.

In spoken dialogues, longer duration of a discussion, high stakes, and social asymmetry between participants associated with more discourse reflexivity. Thus, settings where one participant is responsible for evaluating the other's performance seems to generate more reflexive discourse. Such situations are beset with social uncertainty, which is in line with some observations in earlier chapters. For written dialogue, asynchrony and planning time may be contributing factors since social asymmetry is not relevant.

This brief numerical overview has brought to light several interesting things that do not always reveal themselves clearly in purely qualitative analysis. Where numerical evidence of the distribution of the analytical categories has not been presented for reasons already explained like for thesis defences, it feels like the next step would require including numbers. Most importantly, we find that there is considerable variability in the extent to which spoken discourses resort to discourse reflexivity and that the more we get into detail, the more we find new distinctions, if also unsuspected commonalities. The situational and contextual parameters that have been considered at this stage already suggest what may lie behind the variation, but clearly deserve more research. Amidst all this intriguing variability one dividing line stands firm: the major division between dialogue and monologue. This is important for understanding discourse reflexivity from a perspective that has been virtually neglected in previous research and shows how much more there is to explore. Methodologically, this discovery presents a justification for an exploratory study that adopts what Ädel (2010) calls a 'splitting' approach, but ultimately it is possible, and to be hoped, that this results in amended 'lumping' models.

Chapter 9
Conclusion

In this book I have conceptualised discourse reflexivity, discourse about the ongoing discourse, as an integral part of the discourse that is being co-created by interacting parties. It is a pivotal means of updating and coordinating interacting parties' interpretations of the current state of the discourse and predictions concerning the next state.

To say that dialogic metadiscourse is interactional is perhaps not the best way of putting it, because in effect discourse *is* interaction, and so is metadiscourse as part of it. This is unquestionably so with spoken discourse, which is co-present and embodied.

As humans we are inescapably attuned to other humans, especially human speech. Interaction is a hub of activity for language processing and throws light on how reflexive discourse is likely to be involved in cognition. Perhaps the most relevant concept in this connection is prediction. Contemporary neurocognitive science posits that the brain is an active predictor and generates its own models, which it tests against external stimuli, rather than merely a reactive system that responds to external stimuli as it was previously conceived. Therefore, the notion of the active hearer (Chapter 7) is as important as the active reader (Chapter 2). From this viewpoint, the central contribution of reflexive discourse is in providing a resource for interactants to coordinate and align their representations of the evolving discourse, make prospections and predictions of where it is going, and update predictions in the light of confirming or contradicting evidence. Of course, reflexive discourse is by no means the only facet of language that enables speakers to predict. Quite the contrary, it is likely that we draw on a wide variety of cues and their combinations to construct our situation models via language. Yet it is also clear that reflexive discourse is one of the prominent though less investigated resources that human language possesses for speaker alignment, increasing predictability, and reducing uncertainty in communication.

We have talked about prediction in this book, but equally often we have used the term *prospection*. This suits a discourse analytical context better because prospection is what we can recognise in language, while prediction in neurocognitive research refers to many processes that are inaccessible to linguistic analysis. The timescales of the processes are also different; although speech is fast, it operates on variable timescales from hundreds of milliseconds to seconds, whereas neuronal activity typically operates on a millisecond scale. Speech is rapid and fleeting, but within limits it can make use of variable timescales for prospection, which are likely to affect perceptual processes. Prospection is not only detectable in language, it also falls into the speaker's domain, and as the primary concern in this book has

https://doi.org/10.1515/9783110295498-009

been to discover metadiscourse in interaction, it is important to appreciate the changing speaker-hearer perspectives of interacting parties. In the alternating capacities, both prospection and prediction are needed.

The data analysed are mostly spoken, supplemented by written dialogues. They all relate to academia, which can be seen as a limitation, but has its motivation in a research field which has taken academia into its focus from the start: the current findings can be related to what we already know about metadiscourse, and above all, show how much there is we did - and do - not yet know.

9.1 What have we learned from dialogic data?

The principal insight from this research is the fundamental difference between dialogue and monologue. It was strong enough even to override the difference between speaking and writing, which, as is well known in linguistics, is a crucial divide (e.g. Linell 2001). Even though we only talk about reflexive discourse here, not all language use, it is still noteworthy how essential the dialogue-monologue divide is.

In this section the focus is on *discourse-related* factors. Investigating dialogues reveals the vital importance of reflexive metadiscourse to human interaction, and to the interface of social interaction and cognition. It supports participants' making sense of fast-flowing discourse and coping with the contingencies of dialogue. Co-present interacting speakers use metadiscourse to facilitate coordinating, aligning, and updating their situation models. Reflexive discourse in dialogues is mainly altercentric, oriented to other speakers. It is also predominantly retrieving, mostly referring to what has already been said and fitting the current speaker's turn into this context as a kind of springboard to what they will be saying next. Thus, discourse reflexivity in dialogic interaction indicates the relevance of the speaker's contribution to the dialogue up to the moment of speaking, simultaneously prospecting ahead. Putting it very briefly we could say that the prototypical use of discourse reflexivity in dialogic interaction is talking about what an interlocutor has said and how the speaker takes things forward from there.

Retrospective and prospective orientations are both vital interactional resources, retrospection orienting primarily to the addressee and prospection to the speaker. Both can be seen in terms of recipient design and reduction of uncertainty in interaction, but analyses in this book point to a further function: we can see them as indicating co-construction of new knowledge and understanding. Altercentric retrospection manifests in retrieving reflexive references and performs either or both of two tasks: *construal*, the current speaker's interpretation of what the addressee had said, and *springboard*, the current speaker's contextualisation of their own contribution in the previous speech before taking it forward. It is the springboard function that is particularly intriguing in the joint construction of new knowledge, since it explicitly acknowledges the interlocutor's part in sparking off ideas in the speaker.

Discourse reflexivity is also a resource for matching speaker perspectives, which implies revising interactants' assumptions and adapting their current theories of mind, which lays the ground for advancing mutual understanding. Shared understanding is thus jointly incremented by co-present participants, which can also lead to new ideas. It is probable that many new ideas people spark off each other never show on record, either because they arise in silent participants who simply do not express their new thoughts, or the idea connecting what was heard to something else occurs to hearers only later. Evidence for the processes is therefore hard to uncover. The overt indications of such interactional thought processes in real time that discourse reflexivity offers are thus valuable in providing a methodological handle for studying them.

A second important use that underlines the social significance of discourse reflexivity comes into play when problematic or perplexing situations arise, like differences of opinion, disagreements, or potential misunderstandings. Such points in the interaction show concentrations of reflexive metadiscourse. It seems that speakers are keen to pre-empt misunderstanding by for example clarifications in situations where potentially sensitive issues arise, as well as to redress misunderstandings and attenuate sharply conflicting views. More than the general 'linguistic positivity bias' (Dodds et al. 2015), this would seem to reflect a propensity to consensus in face-to-face conversations (Eggins & Slade 2006 [1997]), and help interlocutors coordinate their situation models (Kurby & Zacks 2015) or align them (Pickering & Garrod 2021). Reflexive metadiscourse thus plays a social role in helping explicate speakers' reasons, intentions, and attitudes towards a degree of mutual understanding despite differences and to avoid disruptive conflicts.

The characteristic dialogic negotiation of viewpoints is also visible in the predominant orientation in dialogues, which set them apart from monologues. While dialogue shows a strong preference for talking about other interactants' talk, monologues primarily orient to speakers' own talk in egocentric orienting references. The difference is more than a directional preference in organising discourse because orienting reflexivity only looks forward from the present, while retrieving reflexivity looks both ways and thus straddles past, present, and future states of the discourse. This renders dialogue interactionally complex and puts different demands on participants' attention compared to monologue. It also enables them to *negotiate* their understanding of what is being said, align their situation models, importantly including new points created during the interaction. Retrieving references in monologues are prevalently egocentric, and prompt listeners to anticipate reformulations of relevant points and adjust their cognitive representations of the talk. In dialogic exchanges, similar references come across more like speakers' assurances of their self-consistency during the discussion, which shows such expressions in a more social than cognitive role.

The different ramifications of discourse reflexivity in dialogues and monologues reflect the *distributed* nature of cognition and discourse in dialogic interaction (see, e.g. Levinson 2013). An example is the *commenting* function in monologues, which comprises clarifications and evaluations, and captures in a single speaker's talk what in dialogue gets jointly constructed, that is, negotiated. The distributed character of dialogic exchanges leads to joint products with unpredictable outcomes. Monologues are not unpredictable at the point of delivery, even if they contain surprises and unexpected turns for listerners. Like dialogues, they undoubtedly give new thoughts and ideas to listeners. The evidence of this came from dialogues, where speakers made connections to talks heard shortly before. Dialogues, however, are imbued with potential for new thoughts, ideas, and knowledge being collaboratively generated in the process. Moreover, they can develop into new, unforeseen directions.

As we have seen, the mode of speaking, that is monologue vs dialogue, showed striking contrasts in metadiscourse uses, which supports and offers a close-up view on findings like those in Zhang's (2022) register-based metadiscourse analysis, which singled out the conversational register. By contrast, the effect of the medium is slight compared to the mode effect: written and spoken dialogues are in most respects very similar in their use of reflexive discourse. This is seen in Figure 9.1, which is constructed by a principle of the least common denominator and comprises both spoken and written dialogues (Chapters 4 and 5). The same categorisation fits without difficulty, and the distributions within the categories are generally alike. In view of previous research on written and spoken monologues this may not be surprising, since modifications to writing-based models have remained small in analyses of spoken monologues, which have led to some new minor categories but nothing substantially new. What makes this particularly interesting is that the findings on written monologues appear very similar independently of the metadiscourse model applied (i.e., 'reflexive' vs 'broad').

9.2 Other interesting findings

9.2.1 Co-presence in speaking

Although the division between dialogue and monologue came out as the most fundamental in the analyses, in one important respect they are closer to each other than either is to written dialogues. This is *co-presence*. It is clearly a constraint of the *external situation*, which manifests itself in subtle but interesting ways in shaping discourse. The physical presence of others in the same space with joint

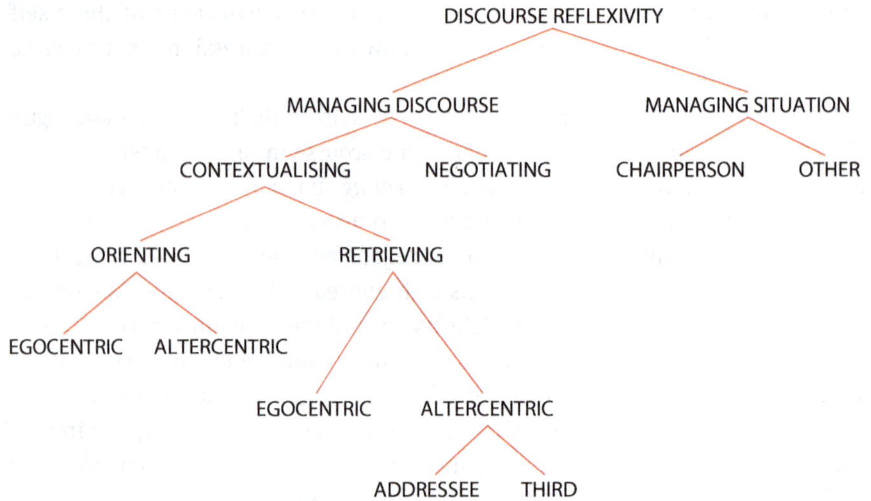

Figure 9.1: Discourse reflexivity in dialogue.

attention on the same discourse affects the unfolding of the event and the use of language, even though co-presence means an audience for monologue but interlocutors for dialogue.

Co-present others mean a wealth of available information to an individual that is missing from disembodied communication like writing: paraverbal and nonverbal cues, such as the tone of voice, prosody, eye contact, or gestures. All humans are sensitive to such cues and respond to them automatically (Hari et al. 2015). In dialogues and monologues alike, we commonly find for example joint laughter, speakers signalling that they are thinking on their feet, or references to the shared experience of the ongoing event, drawing on its affordances in real time. Such talk is specific to the here-and-now situation, where reflexive metadiscourse is involved in managing the discourse as well as the situation. Even in monologues, where situational management is rare and mostly limited to chairpersons' routines, the little that there is indicates awareness of audience presence and its effect on discourse. In practical transitions and minor problem situations speakers make remarks as it were off the record, often generating joint laughter, and listeners occasionally participate with short verbal responses.

Time itself works differently in speech and writing. Interesting indicators of presenters' adaptation to the contingencies of speech situations are ad hoc deviations from a plan, for instance omissions (*I'll skip some of the slides*). They reveal how the transition from a longer to a shorter timescale, from planning to performance, and from an imagined to a real audience impose constraints on speaking which are absent from writing.

Orienting egocentric discourse reflexivity, which dominates monologues, seeks to attune hearers to the presenter's speech at intervals of varying spans. We can roughly discern three spans in what is really a continuum: a global orientation to the whole talk typically occurs at beginnings and endings, local orienting at important junctions along the way, and immediate orientation in rapid micro-level signposting during the talk. It would be interesting to see how the span of orienting reflexivity compares to written texts, because it might tell us more about the effect of co-presence on monologue. Are expressions of orienting reflexivity of different spans more (or perhaps less) frequent in written text, and how similar are their uses in speech and writing?

Monologues do not often employ altercentric retrieving discourse reflexivity, in other words they do not talk much about what others have said. The obvious reason is of course that the others present do not speak, but though silent, they are there, and in conferences and seminars they have participated in the same macro-event with the current speaker. We find altercentric references in monologues to third-person participants in the ongoing macro-event. In social terms, we can see this as enhancing social cohesion by evoking shared experience, but perhaps more importantly, it is a way of co-constructing knowledge by drawing on the macro-event. In making the connection, the speaker also indicates mutual relevance between the larger event and their own speech and builds on that in a manner that is reminiscent of altercentric references to others in dialogic speech. Compared to egocentric references, which only cover the current presentation, altercentric references thus extend the horizon to include a wider context. In different terms, speakers holding a monologue turn to their theory of mind, making assumptions about what others know. They also adapt to those present in other ways, adjusting recipient design on the fly in the light of subtle nonverbal responses from addressees. Co-present interactionality and collaboration therefore make their presence felt in monologue, even if chiefly only by modulating the delivery. The effect is clear though not dramatic and overrides some of the mode divide.

9.2.2 Embodied vs disembodied communication

If co-presence thus softens the contrast between spoken dialogue and monologue, it would seem to have the opposite effect across the medium divide. Reflexive signalling is an essential turn-taking practice, which requires new discourse increments to be contextualised whatever the medium but acquires different practices for speech and writing. The two external constraints that are relevant here again relate to co-presence – or the lack of it – and temporality. In contrast to co-present dialogues, participants in written dialogues mostly do not refer to addressees but to the traces they have left, that is, their texts. As *disembodied* communication, written dialogues lack paraverbal and nonverbal cues, and consequently must allocate a larger share of the communication to linguistic means. Temporal asynchrony moves online participants further away from each other by carrying out the discussion at their separate paces. An additional complication in online communication is that conversations on a given topic do not take place one at a time, but discussion threads become interleaved, which leads to carefully crafted reference practices.

Together with the lack of paralinguistic and nonverbal cues, asynchrony may go a long way towards accounting for the enhanced explicitness observed in online discourses, which can be regarded as a *channel effect*, i.e., what is shared by written digital discussions on the Internet. In the current data, one of its most obvious manifestations is the very high overall incidence of reflexive discourse in written dialogues, higher than in any other event type. The channel effect of the Internet is not of course merely a question of writing. As an open public forum, a blog site does not equal digital dialogues of whatever kind, like emails, text messages, or their variants in closed-group platforms. Some typical open online features, such as a tendency to direct expression of high and often polarised emotional loading separate the blog discussion threads from traditional academic dialogues, together with numerous other features, notably multimodality, which fall outside our focus, but which a large research body into online discourses has unearthed. Blog comment threads align with other online genres in their openness to anyone, anonymity, and relative lack of external regulation, in contrast to co-present academic discussion events. Many of their characteristics imply different social norms from more established academic writing or speaking, which suggests different social action, that is, different genres. At the same time, they also manifest some register similarities with both spoken dialogues and written monologues (Grieve et al.2011; Zhang 2022) but cannot be reduced to a mixture of the two. In respect of spoken co-present dialogue and written monologue, written dialogue is a 'third'.

The thirdness of written online dialogue reflects the relations of speech and writing while it also throws light on the ways in which reflexive discourse adapts to situational parameters. Written dialogue is genuine dialogue, despite being disembodied and produced in solitude like written monologue. In online commentary, unlike written texts, the imaginary reader can turn into an actual reader and become an interacting participant, assuming the writer position in their turn.

9.2.3 Long discussions

Another external constraint points to an unexpected connection: the duration of a discussion turned out to be related to the frequency of discourse reflexivity. Longer discussions not only have a higher aggregate rate of reflexive discourse, as might be expected, but more interestingly, they have a higher proportion of it than short dialogues. The 'longer' dialogues consisted of anything from half an hour upwards, whereas the 'shorter' ones were the typical conference discussion sections following individual papers, of about five minutes. The impression from reading the transcripts is that longer discussions show self-organising tendencies, that is, they take up new angles, make connections with new issues, and shift topics. They thus show similarities to ordinary conversation. If altered time constraints have this effect, the exceptionally low rate of reflexive discourse in conference discussions (2/1,000w) can be better understood against this background, and perhaps the exceptionally high rate (12/1,000w) in blog discussions could to some degree be related to sheer overall duration as well. If long co-present dialogues tend to become more self-organised, and written dialogues are self-organised from the start, it suggests a medium-independent tendency. Clearly, longer discussions at conferences tend to follow not one but several presentations, which might explain some of the difference. The blog discussions, however, would seem to refute this because they follow one topic chain each. Their self-organising is given in the situation, which is of course unregulated. It is beyond the scope of this book to pursue the matter further, but it would be worth more investigation, since there is more than one possible explanation for this. It might, moreover, give something to think about for our practices of organising conferences.

9.2.4 Social asymmetries

Dialogues reveal differences in event types that can be related to their social composition: conference participants make three times more altercentric references than participants in graduate seminars. Conference references typically frame questions with explicit reference to what an addressee has said. It looks like referring and framing practices in academia may well be acquired during secondary socialisation into the role of an academic, which is not relevant to graduate seminars, from which only a few participants are likely to go on to pursue an academic career.

There would seem to be no notable social status asymmetries among conference participants or seminar students. However, even if students in graduate seminars are of equal social status among themselves, the situation holds one source of asymmetry, which is the novice-expert relationship between students and the seminar leader, who also occupies a position in the university hierarchy which implies assessment of the students. Interestingly, status disparity shows in different ways in discourse managing and situation managing. For discourse managing reflexivity, asymmetric status, that is, high *vertical distance* among participants, appears to contribute to an increase in its overall amount, whereas for situation management, vertical asymmetry seems to concentrate management in the hands of higher status participants. Thus, graduate seminar leaders who act as chairs are responsible for nearly 90% of situation management. Comparing this to conferences, where the status hierarchy is negligible, we find that the chairperson accounts for less than 60% of situation management. The status symmetry interpretation is supported by digital discussions, which are on a level with conferences in metadiscourse incidence, and from which status hierarchies are absent.

Other participants than the chair can also take on situation management and they seem to seize the opportunity especially in contexts of low vertical distance, such as in conference and digital dialogues. These spontaneous acts of management are *plane shifts*, which generally either seek to alter turn allocation or initiate a topic change. In contexts of higher vertical distance like graduate seminars, lower-status participants tend not to attempt plane shifts, in other words to control the direction of the discussion. While managing the discourse essentially means contextualising the speaker's own speech, managing the situation implies organising or attempting to organise everyone's speech, much like moderators do (McKeown & Ladegaard 2020). Situation management acts are thus acts of social power in a way that managing the discourse is not. This is what we are witnessing in a seminar leader's situational monopoly, and conversely, where the chairperson role is a temporary allocation like in conferences, other participants remain fairly free to suggest new directions to the discussion, and in non-chaired contexts like blog discussions, any participant is at liberty to do so.

Asymmetries of power and status may also play out somewhat differently when reflexive discourse is involved in knowledge co-construction between participants. This is suggested by observations from doctoral defences, where the status difference between examiners and candidates is obvious but was in many cases ignored in favour of joint construction of knowledge. Similar developments were not seen in graduate seminars, which shows the dynamics of academia in an interesting light. However, these observations are tentative since the data behind them was not compiled to represent power relations but uses of metadiscourse and joint construction of knowledge.

Briefly, then, social factors that seem to predict a high rate of organising discourse reflexivity in spoken dialogues are associated with social uncertainty: high stakes and social asymmetry between participants. Of external factors, longer duration of a discussion is most clearly linked to a high degree of reflexive discourse, in addition to having other consequences for the discourse like enhancing self-organising characteristics and more conversational features.

Online dialogues are in social terms comparatively free from external control, chairpersons, and social asymmetry. The ensuing self-organisation is evident in the blog comment threads. In some respects, comment threads thus resemble spontaneous conversation more than organised academic discussions. External temporal constraints such as asynchrony and planning time may be further contributing factors to a high incidence of reflexive discourse.

9.3 What were the commonalities?

Despite notable variability across event types, media, and modes, the basic understanding of discourse reflexivity as discourse about the currently ongoing discourse remained the recognisable core throughout the data analyses. In addition to variation in discourse-based categories, reflexive metadiscourse also shows sensitivity to external and social constraints, also in evidence in register research (Zhang 2022).

The principal kind of discourse reflexivity consists in what was termed managing the discourse, and a lesser kind is managing the situation. The distinction between these two is not usually made in metadiscourse studies, perhaps because the division pertains only to speech, and does not play a notable role in monologic discourse. Even in dialogic data, where managing the situation was more common, it amounted to only about a quarter of reflexive discourse. However, this may not be an accurate estimate of its incidence even in the present event types since some of it has probably been omitted from the recordings or transcripts. Be that as it may, the uniting feature among all event types is that managing the discourse constitutes the cornerstone of discourse reflexivity.

Speech progresses inexorably in time, and temporality gives the overall backdrop to spoken metadiscourse. Speaking in real time is manifest in both prospective, orienting discourse reflexivity and in retrospective, that is, retrieving discourse reflexivity. For the speaker, the former indicates what they intend to say, the latter relates it to a point or topic in their representation of the discourse so far. For listening fellow participants, both supply material for predicting how the discourse is likely to continue and for confirming or revising their earlier predictions.

Speech takes place in a social context. Co-present others are at the heart of dialogue and exert their influence on spoken monologue as well. The data has many indications of the latter, showing that the transition from an imagined to a real audience alters not only the presenter's position but the discourse.

The core of discourse about the ongoing discourse, then, lies in indicating how what is being said by the current speaker in the moment of speaking relates to the co-text, that is, the rest of the discourse, both past and upcoming. It makes explicit the mutual relevance of past, present, and intended discourse, as evinced throughout the present data. Importantly, it helps speakers negotiate their meanings, the course of interaction, and the sharing and co-construction of new ideas.

9.4 Where next?

Metadiscourse as exclusively a matter of writer-to-reader interaction has been challenged in this book, because embodied spoken interaction is fundamental to humans and crucial for understanding the use of language. The journey through metadiscourse in spoken dialogue has uncovered many new phenomena, but there is much more to be discovered.

The methodological approach here has been what Ädel (2010) calls 'splitting', in other words, taking speech into a special focus while excluding writing. At this exploratory stage, this approach was felt necessary to help understand discourse reflexivity from a perspective that has been virtually neglected in previous research. The split was not complete, however, because written dialogues were included in the data. Cross-comparison between several event types was deliberately adopted to tease out effects of mode and effects of medium. It has paid off, because it has opened our eyes to the great divide in reflexive discourse between dialogue and monologue. We have also discovered that the division was not so dramatic between the spoken and written medium. This has important repercussions for understanding the relationship of interaction and discourse reflexivity in real-time co-present interaction. It also gives a new reading to previous research on spoken and written metadiscourse: since the studies have mainly been concerned with comparing monologues in the two modes, it is not surprising that the same models have seemed applicable to speaking and writing without much difficulty. It was similarly possible to analyse spoken and written dialogues with essentially one model.

Ädel is right, however, in preferring a 'lumping' approach. This ought to be the ultimate aim in metadiscourse studies. The present analyses demonstrate that we need an amended overall model of discourse reflexivity, or metadiscourse, that accounts for dialogic as well as monologic interaction in both speech and writing. As I have argued before (Mauranen 2006b), integrated approaches to language description ought to start from what is most fundamental to language, which is speech.

When we depict speakers in dialogic interaction, where participants alternate in speaker and hearer roles, it is clear that they must continuously process the discourse actively in both capacities. This assumption of equal activity on the listener's part makes sense also in the light of contemporary research on cognition and the brain, which posit an active, predictive brain. It would seem that the same is true of listeners processing monologic speech, and that discourse reflexivity plays an important role in this prospective - predictive discourse activity. The same assumption could be made for the reader. As suggested in Chapter 2, we should posit an active reader, who makes hypotheses about the upcoming discourse based on multiple cues in the text, including metadiscourse. The conceptualisation of the writer guiding, helping, and engaging the (essentially passive) reader may be too writer-centred to be realistic, and has perhaps seen its best days. Reconceptualising readers as actively generating their own representations of the text could extend metadiscourse research further into the reader's domain and above all work towards an integrated model of spoken and written metadiscourse.

The data-driven categorisation that the present study arrived at seems fit for the purpose. It is good to bear in mind, however, that exploratory categorisations tend to focus attention on the broad outlines and perhaps unavoidably overlook what is less common or more detailed but might still have something to offer. Subsequent research must probe nooks and corners that might bring to light valuable new discoveries.

In addition to suggesting a new model, the current findings indicate that further explorations into the territory of dialogic discourse are needed. In general, the situational and contextual parameters considered here suggest what may lie behind the observed variation, but they clearly call for more research and more precise conceptualisations. One of the intriguing findings was that longer discussions tend to become more self-regulated and self-organised, and in this process, show characteristics of ordinary conversation. Moreover, longer duration seems connected to a higher rate of reflexive discourse in dialogues. Time, then, as mere extended duration, seems to constrain the character of the discourse. But how does it happen, what reasons could best explain the tendency of the rate of reflexivity to grow, and is this change entirely gradual or are there temporal thresholds after which discussions begin to organise themselves to a perceptible degree?

Time spans also varied in monologues: at least prospective remarks were made on more global and more local scales in the discourse so that they spanned longer or shorter sections of the talk. This would be interesting to compare to written texts. Are expressions of orienting discourse reflexivity more frequent in speech, and how similar are they to writing? Are there similar span variations in retrieving reflexivity? Answers to questions like these could enlighten us further about the effects of co-presence and the different time scales of spoken and written discourse.

A higher rate of discourse reflexivity was also associated with situations of social asymmetry. Social parameters associated with metadiscourse have not received very much attention in the field (see, however, McKeown & Ladegaard 2020), but as hopefully more studies will take spoken interaction in their focus, social settings should certainly get more prominence, and will be elaborated together with other contextual parameters. It is important to note that many commonly employed parameters like first language, native culture, or disciplinary domain are not omnirelevant categories. In written metadiscourse analysis, we already see effects of contextual parameters through different genres, and since the most salient and important academic genres have been covered from almost every thinkable angle, research is flowing into less obvious genres within and outside academic confines.

We saw in the present data that a distinction between managing the discourse and managing the situation was motivated, but it would be worth studying how it works outside academic discourses, if at all, and whether or how specifically it is relevant to metadiscourse in casual conversations. To what extent do we organise our everyday conversations by metadiscoursal means?

Linguistic analyses can make independent contributions to understanding language processing, despite their limitations in tackling the mechanisms directly. Speech processing in individuals is inseparably intertwined with social interaction, which is accessible to linguistic observation and without which, much would probably go unnoticed otherwise. For example, with regard to temporal aspects of metadiscourse, questions arose that would be intriguing to ask in collaboration with experimental cognitive research, for example what happens when there is a delay between an explicit discourse reflexive prospection and the prospected speech act. How long do predictions stay intact, get revised, or just fade? Can we detect linguistic cues that trigger one of these, or is it simply a matter of time? Are there scales of strength that can be determined from linguistic cues?

Taking the co-construction of knowledge on board as manifest in reflexive metadiscourse was a new opening in this book. More research into that would be welcome, perhaps most fruitfully from the perspective of complex dynamic systems. Dialogic interaction between humans can be conceived of as a complex system, where the outcome is not predetermined. One of its possible outcomes, though not the only one, is that interacting individuals produce something new between them. Comparing situations outside academia could throw more light on what the principal determinants are of such processes, and what roles metadiscourse plays in them.

Aspects of speech and discourse reflexivity that were not addressed in this book include sound and multimodality. Prosodic features such as intonation, pitch, loudness, and rhythmic changes amount to an important interactional resource that humans spontaneously produce and understand. How they combine with reflexive discourse would throw more light on the processes of communication. The same can be said about paraverbal communication, like gestures. Investigating multimodality has been an obvious gap in the field, but it has begun to be addressed in metadiscourse research (see e.g. Liu 2021; Ädel 2021; Biri 2021).

This book has sought to contribute to the 'reflexive turn' in metadiscourse studies. It has not counted 'markers' of reflexive metadiscourse but explored how speakers use discourse reflexivity and what they use it for. The research arose out of an interest in metadiscourse in face-to-face interaction as an alternative to the usual attention to a solitary writer and their imagined audience. The approach has yielded new insights by showing how embodied communication takes place in real time with co-present others, how metadiscourse shapes interaction, and how context shapes metadiscourse. Discourse reflexivity concentrates in places where speakers are faced with a multiplicity of perceptions, interests, and purposes in fast-moving discourse, negotiating and matching perspectives, managing the situation along with the discourse. Moreover, reflexive metadiscourse indicates real-time joint construction of emerging knowledge. Discourse reflexivity is pivotal in carrying out participants' deeply collaborative negotiation and weighing of each other's arguments, evidence, methods, or premises. Discourse reflexivity structures episodes, navigates debates forward or tones them down, and helps catalyse or manoeuvre the development of arguments.

By indicating our awareness of our talk, we share it with our interlocutors.

Reflexive language contributes significantly to our conceptualisations of language, and what is specifically human about it. It generates intersubjectivity by shaping conversationalists' mutual understanding of how to relate to the discourse that is being co-constructed. In this way, discourse reflexivity contributes to the two fundamental uses that language has: sharing experience and negotiating interaction.

List of figures

Figure 2.1 Discourse reflexivity as discourse about the ongoing discourse —— **27**
Figure 4.1 Discourse reflexivity in spoken dialogue —— **81**
Figure 5.1 Discourse reflexivity in written dialogue —— **106**
Figure 7.1 Discourse reflexivity in spoken monologue —— **180**
Figure 9.1 Discourse reflexivity in dialogue —— **208**

https://doi.org/10.1515/9783110295498-010

References

Corpora used

ELFA 2008. The Corpus of English as a Lingua Franca in Academic Settings. Director: Anna Mauranen. http://www.helsinki.fi/elfa/elfacorpus.www.helsinki.fi/elfa

WrELFA 2015. The Corpus of Written English as a Lingua Franca in Academic Settings. Director: Anna Mauranen. Compilation manager: Ray Carey. http://www.helsinki.fi/elfa/wrelfa.html.

Bibliography

Ädel, Annelie. 2006. *Metadiscourse in L1 and L2 English*. Amsterdam: John Benjamins.

Ädel, Annelie. 2010. Just to give you kind of a map of where we are going: A Taxonomy of Metadiscourse in Spoken and Written English. *Nordic Journal of English Studies* 9(2). *Metadiscourse* [Special Issue]. 69–97.

Ädel, Annelie & Anna Mauranen 2010. Metadiscourse: Diverse and divided perspectives. *Nordic Journal of English Studies* 9(2). *Metadiscourse* [Special Issue].1–11.

Ädel, Annelie. 2018. Variation in metadiscursive 'you' across genres: From research articles to teacher feedback. *Educational Sciences: Theory & Practice* 18(4). 777–796.

Ädel, Annelie. 2021. Reflections on Reflexivity in Digital Communication: Towards a Third Wave of Metadiscourse Studies. In Larissa D'Angelo, Anna Mauranen & Stefania Maci (eds.), *Metadiscourse in Digital Communication. New Research, Approaches, and Methodologies*, 37–64. Cham: Palgrave MacMillan.

Ahn, Ruth & Mary Class. 2011. Student-Centered Pedagogy: Co-Construction of Knowledge through Student-Generated Midterm Exams. *International Journal of Teaching and Learning in Higher Education* 23(2). 269–281 http://www.isetl.org/ijtlhe/

Ankener, Christine S, Mirjana Sekicki & Maria Staudte. 2018. The influence of visual uncertainty on word surprisal and processing effort. *Frontiers in Psychology* 9. https://doi.org/10.3389/fpsyg.2018.02387

Arvaja, Maarit. 2005. *Collaborative knowledge construction in authentic school contexts*. Jyväskylä: University of Jyväskylä Institute for Educational Research: Research Reports 14.

Auer, Peter. 2005. Projection in interaction and projection in grammar. *Text* 25. 7–36.

Baggio, Giosué. 2018. *Meaning in the Brain*. MIT Press. Cambridge, MA.

Bandura, Albert. 2000. Self-efficacy: The foundation of agency. In Walter J. Perrig & Alexander Grob (eds.), *Control of Human Behavior, Mental Processes, and Consciousness*, 17–33. Mahwah, N.J. Lawrence Erlbaum.

Becher, Tony & Paul Trowler. 2001. *Academic Tribes and Territories: intellectual enquiry and the cultures of disciplines*. Buckingham: Open University Press /SRHE.

Berkenkotter, Carol & Tom Huckin. 1995. *Genre Knowledge in Disciplinary Communication*. Hillsdale, N.J.: Lawrence Erlbaum.

Biber, Douglas. 1988. *Variation across Speech and Writing*. Cambridge: Cambridge University Press.

Biber, Douglas, Ulla Connor & Thomas A. Upton. 2007. *Discourse on the Move: Using Corpus Analysis to Describe Discourse Structure*. Amsterdam: John Benjamins.

https://doi.org/10.1515/9783110295498-011

Biber, Douglas & Susan Conrad. 2009. *Register, Genre, and Style*. Cambridge: Cambridge University Press.

Biber, Douglas & Jesse Egbert. 2018. *Register Variation Online*. Cambridge: Cambridge University Press.

Biri, Ylva. 2021. Metadiscourse in Social Media: A Reflexive Framework. In Larissa D'Angelo, Anna Mauranen & Stefania Maci (eds.), *Metadiscourse in Digital Communication. New Research, Approaches, and Methodologies*, 133–154. Cham: Palgrave MacMillan.

Bolander, Brook. 2012. Disagreements and agreements in personal/diary blogs: A closer look at responsiveness. *Journal of Pragmatics* 44. 1607–1622.

Bondi, Marina. 2018. "Try to prove me wrong": Dialogicality and audience involvement in economics blogs. *Discourse, Context & Media* 24. 33–42.

Bouziri, Basma. 2021. A tripartite interpersonal model for investigating metadiscourse in academic lectures. *Applied Linguistics* 42(5). 970–989.

Brazil, David. 1995. *A Grammar of Speech*. Oxford: Oxford University Press.

Bruffee, Kenneth A.1998. *Collaborative Learning: Higher Education, Interdependence, and the Authority of Knowledge*. Second Edition. The British Psychological Society.

Buszáki, György. 2019. *The Brain from Inside Out*. Oxford: Oxford University Press.

Butler, Cristopher S. 2008. The subjectivity of basically in British English – a corpus-based study. In Jesús Romero-Trillo (ed.), *Pragmatics and Corpus Linguistics: A Mutualistic Entente*, 37–62. Boston/Berlin: Mouton de Gruyter.

Canagarajah, Suresh. 2018. Translingual Practice as Spatial Repertoires: Expanding the Paradigm Beyond Structuralist Orientations. *Applied Linguistics* 39(1). 31–54.

Canagarajah, Suresh. 2021. Materialising semiotic repertoires: Challenges in the interactional analysis of multilingual communication. *International Journal of Multilingualism* 18(2). 206–225.

Carey, Ray. 2013. On the other side: formulaic organizing chunks in spoken and written academic ELF. *Journal of English as a Lingua Franca*. 2(2). 207–228. https://doi.org/10.1515/jelf-2013-0013

Carter, Ronald. 2004. *Language and Creativity. The Art of Common Talk*. London: Routledge.

Chafe, Wallace (ed.). 1980. *The Pear Stories: Cognitive, Cultural, and Linguistic Aspects of Narrative Production*. Norwood, N.J: Ablex.

Chafe, Wallace. 1994. *Discourse, Consciousness, and Time: The Flow and Displacement of Conscious Experience in Speaking and Writing*. Chicago: The University of Chicago Press.

Chafe, Wallace. 1998[2014]. Language and the flow of thought. In Michael Tomasello (ed.), *The New Psychology of Language*. Vol.1. Mahwah, N.J.: Lawrence Erlbaum. Republished 2014, 87–104. New York: Psychology Press.

Chafe, Wallace. 2018. *Thought-based Linguistics. How Languages Turn Thoughts into Sounds*. Cambridge: Cambridge University Press.

Channell, Joanna. 1994. *Vague Language*. Oxford: Oxford University Press.

Cheng, Winnie, Christopher Greaves, John McH. Sinclair & Martin Warren. 2009. Uncovering the extent of the phraseological tendency: Towards systematic Analysis of concgrams. *Applied Linguistics* 30(2). 236–52.

Christiansen, Morten H. & Nick Chater. 2016. The Now-or-Never Bottleneck: A Fundamental Constraint on Language. *Behavioral and Brain Sciences, FirstView*.1–52. https://doi.org/10.1017/S0140525X1500031X

Chu, S. Kai Wai & David M. Kennedy. 2011. Using online collaborative tools for groups to co-construct knowledge. *Online Information Review* 35(4). 581–597.

Clark, Andy. 1997. *Being There: Putting Brain, Body, and World Together Again*. Cambridge, MA/London: The MIT Press.

Clark, Andy. 2013.Whatever next? Predictive brains, situated agents, and the future of cognitive science. *Behavioral and Brain Sciences* 36(3). 181–204.
Clark, Herbert H. & Jean E. Fox Tree. 2002. Using *uh* and *um* in spontaneous speech. *Cognition* 84. 73–111.
Craig, Robert T. & Alena L. Sanusi. 2000. 'I'm just saying . . .' Discourse Markers of Standpoint Continuity. *Argumentation* 14(4). 425–445.
Crismore, Avon. 1983. *Metadiscourse: What is it and how is it used in school and non-school social science texts*. Urbana-Champaign: University of Illinois.
Crismore, Avon. 1989. *Talking with Readers. Metadiscourse as a Rhetorical Act*. American University Studies, Series XIV (17). New York: Peter Lang.
Crismore, Avon & Robert Farnsworth. 1990. Metadiscourse in popular and professional science discourse. In Walter Nash (ed.), *The Writing Scholar*, 118–136. London: Sage
Couper-Kuhlen, Elizabeth & Margaret Selting. 2018. *Interactional Linguistics: An Introduction to Language in Social Interaction*. Cambridge University Press.
Cutting, Joan. 2007. *Vague Language Explored*. Basingstoke: Palgrave Macmillan.
Daneš, Frantisek (ed.). 1974. *Papers on Functional Sentence Perspective*. Janua Linguarum, Series Minor, 147. The Hague: Mouton.
D'Angelo, Larissa, Anna Mauranen & Stefania Maci (eds.). 2022. *Metadiscourse in Digital Communication. New Research, Approaches and Methodologies*. Cham: Palgrave Macmillan.
Delibekovic Dzanic, Nihada & Sanja Berberovic 2021. Lemons and Watermelons: Visual Advertising and Conceptual Blending. In Larissa D'Angelo, Anna Mauranen & Stefania Maci (eds.), *Metadiscourse in Digital Communication. New Research, Approaches and Methodologies*, 115–132. Cham: Palgrave Macmillan.
Dobrego, Aleksandra, Alena Konina & Anna Mauranen. 2022. Continuous Speech Segmentation by L1 and L2 Speakers of English: The Role of Syntactic and Prosodic Cues. *Language Awareness*. Doi:10.1080/09658416.2022.213801.
Dodds, Peter S., Eric M. Clark, Suma Desu, Morgan R. Frank, Andrew J. Reagan, Jake R. Williams, Lewis Mitchell, Kameron D. Harris, Isabel M. Kloumann, James P. Bagrow, Karine Megerdoomian, Matthew T. McMahon, Brian F. Tivnan & Cristopher M. Danforth. 2015. Human language reveals a universal positivity bias. *PNAS* 112(8). 2389–2394.
Du Bois, John W. 2014. Towards a Dialogic Syntax. *Cognitive Linguistics* 25(3). 359–410.
Edge, Julian. 1986. Towards a Professional Reading Strategy for EFL Teacher Trainees. Birmingham: PhD thesis, University of Birmingham.
Eggins, Susan & Diane Slade. 1997[2006]. *Analysing Casual Conversation*, 2nd edn. London: Equinox.
Ehret, Katharina & Maite Taboada. 2020. Are online news comments like face-to-face conversation? A multi-dimensional analysis of an emerging register. *Register Studies* 2(1).1–36.
Ellis, Nick. 2007. Cognitive perspectives on SLA: The associative-cognitive CREED. *AILA Review* 19(1).100–121.
Ericsson, K. Anders & Walter Kintsch. 1995. Long-term working memory. *Psychological Review* 102(2). 179–211.
Evans, Vyvyan. 2014. *The Language Myth: Why Language is Not an Instinct*. Cambridge: Cambridge University Press.
Fernández-Polo, Francisco Javier. 2018. Functions of "you" in conference presentations. *English for Specific Purposes* 49. 14–25. DOI: 10.1016/j.esp.2017.10.001
Firth, John Rupert. 1957[1968]. A Synopsis of Linguistic Theory, 1930–55. *Studies in Linguistic Analysis*. Special volume of the Philological Society, 1–31. Oxford, 1957. Reprinted in F.R.Palmer, 1968. *Selected Papers of J.R. Firth 1952–59*, 168–205. London: Longman.

Fleming, Stephen M. & Cristopher D. Frith, (eds.). 2014. Metacognitive Neuroscience: An Introduction. In Stephen M. Fleming & Cristopher D. Frith (eds.), *The Cognitive Neuroscience of Metacognition*, 1–6. Berlin: Springer Nature.

Flowerdew, John & Steve Tauroza. 1995. The effect of discourse markers on second language lecture comprehension. *Studies in Second Language Acquisition* 17(4). 435–458. https://doi.org/10.1017/S0272263100014406

Frank, Stefan L. 2013. Uncertainty reduction as a measure of cognitive load in sentence comprehension. *Topics in Cognitive Science* 5. 475–494.

Franzmann, Andreas, Axel Jansen & Peter Münte. 2015. Legitimizing Science: Introductory Essay. In Axel Jansen, Andreas Franzmann & Peter Münte (eds.), *Legitimizing Science: National and Global Publics (1800–2010)* 11–34. Chicago: University of Chicago Press.

Friston, Karl. 2010. The free-energy principle: a unified brain theory?. *Nat Rev Neurosci,* 11(2). 127–138. doi:10.1038/nrn2787

Gilbert, G. Nigel & Michael Mulkay 1984. *Opening Pandora's Box. A sociological analysis of scientists' discourse*. Cambridge: Cambridge University Press.

Glenn, Philip. 2003. *Laughter in Interaction*. Cambridge: Cambridge University Press.

Gozdz-Roszkowski, Stanislaw & Susan Hunston. 2016. Corpora and beyond – investigating evaluation in discourse: Introduction to the special issue on corpus approaches to evaluation. *Corpora* 11(2). 131–141.

Goffman, Erving. 1981. *Forms of Talk*. Philadelphia: University of Pennsylvania Press.

Goldberg, Adele E. 2019. *Explain Me This: Creativity, Competition, and the Partial Productivity of Constructions*. Princeton University Press.

Grice, H. Paul. 1975. Logic and conversation. In Peter Cole & Jerry L. Morgan (eds.), *Syntax and Semantics*, Vol 3, 41–58. New York: Academic Press.

Gries, Stefan Th. 2010. Methodological skills in corpus linguistics: a polemic and some pointers towards quantitative methods. In Tony Harris & María Moreno Jaén (eds.), *Corpus linguistics in language teaching*, 121–146. Frankfurt a.M.: Peter Lang.

Grieve Jack, Douglas Biber, Eric Friginal & Tatiana Nekrasova. 2011. Variation among blog text types: A multi-dimensional analysis. In Alexander Mehler, Serge Sharoff & Marina Santini (eds.), *Genres on the Web. Computational Models and Empirical Studies*, 303–322. New York: Springer-Verlag.

Gunawardena, Charlotte N., Constance A. Lowe & Terry Anderson. 1997. Analysis of a global online debate and the development of an interaction analysis model for examining social construction of knowledge in computer conferencing. *Journal of Educational Computing Research* 17. 397–431.

Gweon, Gahgene. 2012. *Assessment and support of the idea co-construction process that influences collaboration*. PhD thesis, Pittsburgh, Pennsylvania: Carnegie Mellon University Human Computer Interaction Institute School of Computer Science.

Hafner, Cristopher A. & Jack Pun. 2020. Introduction to this special issue: English for academic and professional purposes in the digital era. *RELC Journal* 51(1). 3–13. https://doi.org/10.1177/0033688220917472

Halliday, Michael A. K. 1985. *Introduction to Functional Grammar*. London: Edward Arnold.

Halliday, Michael A.K. & Ruqaiya Hasan. 1976. *Cohesion in English*. London: Longman.

Hanski, Ilkka. 1999. *Metapopulation Ecology*. Oxford: Oxford University Press.

Hari, Riitta. 2007. Human mirroring systems: On assessing mind by reading brain and body during social interaction. In Stein Bråten (ed.), *On being moved: From mirror neurons to empathy*, 89–100. Amsterdam: John Benjamins.

Hari, Riitta, Linda Henriksson, Sanna Malinen & Lauri Parkkonen. 2015. Centrality of Social Interaction in Human Brain Function. *Neuron* 88, October 7. 201–192.

Hari, Riitta., Mikko Sams & Lauri Nummenmaa. 2016. Attending to and neglecting people: bridging neuroscience, psychology and sociology. *Phil. Trans. R. Soc.* B 371: 20150365. http://dx.doi.org/10.1098/rstb.2015.0365

Heilbron, Micha, Kristijan Armeni, Jan-Mathjis Schoffelen & Floris P. de Lange. 2022. A hierarchy of linguistic predictions during natural language comprehension. *PNAS* 119(32). https://doi.org/10.1073/pnas.2201968119

Herring, Susan C. 2007. A faceted classification scheme for computer-mediated discourse. *Language @internet.* http://www.languageatinternet.org/articles/2007/761

Hoey, Michael. 1983. *On the Surface of Discourse*. London: George Allen & Unwin.

Hoey, Michael. 2001. *Textual Interaction.* London & New York: Routledge.

Hoey, Michael. 2005. *Lexical Priming.* London: Routledge.

Hopper, Paul J. & Elizabeth C. Traugott 1994[2003]. *Grammaticalization* (2nd edn). Cambridge: Cambridge University Press.

Hull, Darrell M. & Terrill F. Saxon. 2009. Negotiation of meaning and co-construction of knowledge: An experimental analysis of asynchronous online instruction. *Computers & Education* 52(3). April 2009. 624–639.

Hyland, Ken. 2005. *Metadiscourse. Exploring Interaction in Writing*. London: Continuum.

Hyland, Ken. 2015. *Academic Publishing: Issues and Challenges in the Construction of Knowledge*. Oxford: Oxford University Press.

Hyland, Ken. 2017. Metadiscourse: What is it and where is it going? *Journal of Pragmatics*, 113.16–29. https://doi.org/10.1016/j.pragma.2017.03.007

Hyland, Ken & Hang Zou. 2020. "I believe the findings are fascinating": Stance in three-minute theses. *Journal of English for Academic Purposes* 43. https://doi.org/10.1016j.jeap.2019.100809.

Hyland, Ken & Hang Zou. 2022. Pithy persuasion: Engagement in 3-minute thesis presentations. *Applied Linguistics* 43(1). 21–44.

Ilie, Cornelia. 2003. Discourse and Metadiscourse in Parliamentary Debates. *Journal of Language and Politics* 2(1). 71–92.

Jenkins, Jennifer. 2000. *The phonology of English as an international language*. Oxford: Oxford University Press.

Jenkins, Jennifer. 2014. *English as a Lingua Franca in the International University.* London: Routledge.

Jenkins, Jennifer. 2015. Repositioning English and multilingualism in English as a lingua franca. *Englishes in Practice* 2(3). 49–85.

Jenkins, Jennifer & Anna Mauranen (eds.). 2019. *Linguistic Diversity on the EMI Campus; Insider accounts of the use of English and other languages in ten universities within Asia, Australasia and Europe* London: Routledge.

Kastberg, Peter. 2010. Knowledge Communication – Formative Ideas and Research Impetus. *Programmatic Perspectives* 2(1). 59–71.

Kintsch, Walter. 1974. *The Representation of Meaning in Memory.* Hillsdale, N.J: Lawrence Erlbaum Associates.

Komori-Glatz, Miya & Ute Smit. 2022. Exploratory Interactive Explaining (EXINTEX): constructing disciplinary knowledge in two university settings. *Applied Linguistics* 43(2). 271–292. https://doi.org/10.1093/applin/amab023

Kurby, Christopher A. & Jeffrey M. Zacks. 2008. Segmentation in the perception and memory of events. *Trends in Cognitive Sciences* 12. 72–79.

Kurby, Christopher A. & Jeffrey M. Zacks. 2015. Situation models in naturalistic comprehension. In Roel M. Willems (ed.), *Cognitive Neuroscience of Natural Language Use*, 59–76. Cambridge: Cambridge University Press.

Kuteeva, Maria & Anna Mauranen (guest eds.). 2018. *Digital academic discourse*. [Special Issue] *Discourse Context & Media.*

Kuter, Sitkiye, Zehra Altinay Gazi & Fahriye Altinay Aksal. 2012. Examination of Co-construction of Knowledge in Videotaped Simulated Instruction. *Educational Technology & Society 15*(1). 174–184.

Laitinen, Mikko & Jonas Lundberg 2021. ELF, language change and social networks: Evidence from real-time social media data. In Anna Mauranen & Svetlana Vetchinnikova (eds.), *Language Change: The Impact of English as a Lingua Franca*, 179–204. Cambridge: Cambridge University Press.

Lakoff, George. 1987. *Women, Fire, and Dangerous Things*. Chicago: The University of Chicago Press.

Latour, Bruno & Steve Woolgar. 1986. *Laboratory Life. The Construction of Scientific Facts*. Princeton: Princeton University Press.

Lave, Jean & Etienne Wenger. 1991. *Situated Learning. Legitimate peripheral participation*. Cambridge: Cambridge University Press

Lee, Joseph J. & Nicholas C. Subtirelu. 2015. Metadiscourse in the classroom: A comparative analysis of EAP lessons and university lectures. *English for Specific Purposes* 37. 52–62. https://doi.org/10.1016/j.esp.2014.06.005

Lee, Namhee, Lisa Mikesell, Anna Dina L. Joaquin, Andrea W. Mates & John H. Schumann 2009. *The Interactional Instinct*. Oxford: Oxford University Press.

Levinson, Stephen C. 2013. Recursion in pragmatics. *Language* 89.149–62.

Lillis, Teresa & Mary Jane Curry. 2010. *Academic writing in a global context: The politics and practices of publishing in English*. London and New York: Routledge.

Linell, Per. 2001. *Approaching Dialogue: Talk, Interaction and Contexts in Dialogical Perspectives*. John Benjamins.

Liu, Yanhua. 2021. *Investigating Metadiscursive and Visual Features in Three Minute Thesis Presentations*. Unpublished PhD thesis, Nanyang Technological University, Singapore.

Luukka, M. R. 1994. 'Metadiscourse in Academic Texts'. In Gunnarson, B.-L., Linell, P. & Nordberg, B. (eds.), *Text and Talk in Professional Contexts*. The Swedish Association of Applied Linguistics. Uppsala: ASLA.

Luukka, Minna-Riitta. 1995. *Puhuttua ja kirjoitettua tiedettä: funktionaalinen ja yhteisöllinen näkökulma tieteen kielen interpersonaalisiin piirteisiin*. PhD thesis. Jyväskylä: University of Jyväskylä.

Luzón, Maria José. 2011. "Interesting Post, But I Disagree": Social presence and antisocial behaviour in academic weblogs. *Applied linguistics*, 32(5). 517–540.

Luzón, Maria José. 2012. "Your argument is wrong": a contribution to the study of evaluation in academic weblogs. *Text and Talk* 32(2). 145–165.

Luzón, Maria José. 2013a. Public communication of science in blogs: recontextualizing scientific discourse for a diversified audience. *Written Communication*, 30(4). 428–457.

Luzón, Maria José. 2013b. "This is an erroneous argument": conflict in academic blog discussions. *Discourse, Context & Media*, 2(2). 111–119.

Luzón, Maria José. 2018. Constructing academic identities online: Identity performance in research group blogs written by multilingual scholars. *Journal of English for Academic Purposes* 33. 24–39.

Lyons, John. 1977. *Semantics*. Vol.1. Cambridge: Cambridge University Press.

Mahrt, Merja & Cornelius Puschmann. 2014. Science blogging: An exploratory study of motives, styles, and audience reactions. *Journal of Science Communication*, 13(3), A05. doi: 10.22323/2.13030205.

Malmströn, Hans. 2014. Engaging the Congregation: The Place of Metadiscourse in Contemporary Preaching. *Applied Linguistics* 37(4). 561–582.

Mandel, Anne, Siiri Helokunnas, Elina Pihko & Riitta Hari. 2015. Brain responds to another person's eye blinks in a natural setting – the more empathetic the viewer the stronger the responses *European Journal of Neuroscience*.Oct;42(8): 2508–14. DOI: 10.1111/ejn.13011

Matlin, Margaret W. 2016. Pollyanna Principle. In Rüdiger F. Pohl (ed.), *Cognitive Illusions: Intriguing Phenomena in Judgement, Thinking and Memory*, 315–333. Hove: Psychology Press.

Mauranen, Anna. 1993a. *Cultural Differences in Academic Rhetoric. A Textlinguistic Study*. Frankfurt: Peter Lang.

Mauranen, Anna. 1993b. Contrastive ESP Rhetoric: Metatext in Finnish – English Economics texts. *English for Specific Purposes* 12(1). 3–22.

Mauranen, Anna. 1994. Two Discourse Worlds: Study genres in Britain and Finland. In Anna Mauranen & Raija Markkanen (eds.), *Students abroad. Aspects of exchange students' language*,1–40. Jyväskylä: Korkeakoulujen kielikeskus.

Mauranen, Anna. 1997. Hedging and modality in revisers' hands. In Raija Markkanen & Hartmut Schröder (eds.), *Hedging and Discourse. Approaches to the Analysis of a Pragmatic Phenomenon*, 115–133. Berlin: de Gruyter.

Mauranen, Anna. 2001. Reflexive Academic Talk: Observations from MICASE. In Rita Simpson & John M. Swales (eds.), *Corpus Linguistics in North America*, 165–178. Ann Arbor: University of Michigan Press.

Mauranen, Anna. 2002. "A Good Question". Expressing Evaluation in Academic Speech. In Giuseppina Cortese & Philip Riley (eds.), *Domain-specific English. Textual Practices across Communities and Classrooms*, 115–140. Frankfurt: Peter Lang.

Mauranen, Anna. 2003. "But here's a flawed argument". Socialisation into and through metadiscourse. In Pepi Leistyna & Charles F. Meyer (eds.), *Corpus Analysis. Language Structure and Language Use*, 19–34. Amsterdam: Rodopi.

Mauranen, A. 2004. "They're a little bit different". Observations on hedges in academic talk. In Karin Aijmer & Anna-Brita Stenström (eds.) *Discourse Patterns in Spoken and Written Corpora*, 173–198. Amsterdam: John Benjamins,

Mauranen, Anna. 2006a. Speaking the Discipline. In Ken Hyland & Marina Bondi (eds.), *Academic Discourse Across Disciplines*, 271–294. Bern: Peter Lang.

Mauranen, Anna. 2006b. Spoken discourse, academics and global English: a corpus perspective. In Rebecca Hughes (ed.), *Spoken English, TESOL and Applied Linguistics. Challenges for Theory and Practice*, 143–158. London: Palgrave Macmillan.

Mauranen, Anna. 2010. Discourse Reflexivity – a Discourse Universal? The case of ELF. *Nordic Journal of English Studies* 9 (2).*Metadiscourse*. [Special Issue]. 13–40.

Mauranen, Anna. 2012. *Exploring ELF. Academic English shaped by non-native speakers*. Cambridge: Cambridge University Press.

Mauranen, Anna. 2013a. Hybridism, edutainment, and doubt: science blogging finding its feet. *Nordic Journal of English Studies* 12(1). 7–36.

Mauranen, Anna. 2013b. "But then when I started to think . . ." Narrative Elements in Conference Presentations. In Maurizio Gotti & Carmen Sancho Guinda (eds.), *Narratives in Academic and Professional Genres*, 45–66. Frankfurt: Peter Lang.

Mauranen, Anna. 2013c. Speaking professionally in an L2 – Issues of corpus methodology. In Gianna Diani, Julia Bamford & Silvia Cavalieri (eds.), *Variation and change in spoken and written discourse*, 5–31. Corpus Linguistic approaches. Amsterdam: John Benjamins.

Mauranen, Anna. 2021a. ELF and Translation as Language Contact. In Anna Mauranen & Svetlana Vetchinnikova (eds.), *Language Change: The impact of English as a Lingua Franca*, 95–122. Cambridge: Cambridge University Press.

Mauranen, Anna. 2021b. "Gonna write about it in my blog too". Metadiscourse in Research Blog Discussions. In Larissa D'Angelo, Anna Mauranen & Stefania Maci (eds.), *Metadiscourse in Digital* Communication. *New Research, Approaches and Methodologies*, 11–35. Cham: Palgrave Macmillan.
McCarthy, Michael. 2001. *Issues in applied linguistics*. Cambridge: Cambridge University Press.
McGrath, Lisa. 2015. *Writing for publication in four disciplines: insights into text and context*. PhD thesis, University of Stockholm.
McKeown, James, & Hans J. Ladegaard. 2020. Exploring dominance-linked reflexive metadiscourse in moderated group discussions. Journal of Pragmatics, 166. 15–27. https://doi.org/10.1016/j.pragma.2020.05.007
Mercier, Hugo & Dan Sperber 2017. *The Enigma of Reason. A New Theory of Human Understanding*. Cambridge, MA: Harvard University Press.
Miller, Carolyn. 1984. Genre as Social Action. – *Quarterly Journal of Speech* 70. 151–167.
Miller, Carolyn & Dawn Shepherd. 2004. Blogging as social action: a genre analysis of the weblog. In Laura Gurak, Smiljana Antonijevic, Laurie Johnson, Clancy Ratliff, & Jessica Reyman (eds.), *Into the Blogosphere: Rhetoric, Community, and the Culture of Weblogs*. Minneapolis: University of Minnesota Press. (http://conservancy.umn.edu/handle/11299/172818)
Miller, Carolyn & Dawn Shepherd. 2009. Questions for genre theory from the blogosphere. In Janet Giltrow & Dieter Stein (eds.), *Genres in the Internet: Issues in the Theory of Genre*, 263–290. Amsterdam: John Benjamins.
Monschau, Jacqueline, Rolf Kreyer & Joybrato Mukherjee. 2004. Syntax and semantics at tone unit boundaries. *Anglia-Zeitschrift für Englische Philologie* 121(4). 581–609.
Morgan, Jerry L. & Manfred B. Sellner. 1980. Discourse and Linguistic Theory. In Rand J. Spiro, Bertram C. Bruce & William F. Brewer (eds.), *Theoretical Issues in Reading Comprehension. Perspectives from Psychology, Linguistics, Artificial Intelligence, and Education*, 165–200. Hillsdale, NJ: Lawrence Erlbaum.
Mukherjee, Joybrato. 2001. *Form and Function of Parasyntactic Presentation Structures. A corpus-based Study of Talk Units in Spoken English*. Amsterdam: Rodopi.
Myers, Greg. 1989. Pragmatics of politeness in scientific articles. *Applied Linguistics* 10. 1–35.
Myers, Greg. 2003. Discourse studies of scientific popularization: Questioning the boundaries. *Discourse Studies*, 5(2). 265–279. https://doi.org/10.1177/1461445603005002006
Myers, Greg. 2010. *The Discourse of Blogs and Wikis*. London: Continuum.
Myhill, Debra, Ruth Newman & Annabel Watson. 2020. Going meta: Dialogic talking in the writing classroom. In Christine Edwards-Groves & Christina Davidson (guest eds.), *Australian Journal of Language and Literacy*. [Special Issue] DOI: 10.5565/rev/jtl3.870.
Myhill, Debra & Ruth Newman. 2016. Metatalk: Enabling metalinguistic discussion about writing. *International Journal of Educational Research* 80. 177–187. http://dx.doi.org/10.1016/j.ijer.2016.07.007
Ng, Connie Siew Ling, Wing Sum Cheung & Khe Foon Hew. 2012. Interaction in asynchronous discussion forums: Peer facilitation techniques. *Journal of Computer Assisted Learning*, 28(3). 280–294.
Northoff, Georg. 2018. *The Spontaneous Brain: From the Mind-Body to the World-Brain Problem*. Cambridge, Mass.: The MIT Press.
Partington, Alan. 2006. *The Linguistics of Laughter: A Corpus-assisted Study of Laughter Talk*. London: Routledge.
Pekarek Doehler, Simona. 2011. Clause-combining and the sequencing of actions: projector constructions in French conversation. In Ritva Laury & Ryoko Suzuki (eds.), *Subordination in Conversation: A cross-linguistic perspective*, 103–148. Amsterdam: John Benjamins.

Pennycook, Alistair. 2017. *Posthumanist Applied Linguistics*. London: Routledge.
Pérez-Llantada, Carmen. 2006. Signalling Speaker's Intentions: Toward a Phraseology of Textual Metadiscourse in Academic Lecturing. In Carmen Pérez-Llantada & Gibson R. Ferguson (eds.), *English as a Glocalisation Phenomenon: Observations from a Linguistic Microcosm*, 59–88. Valencia: University of Valencia.
Pickering, Michael J. & Simon Garrod. 2004. Towards a mechanistic psychology of dialogue. *Behavioural and Brain Sciences* 27(2). 169–225.
Pickering, Michael J. & Simon Garrod. 2017. Priming and language change. In Marianne Hundt, Sandra Mollin & Simone E. Pfenninger (eds.), *The Changing English Language. Psycholinguistic Perspectives*, 173–190. Cambridge: Cambridge University Press.
Pickering, Michael J. & Simon Garrod. 2021. *Understanding Dialogue: Language use and Social Interaction*. Cambridge: Cambridge University Press.
Pitzl, Marie-Luise. 2015. *Creativity in English as a Lingua Franca: Idiom and Metaphor*. Berlin: DeGruyter Mouton.
Poeppel, David. 2004. The analysis of speech in different temporal integration windows: Cerebral lateralization as 'asymmetric sampling in time'. *Speech Communication* 41. 245–55.
Puschmann, Cornelius. 2013. Blogging. In Susan Herring, Dieter Stein & Tuija Virtanen (eds.), *Pragmatics of Computer-Mediated Communication*, 83–108. Boston/ Berlin: DeGruyter Mouton.
Qian, Hua, & Craig R. Scott. 2007. Anonymity and self-disclosure on weblogs. *Journal of Computer-Mediated Communication* 12(4). 1428–1451.
Qiu, Xuyan & F. Kevin Jiang. 2021. Stance and engagement in 3MT presentations: How students communicate disciplinary knowledge to a wide audience. *Journal of English for Academic Purposes* 51. https://doi.org/10.1016/j.jeap.2021.100976
Radvansky, Gabriel. A. & Jeffrey M. Zacks. 2014. *Event Cognition*. Oxford: Oxford University Press.
Reagle, Joseph M. 2015. *Reading the comments: Likers, haters, and manipulators at the bottom of the web*. Cambridge: MIT Press.
Rosch, Eleanor. 1978. Principles of Categorization. In Eleanor Rosch & Barbara B. Loyd (eds.), *Cognition and Categorization*, 27–48. Hillsdale, NJ: Lawrence Erlbaum.
Rowley-Jolivet, Elizabeth & Shirley Carter-Thomas. 2005. Genre awareness and rhetorical appropriacy: Manipulation of information structure by NS and NNS scientists in the international conference setting. *English for Specific Purposes* 24(1). 41–64. https://doi.org/10.1016/j.esp.2003.09.003
Rumelhart, David E. 1975. Notes on a Schema for Stories. In Daniel G. Bobrow, & Allan M. Collins (eds.), *Representation and Understanding: Studies in Cognitive Science*, 211–36. New York: Academic Press.
Sacks, Harvey & Emanuel Schegloff. 1974. A simplest systematics for the organization of turn-taking for conversation, *Language* 50. 696–735.
Salmon, Gilly. 2003. *E-moderating: the key to teaching and learning online*. New York: Routledge Falmer, 2003.
Sancho-Guinda, Carmen. 2021. This has changed: 'Out-of-the-box' metadiscourse in scientific graphical abstracts. In Larissa D'Angelo, Anna Mauranen & Stefania Maci (eds.), *Metadiscourse in Digital Communication. New Research, Approaches, and Methodologies*, 81–114. Cham: Palgrave MacMillan.
Sanford, Anthony J. & Simon Garrod. 1981. *Understanding Written Language: Explorations in comprehension beyond the sentence*. Hoboken, NJ: John Wiley.

Scardamalia, Marlene & Carl Bereiter. 2006. Knowledge building: Theory, pedagogy, and technology. In R. Keith Sawyer (ed.), *Cambridge Handbook of the Learning*, 97–118. New York: Cambridge University Press.

Schegloff, Emanuel A. 2013. Ten operations in self-initiated, same-turn repair. In Makoto Hayashi, Geoffrey Raymond & Jack Sidnell (eds.), *Conversational repair and human understanding*, 41–70. Cambridge: Cambridge University Press.

Seidlhofer, Barbara. 2011. *Understanding ELF*. Oxford: Oxford University Press.

Seth, Anil. 2021. *Being You: A New Science of Consciousness*. London: Faber & Faber.

Sinclair, John McH. 1966. Beginning the study of lexis. In Charles E. Bazell, Ian Catford, Michael A.K. Halliday & Robert H. Robins (eds.), *In Memory of J.R. Firth*, 410–30. London: Longman.

Sinclair, John McH. 1985 [2004]. On the integration of linguistic description. In Teun Van Dijk (ed.), *Handbook of Discourse Analysis* Vol. 2, 13–28. London: Academic Press. Reprinted in John McH Sinclair & Ron Carter (eds.), *Trust the text*, 67–81. London, Routledge.

Sinclair, John McH. 1993 [2004]. Written discourse structure. In Michael Hoey, John McH. Sinclair & Gwyneth Fox (eds.), *Techniques of Description: Spoken and Written Discourse*. London: Routledge., 6–31. Reprinted in John McH. Sinclair & Ron Carter (eds.), *Trust the text*, 82–101. London, Routledge.

Sinclair, John McH. 2004. Trust the text. In John McH Sinclair & Ron Carter (eds.), *Trust the Text. Language, Corpus and Discourse*, 9–23. London, Routledge.

Sinclair, John McH. 2005. Corpus and Text – Basic Principles. In Martin Wynne (ed.), *Developing Linguistic Corpora: a Guide to Good Practice*, 1–16. Oxford: Oxbow BooksAvailable online from http://ahds.ac.uk/linguistic-corpora/.

Sinclair, John McH. 2007. Collocation Reviewed. Unpublished manuscript. The Tuscan Word Centre.

Sinclair, John McH & R. Malcolm Coulthard. 1975. *Towards an Analysis of Discourse: The English Used by Teachers and Pupils*. Oxford: Oxford University Press.

Sinclair, John McH & Anna Mauranen. 2006. *Linear Unit Grammar. Integrating Speech and Writing*. Amsterdam: John Benjamins.

Snyder, William. 2000. An experimental investigation of Syntactic Satiation effects. *Linguistic Inquiry* 31(3). 575–582.

Smart, Cameron. 2016. *Discourse Reflexivity in Linear Unit Grammar*. Amsterdam: John Benjamins.

Stubbs, Michael. 1996. *Corpus and Text Analysis*. Oxford: Blackwell

Swales, John M. 1990. *Genre Analysis. English in Academic and Research Settings*. Cambridge: Cambridge University Press.

Tadros, Angela. 1985. *Prediction in Text*. Discourse Analysis Monograph 10. Birmingham: English Language Research, University of Birmingham.

Tantucci, Vittorio & Aiqing Wang. 2022. Resonance as an Applied Predictor of Cross-Cultural Interaction: Constructional Priming in Mandarin and American English Interaction. *Applied Linguistics* 43(1). 115–46. https://doi.org/10.1093/applin/amab012

Tantucci, Vittorio. 2021. *Language and Social Minds: The Semantics and Pragmatics of Intersubjectivity*. Cambridge: Cambridge University Press.

Thompson, Geoff. 2001. Interaction in academic writing: learning to argue with the reader. *Applied Linguistics* 22(1). 58–78.

Thompson, Geoff & Puleng Thetela. 1995. The sound of one hand clapping: the management of interaction in written discourse. *TEXT* 15(1). 103–127.

Thompson, Geoff & Susan Hunston. 2000. Evaluation: An Introduction. In Susan Hunston & Geoff Thompson (eds.), *Evaluation in Text*, 1–27. Oxford: Oxford University Press.

Tognini-Bonelli, Elena. 2001. *Corpus Linguistics at Work*. Amsterdam: John Benjamins

Tomasello, Michael. 2003. *Origins of Human Communication*. Cambridge, MA: MIT Press.

Tomasello, Michael. 2014. *A Natural History of Human Thinking*. Cambridge, M.A. Harvard University Press.

Tomasello, Michael (ed.). 1998 [2014]. *The New Psychology of Language*. Vol.1. Mahwah, N.J.: Lawrence Erlbaum. Republished 2014, New York: Psychology Press.

Tomasello, Michael (ed.). 2003/2014. *The New Psychology of Language*. Vol.2. Mahwah, N.J.: Lawrence Erlbaum. Republished 2014, New York: Psychology Press.

Van Dijk, Teun A. 1972. *Some Aspects of Text Grammars*. The Hague: Mouton.

Van Dijk, Teun A. & Walter Kintsch. 1983. *Strategies of Discourse Comprehension*. New York: Academic Press.

Vande Kopple, William J. 1985. Some exploratory discourse on metadiscourse. *College Composition and Communication* (36). 82–93.

Ventola, Eija 1987. *The Structure of Social Interaction. A Systemic Approach to the Semiotics of Service Encounters*. London: Frances Pinter.

Vetchinnikova, Svetlana. 2014. *Second Language Lexis and the Idiom Principle*. PhD thesis. Helsinki: University of Helsinki.

Vetchinnikova, Svetlana. 2019. *Phraseology and the Advanced Language Learner*. Cambridge: Cambridge University Press.

Wächter, Bernd & Friedhelm Maiworm. 2014. *English-Taught Programmes in European Higher Education: The State of Play in 2014*. Bonn: Lemmens, ACA.

Walton, Douglas N. 1997. *Appeal to Expert Opinion. Arguments from Authority*. Pennsylvania: Pennsylvania State University Press.

Webber, Pauline. 2005. Interactive features in medical conference monologue. *English for Specific Purposes*, 24(2). 157–181. https://doi.org/10.1016/j.esp.2004.02.003

Wen, Ju & Lei Lei. 2022. Linguistic positivity bias in academic writing: A large-scale diachronic study in life sciences across 50 years. Applied Linguistics, 43(2). 340–364. https://doi.org/10.1093/applin/amab037

Willems, Roel M. (ed.). 2015. *Cognitive Neuroscience of Natural Language Use*. Cambridge: Cambridge University Press.

Willems, Roel M., Stefan L. Frank, Annabel D. Nijhof, Peter Hagoort & Antal van den Bosch. 2015. Prediction During Natural Language Comprehension. *Cerebral Cortex* 26(6). 1–11.

Williams, Joseph M. 1981. *Style: Ten Lessons in Clarity and Grace*. Boston: Scott Foresman.

Winter, Eugene. 1977. A clause relational approach to English texts: a study of some predictive lexical items in written discourse. *Instructional Science*, 6(1), 1–92.

Zareva, Alla. 2011. 'And so that was it: Linking adverbials in student academic presentations. *RELC Journal*, 42(1). 5–15. https://doi.org/10.1177/0033688210390664

Zhang, Man. 2022. Variation in Metadiscourse across Speech and Writing: A Multidimensional Study. *Applied Linguistics* https://doi.org/10.1093/applin/amac012

Zou, Hang J., & Ken Hyland. 2020. "Think about how fascinating this is": Engagement in academic blogs across disciplines. *Journal of English for Academic Purposes*, 43. https://doi.org/10.1016/j.jeap.2019.100809

Index

Ädel 1, 3, 5, 11, 26, 29, 45, 108, 152, 155, 167, 175, 181, 183, 185, 200, 203, 214, 216
Ahn 112
altercentric 59, 62, 64, 68–69, 71–73, 75, 81–82, 96–97, 99, 101, 107, 119, 127, 137, 142, 149, 155, 167–168, 181–182, 193–197, 199, 201–202, 205, 209, 211
Anderson 83
Ankener 13
Arvaja 112
Auer 14, 158

Baggio 19, 116, 153
Bandura 10
Becher 116
Berberovic 3, 108
Bereiter 113
Berkenkotter 86
Biber 37, 86–88
Biri 2–3, 83, 93, 100, 109, 195, 216
Bolander 85, 95, 110, 131, 201
Bondi 83
bottom-up processing 15
Bruffee 112
Buszáki 16
Butler 29

Canagarajah 113
Carter 46
Carter-Thomas 2
Chafe 14–15, 17, 22
channel effect 201, 210
Channell 99
Chater 64
Cheng 29
Cheung 113
Christiansen 64
Chu 113
Clark, A 16, 22
Clark, H 25
Class 112
Connor 86
Conrad 37, 87
construal 65, 69–71, 81, 205
context-creating 28–29, 45, 159
  See context-dependent
context-dependent 26, 28–29, 45–46, 159
contextualising
– orienting 55–56, 61, 64, 68, 75, 80–81, 94, 97, 155–157, 163, 168–169, 181, 192, 201, 212
– retrieving 56, 60, 64–66, 68, 80–82, 94, 97, 99, 101, 107, 117, 119, 124–125, 132, 142, 144, 146, 148–149, 155–157, 164, 166–168, 170, 180–182, 192–194, 196, 200–202, 205–206, 209, 213, 215
co-presence 7, 60, 106, 153, 177, 179, 182–183, 207, 209, 215
– co-present 5–6, 20–22, 25, 30, 32, 75, 82, 90, 96, 105, 107–108, 110, 119, 135, 142, 153, 167, 171, 176, 189, 197, 199–202, 204, 206, 209–211, 214, 217
Couper-Kuhlen 14, 19, 69, 115, 158
Craig, R. 67
Crismore 3, 5, 11, 20, 152
Curry 34
Cutting 99

D'Angelo 83
Daneš 15
de dicto 11
de re 11
Delibekovic Dzanic 3, 108
discourse-related 7, 186, 188, 201, 205
distributed 22, 207
Dobrego 4
Dodds 70, 100, 206
Du Bois 22

Egbert 86, 88
Eggins 116
egocentric 59, 62, 64–68, 73, 81, 96–98, 107, 119, 127, 140, 149, 155, 164–168, 181–182, 193, 195, 201, 206, 209
Ehret 88, 93, 100
Ellis 112

https://doi.org/10.1515/9783110295498-012

embodied 3, 6, 24–25, 32, 107–108, 118, 204, 214, 216
Ericsson 27
evaluation
- evaluative 50, 66, 70–71, 75, 99, 109–110, 118, 123, 125, 132, 156, 169–170, 174–176, 192, 199, 202
Evans 8
event model. See situation model
external constraints 6–7, 51, 186, 188, 200, 202, 209

Firth 55, 156
Fleming 10
Flowerdew 2, 158
Fox Tree 25
Frank 18
Franzmann 34
Friston 16
Frith 10

Garrod 3, 15–17, 22, 24, 45, 55, 112, 114, 206
Gilbert 4
Glenn 59
Goffman 20, 153
Goldberg 22
Gozdz-Roszkowski 169
Grice 153
Gries 45
Grieve 37, 42, 88, 110, 210
Gunawardena 83
Gweon 114

Hafner 84
Halliday 11, 13–15
Hari 16, 22–24, 55, 90, 208
Herring 83
Hew 113
Hoey 13, 19
Hopper 29
Huckin 86
Hull 113
Hunston 169
Hyland 2, 5, 11, 19–20, 21, 26, 34, 46, 65, 83, 152, 164, 167, 175, 185, 200

Ilie 3
imagined reader 19, 167

Jansen 34
Jenkins 4, 34
Jiang 167

Kastberg 112, 115, 149
Kennedy 113
Keryer 158
Kintsch 15–16, 27
Komori-Glatz 112
Konina 4
Kurby 16, 206
Kuteeva 83
Kuter 113

Ladegaard 2, 21, 26, 179, 212, 215
Laitinen 4
Lakoff 49
Latour 21
Lee, J. 152
Lei 70
Levinson 22, 207
Lillis 34
Linell 205
Liu 2, 108, 152, 164, 183, 185, 194, 216
Lowe 83
Lundberg 4
Luzón 83, 85–86, 95, 98, 100, 143, 145

Maci 83
macro event 36, 137, 187
Mahrt 38, 85, 95, 105, 143, 145
Maiworm 4, 34
Malmström 3
Mandel 25
Matlin 70
Mauranen 1–2, 4–5, 11, 14, 21, 23, 26, 29, 31, 34–35, 42, 45–46, 51, 57, 64, 69–70, 76, 83–84, 86–87, 98, 112, 114, 167, 172, 175, 180, 214
McCarthy 5
McGrath 85, 142

McKeown 2, 21, 26, 179, 212, 215
Mercier 8, 24
metalanguage 9–11, 26, 31, 113, 172
Miller 84, 86–87
Monschau 158
Morgan 15
Mukherjee 158
Mulkay 4
Münte 34
Myers 83, 85, 116
Myhill 9, 113

N. Lee 8, 22
Newman 113
Ng 113
Northoff 16

Partington 30
Pekarek Doehler 14
Pennycook 8
Pérez-Llantada 2
Pickering 3, 16–17, 22, 24, 45, 55, 112, 114, 206
Pitzl 30, 46, 112
plane-shift 76–79, 102, 121–122, 134, 198
Poeppel 118
polyadic 22, 135, 191
prediction 15–16, 17, 28, 32, 164, 204
- predictive 14, 16–17, 56, 156–159, 164, 214
primed 13
priming 112
prospection 14–15, 16, 30, 60, 65, 80, 158, 204–205, 216
prototypical 26–27, 31, 33, 35, 44, 47, 49, 56, 68, 157, 205
Pun 84
Puschmann 38, 85, 95, 105, 143, 145

Qian 98
Qiu 2, 164, 167

Radvansky 16–17, 56
Reagle 90
Rosch 26, 49, 87, 181
Rowley-Jolivet 2
Rumelhart 15

Sacks 19, 153
Salmon 113
Sancho-Guinda 108
Sanford 15
Sanusi 67, 164
Saxon 113
Scardamalia 113
Schegloff 14, 19, 153, 158
Scott 98
Seidlhofer 4
Sekicki 13
self-regulation
- self-regulated 52, 187, 202, 215
Sellner 15
Seltig 158
Seth 16
Shepherd 84, 87
Sinclair 10, 12, 14, 16, 29, 35, 84
situation model 16–17, 25, 56, 62, 72, 114, 167, 204–206
Slade 116, 206
Smart 2–3, 5, 11, 26, 29, 37, 83, 91, 93–94, 100–101, 110, 175, 200
Smit 112
social asymmetry 190, 199, 203, 212, 215
social constraints 213
social factors 85, 212 *See* external factors
- horizontal distance 187, 190
- vertical social distance 187–188
span 28, 49, 158, 162–163, 167, 181, 184, 209, 215
Sperber 8, 24
springboard 67, 69, 73, 77, 81, 137, 140, 151, 205
Staudte 13
Stubbs 86
Subtirelu 2, 152
Swales 86–87

Taboada 88, 93, 100
Tadros 13
Tantucci 22, 112
Tauroza 158
theory of mind
- recipient design 1, 19–20, 96, 153, 169, 209
Thompson 18, 169
Tognini-Bonelli 45
Tomasello 8, 17, 22

top-down 6, 15–16, 48, 89
Traugott 29
Trowler 116

Upton 86

van Dijk 15
Vande Kopple 3, 5, 20, 152
Ventola 86
Vetchinnikova 29–30

Wächter 4, 34
Walton 121
Wang 22
Watson 113
Webber 2, 162
Wen 70
Willems 16
Winter 13
Woolgar 21

Zacks 16–17, 56, 206
Zareva 2
Zhang 2–3, 26, 37, 45, 110, 207, 210, 213
Zou 2, 83, 164

www.ingramcontent.com/pod-product-compliance
Lightning Source LLC
Chambersburg PA
CBHW050522170426
43201CB00013B/2049
* 9 7 8 3 1 1 1 6 1 9 9 4 1 *